In a Waking State

THE EDGAR CAYCE LECTURES

Compiled and Edited by
Richard O. Peterson

With a Foreword by
Charles Thomas Cayce

ARE
PRESS

ASSOCIATION FOR
RESEARCH AND
ENLIGHTENMENT

A.R.E. Press • Virginia Beach • Virginia

A.R.E. Press
215 67th Street
Virginia Beach, VA 23451-2061

Library of Congress Cataloguing-in-Publication Data
Cayce, Edgar, 1877–1945.
    In a waking state : Edgar Cayce lectures / compiled by Richard O. Peterson : foreword by Charles Thomas Cayce.
        p.   cm.
    Includes bibliographical references.
    ISBN 0-87604-489-5 (trade pbk.)
    1. Parapsychology. 2. Occultism. I. Peterson, Richard, 1928– II. Title.
    BF1031.C47 2004
    133.8–dc22
                                                2004025019

Cover design by Richard Boyle

In a Waking State

THE EDGAR CAYCE LECTURES

2005

In A Waking State
Edgar Cayce Lectures

CONTENTS

Foreword

The spiritual wisdom of my grandfather, Edgar Cayce, has been largely assembled and disseminated from the information and ideas recorded during his psychic readings between 1900 and 1945. Most of the books and articles about his work and philosophy are based on that information, channeled through him during a sleep-like trance. He did not consciously hear the information at the time the readings were given nor did he later recall it.

Yet he developed his own personal belief system—not only from his study of the recorded readings, but also from his faithful study of the Bible and other resources, from his own challenging life experiences, and from his interactions with those he encountered around him. Perhaps the most complete expression of his personal beliefs is represented in his public lectures—especially those given frequently during the period that included both the realization of his dream of a hospital and the subsequent loss of that hospital amidst much conflict and personal sacrifice. Perhaps coincidentally, his lecturing virtually ceased when he began an outreach alternative that resulted in a ten-year series of readings on lessons for developing personal spirituality through *A Search for God*.

This book contains most of the known public lectures delivered by Edgar Cayce. These lectures—thirty in all—were delivered between 1929 and 1935, most of them on Sunday afternoons during the crucial period of his life and work from late 1929 through 1931. The lectures present many of the spiritual and metaphysical ideas now considered the foundation of "the work" of Edgar Cayce.

The lectures do more than summarize key principles and ideas. In fact, these lectures are the best expression we have of Edgar Cayce's personal understanding and beliefs about these fundamental ideas and issues. You will sense that Cayce is not just presenting information in a tutorial style. In his desire to help his listeners change their lives for the better, Cayce frequently urges them to take the information to heart and apply it in their own lives. He is clearly an enthusiastic advocate for the life-shaping principles.

What he is advocating to his listeners during this period is significantly different from what he would have said to them before 1923 when his own spiritual views were challenged by startling information that began to appear that year. Readings requested by friend Arthur Lammers included information on such topics as reincarnation, the soul and its destiny, psychic ability and psychic phenomena, astrology, levels of consciousness, and dreams. Another friend of the work, Morton Blumenthal, not only became fascinated by these topics, but requested personal readings on many of them—especially in 1925. The information from the Lammers and Blumenthal readings was elaborated upon over the rest of Cayce's life, often in readings requested for another purpose including those that came to be called "life readings." Thus, the lectures in this collection summarize Cayce's beliefs regarding these fascinating topics during this critical period of his work.

When he gave his first lectures in 1929, Edgar Cayce was a novice at lecturing—and I believe that shows in these transcripts. We have retained the "flavor" of the original lectures (most recorded by unspecified persons), while reducing some of the confusion of self-interruption, unintentional repetition, and probable misunderstanding of words by the unnamed "reporters."

Throughout most of his life, Edgar Cayce relied deeply on his beloved Bible. In his lectures, he frequently referred to biblical people and events to help explain or illustrate his ideas. We have added Bible citations for most of the references in his lectures, so the interested reader may go to the Bible to review the complete story and context.

This is the third book presenting Edgar Cayce "in his own words"—as separate from the readings themselves. The two previous books are:

- *Edgar Cayce—My Life As a Seer: The Lost Memoirs*
- *The Work of Edgar Cayce As Seen Through His Letters*

I hope you enjoy reading what the "awake" Edgar Cayce said about these timeless ideas. I hope these lectures will stimulate you to read (or reread) other material on the subject that will help make these ideas meaningful and useful in your own life.

Charles Thomas Cayce
Executive Director, Association for Research and Enlightenment, Inc., and President, Edgar Cayce Foundation

Introduction

Edgar Cayce, the Lecturer

In 1929, when Edgar Cayce began giving a series of Sunday afternoon lectures at his new hospital in Virginia Beach, lecturing was a relatively new experience for him. He was now on his feet—literally or figuratively—expressing to a public audience many of the spiritual and metaphysical ideas he had formulated in his conscious mind from his study of the readings and of the Bible, as well as from other sources. Lecturing contrasted with his usual reading session during which he reported what he received as an unconscious channel while lying in a prone position in front of a small group of interested people. Before this series of lectures, he had occasionally talked to groups of interested members, especially when he traveled, but he never took on the formal role of "lecturer" until 1929.

Cayce reported having had a dream that seemed to "foretell" (his word) his lecture activity:

> **The dream was about a baby who was very remarkable, talking before an audience that was spellbound. It was being examined to see that it wasn't just a midget, but a prodigy, and no one could find fault. The dream was interpreted as symbolic of conditions that would arise in the giving of speeches and activities, the baby suggesting what I felt as being little, or of no purpose in its environs; but the baby grows so as to make the hearts and souls of men of that turn which brings Life itself. The baby represented truth itself. It was a good dream. (from *Edgar Cayce—My Life As a Seer: The Lost Memoirs*, p. 222; the dream interpretation is a part of reading 294-159)**

As you read Cayce's lectures in this book, you will notice his unassuming approach to lecturing—even reticence at times.

The first twenty-four lectures represent Cayce's first public outreach with this unique spiritual and metaphysical information. Apparently his original intent was to schedule a lecture every Sunday afternoon at the new hospital—alternating weeks between Edgar Cayce and Morton Blumenthal, the president of the official association for the readings activity, the Association for National Investigators (ANI).

In late 1931 when Cayce began a series of readings to formulate lessons for *A Search for God* (the material that would form the basis of the "study group" program), the Sunday lectures stopped. After that, he lectured occasionally locally and at annual Congresses, and a few times in other cities, but never again in an extended series. This can be considered in light of the repeated guidance about the outreach of his work. For example, a 1927 reading on "the work" says:

> . . . for, as has been given, first individual, then as groups, as classes, as masses. In the first, this may possibly be misunderstood. Individual is as the work or application alone, and is of necessity the basis of all truth, for no individual or entity accepts as truth any truth save as that truth relates to its, the entity's, individual needs . . . and the groups meaning the various phases of those elements necessary to bring the truth of phases necessary for development of individuals, groups, classes, masses, nations.   254-34

One can hypothesize that Cayce's outreach shifted emphasis from lectures for "classes and masses" to that of "groups" through the study group approach—and of course always reaching out to the "individuals" in those groups as well as through the ongoing readings.

As one reads a Cayce lecture, which may include words and phrases typical of his conscious style of expression, one can almost imagine his voice and picture his presence in front of a group of interested listeners. Words and phrases Cayce frequently used, the structure of his sentences, his repetition and rephrasing of key ideas, his emphasis on certain words (as recorded at the time)—all these contribute to the essence of the man's spoken presentation. In editing the lectures for this book, I retained most of the language and stylistic "markers" typical of a Cayce presentation. For example, in place of the word "built," he generally used the word "builded," and these transcripts honor that preference.

The Readings as a Resource

When we consider Cayce as a lecturer, focusing on topics mentioned in his readings, we might mistakenly assume he could draw upon the original information stored somewhere in his mind and memory. To the contrary, Edgar Cayce himself told an audience, "I have been in the unconscious state . . . about 2500 times in the last thirty-one years, yet I have never heard a single reading." (See his 1933 lecture, "What Is a Reading?") He had no conscious awareness of the information as it was being provided or any memory of it after the reading. He was a channel for the information—not even an observer in the usual sense of the word, as were his secretary, Gladys Davis, and his wife, Gertrude, during most readings.

Thus, his mental assimilation of the information in the readings came only through his subsequent review and study of the transcripts typed from notes or shorthand recorded by someone present at the reading. (From 1923 to 1945, that recorder was most frequently Gladys Davis.) And certainly, information and concepts in many readings were the frequent subject of discussion with his family, close friends, and associates.

Occasionally, in preparing for a lecture, he requested information or guidance during a reading, and in a few lectures, he quotes extensively from an earlier reading. But for most lectures, he drew upon information and ideas assimilated over a period of time through his conscious study of readings.

In brief, Edgar Cayce had to prepare for his lectures as might almost anyone with access to the transcripts. Thus, the lectures collected in this book represent Edgar Cayce's own "conscious mind" assimilation and organization of ideas and principles in his readings. These truly represent "snapshots in time" of his beliefs and understandings about these subjects.

Two specific groups of readings given years earlier provided a foundation for many of the concepts and ideas in these lectures:

- In 1923–24, Arthur Lammers—whose personal reading in 1923 opened the door to the life readings—had a special series of readings (3744-1 to 3744-5) in which questions were asked or information offered by the Source about many of these topics—e.g., the soul, the subconscious, psychic phenomena, faith, personality, and dreams.
- In 1925, Morton Blumenthal—who later became the president of the organization that preceded the A.R.E. and even lectured at the Cayce Hospital on alternate Sundays—began requesting readings in which he asked questions about many of these same topics. (See especially these in 1925: 900-19 through 900-25, plus 900-31, -56, and -66.) Blumenthal's questions related to, for example: death, destiny of the soul, fate, vibrations, spirit entities, and the mind.

Between 1923 and the first lectures in 1929, other readings enriched and extended this information, as they continued to do throughout the rest of Cayce's life.

The Sequence of the Lectures in This Collection

The archival records relating to these lectures are incomplete and occasionally ambiguous. For example, two different dates are associated with a few lectures, implying that such lectures were given on both dates to different audiences. (One lecture was clearly delivered in three different cities.) Also the location for a few of the lectures is not specified in the records.

The lectures are presented here in chronological sequence (rather than being grouped according to broad topics, for example). In the comments preceding most lectures, date ambiguities are noted.

The lectures are grouped into three parts, which in themselves are essentially chronological:
- Sunday Lectures at the Cayce Hospital (1929–1931)
- Sunday Lectures After the Hospital Closing (1931)
- Other Public Lectures (1933–1935)

At the end of some lectures—especially the later ones—questions from the audience and Cayce's responses were recorded. Such questions were sometimes unrelated to the topic of the lecture. All substantive questions and answers have been included at the end of the lectures. In a few cases (and these are so noted), a question and answer from one lecture is appended to a different lecture where the topic is more relevant.

The Bible as a Resource

Throughout most of his lectures, Cayce "evaluated," explained, and illustrated ideas gathered from his readings against the framework of his deep and abiding knowledge of the Bible, both Old and New Testaments. As many readers know, Cayce read the Bible through once a year, he conducted Bible classes at a local church, and later he formed and led an A.R.E. Bible Study Group. His lectures are filled with direct and indirect references to the Bible.

Citations to book, chapter, and verse of the King James Version of the Bible have been inserted in the lecture texts following most of Cayce's biblical quotations and paraphrases. A direct biblical quote is cited as, for example: (John 8:15)—the gospel of John in the New Testament, chapter 8, verse 15. Indirect and paraphrased references are cited as, for example: (see Gen. 1:5-9). These citations can help the reader appreciate the breadth of Cayce's biblical foundation and allow the curious reader to look up the original source and discover the background and context for the reference.

The Lectures "in Context"

During my work with the lectures, I concluded that the reader would appreciate many of them even more by considering them in the context of Cayce's life and the world around him. For example, in general terms:

• His readings for individuals continued on an almost daily basis, sometimes in considerable numbers while the hospital was in operation.

• More than half of these lectures were delivered during the most turbulent year of Edgar Cayce's life and work—1931. That year included the closing of the Cayce Hospital, a forced move of the Cayce home (twice more the following year), and the arrest in New York of Edgar, Gertrude, and Gladys for "fortune telling." Probably the most positive event of that same year was the start of the reading series for the study group work called *A Search for God*, as well as the readings that initiated the prayer healing group that continues to this day.

• Several of Cayce's close friends and associates were sources of great interpersonal challenge for him and for the work during this period. In fact, the hospital closing in 1931 came after considerable controversy and miscommunication among Cayce, the Blumenthals, and others of the "inner circle."

• The small seaside community of Virginia Beach was meanwhile undergoing significant changes during this period. One is reminded that Cayce was repeatedly urged to locate and keep his work in Virginia Beach.

• The nation—and indeed the world—experienced the crash of the financial markets during this period and, with it, the beginnings of the Great Depression, which immediately reduced financial support for the Cayce work. Putting this into context of the time: Even before the crash in 1929, the government estimated that an income of $2,000 a year was needed to provide a basic living for an average small family, and 60 percent of Americans were below that. A contribution of even $5 was a significant expenditure for many individuals and families—a situation that only got worse after the crash.

• The world was experiencing events that we now see, in hindsight, were early warning signs of World War II, which would begin in less than ten years.

To help the reader be aware of such context, most of the lectures in this book are preceded by a digest of facts and events at the time, including information relating to significant readings of the period. These introductory segments may also include comments or facts about the upcoming lecture.

Various "Editions" of the Lectures, Including This One

Many of the early lectures were apparently published or summarized in issues of the *Virginia Beach News*, a weekly newspaper. Copies of those issues have not been found, however, even in local libraries.

Several of the lectures have been published in whole or in part in prior publications, such as *The New Tomorrow* (1929–30), *The Bulletin* (1934–47), *The Searchlight* (1949–62), *The Edgar Cayce Reader* (1969), *The A.R.E. News* (1981), and *The Lost Memoirs of Edgar Cayce: Life As a Seer* (1997). Some of these versions consist of excerpts and paraphrases of the lectures.

In this book, the texts of lectures adhere closely to the complete, originally (and anonymously) recorded transcripts. "Cautious" editing has tried to preserve the clarity of Cayce's ideas while reducing confusion caused by his interruptions of himself, by repetitions and restatements that seem unnecessary in written form, and by judiciously subdividing and re-punctuating very long sentences and paragraphs. After all, the punctuation was imposed by the unknown recorder, rather than by Cayce himself.

We hope you enjoy reading Cayce "in a waking state," expressing his understanding, his beliefs, and his enthusiasm regarding most of the major spiritual and metaphysical topics in "the work."

Richard O. Peterson
Compiler and Editor

Part One

Sunday Lectures at the Cayce Hospital

1929-1931

It is Sunday, September 15, 1929, in Norfolk, Virginia. As you pick up your copy of the Sunday Virginian-Pilot, *you relish the pleasant morning temperature and clear skies of this autumn day. How pleasant it would be this afternoon to jump on the train over to the village of Virginia Beach! You and your family could enjoy the beach and the ocean, perhaps for one of the last warm days of the fall.*

As you glance at the newspaper before church, you see an announcement about an afternoon lecture at that new hospital in Virginia Beach. The lecture is free, it's right at the hospital, and the speaker will be Mr. Edgar Cayce himself, the man after whom the hospital is named. That might be interesting. The topic of the lecture is "What Is the Holy Ghost?" That sounds appropriate for a Sunday afternoon—although you're not really looking for a second sermon today. But it will give you an excuse to visit the beach and see what this new hospital is all about. You have heard it's not just a regular hospital like St. Vincent DePaul in Norfolk. So, to your family you announce a little afternoon excursion on the train. (You can tell them about the lecture later . . .)

INTRODUCTION TO THE SUNDAY LECTURES AT THE CAYCE HOSPITAL

Thomas Sugrue, author of *There Is a River*, provided this history of Edgar Cayce's vision of a hospital:

"It was natural that Mr. Cayce should conceive of a hospital or sanitarium, where the people he diagnosed could be treated as he prescribed, under physicians in accord with the work; and it was natural that he should go to his own peculiar source of information for advice concerning it. The first reading taken on the establishing of a hospital approved of the idea and outlined the method of going about such a venture. On February 11, 1911, it advised Virginia Beach as a site for this hospital. On June 19, 1928, the first ground was broken for the Cayce Hospital . . .

"It is a long time between the idea and the creation, the dream and the reality. In 1911 Edgar Cayce began working toward the establishment of a hospital. On February 11, 1929, the first patient was treated in the Cayce Hospital at Virginia Beach." (From an editorial by Thomas Sugrue in the first issue of *The New Tomorrow*, December 1929; reprinted in full in *The Work of Edgar Cayce As Seen Through His Letters*, p. 173)

It was eighteen years to the day between that first reading and the first patient!

Six months after the hospital was in operation—in August 1929—Cayce initiated a series of Sunday afternoon "educational lectures" at the Hospital. According to biographer Sidney Kirkpatrick:

For thirty years, Edgar Cayce had delivered his message lying on his back while in trance. In Virginia Beach, in August 1929, prompted by Morton Blumenthal and Tim Brown, he stood on his feet, in front of an audience, and consciously presented the first of more than thirty lectures he would deliver on topics such as karma, astrology, auras, mental telepathy, and evolution. (from *Edgar Cayce: An American Prophet*, p. 412)

In the Months and Weeks Before the Lecture on "What Is the Holy Spirit" (Sept. 15, 1929) . . .

Around the world: The peace declared at the end of World War I is increasingly at risk. Germany finally signs the "Pact of Paris," optimistically outlawing war, while Hitler's National Socialists win their first majority in Bavaria. Violence between Arabs and Jews in the British mandate of Palestine results in hundreds of deaths. India is increasingly defiant under British rule, and Mahatma Gandhi is emerging as a leader of the movement toward independence. The U.S. Marines in Haiti put down a revolt against American control, and hundreds of Marines are still trying to "protect American interests" in Nicaragua.

At a time when many Christian and Jewish organizations are seeking ways to emphasize their common goals and beliefs, Pope Pius XI issues a Vatican encyclical condemning "Pan-Christian unity" and efforts aimed at increasing ecumenism.

In the U.S.: In January 1929, Albert Einstein proposes a new theory he claims demonstrates that gravity, electricity, and magnetism are all just different manifestations of the same basic force. Many scientists are skeptical.

Over 70 percent of American families have incomes below $2,500 a year. The average weekly wage is $28 (less than $1,500 a year). Meanwhile, the number of millionaires has increased dramatically. Newly elected President Herbert Hoover has promised "a chicken in every pot, and a car in every garage" while he sees America moving "nearer the final triumph over poverty."

The stock market experiences new highs, new volumes, wild swings, and even a suspension of operations to catch up on record-keeping. It becomes the subject of conversation among Americans everywhere. Many investors large and small have little understanding of the stock market. They crowd brokerage offices everywhere to watch the boards posting current prices, many buying stocks on credit. The bull market peaks on September 3 and two days later, Roger Babson—"father" of the long line of market prognosticators—predicts an imminent crash.

In Virginia Beach: Just before the new hospital building is finished in 1928, Morton Blumenthal calls a halt to the construction and flies from New York to confront the contractors and Cayce about cost overruns—reflecting Morton's increasing distrust of Cayce's financial management skills.

The Cavalier Hotel opens its Beach Club in 1929, making it one of the most exclusive resorts on the East Coast. It is now possible to board a Pullman sleeping car in Chicago, for example, and get off right at the Cavalier Hotel.

From January 1 through September 14, 1929, Cayce gives a total of 399 readings, including 47 for Morton and Edwin Blumenthal, 17 for David Kahn, and 13 for Tim Brown. A March 1929 reading for the Blumenthals (900–425) urges caution about the stock market in general as well as about specific investments. " . . . Throughout the summer and fall of 1929, Morton and his brother received numerous readings suggesting that an upheaval in the market was imminent" (from Kirkpatrick's *Edgar Cayce: An American Prophet*, p. 425). They later denied ever receiving this guidance.

About the lecture on "What Is the Holy Spirit?": Morton Blumenthal had lectured the preceding Sunday. The title of this first recorded Cayce lecture has sometimes been listed as "What Is the Holy Ghost?" This is the only lecture known to have been recorded by Gladys Davis, who had worked with him on its preparation for several days. This lecture is the longest of the recorded Cayce lectures.

Before he begins the lecture, Cayce says:

> You possibly wonder why I have kept you waiting these few minutes, but someone phoned and asked me to wait until they got here. I think that is doing one of the things we are often commanded to do—"Tarry yet one for another, and so fulfill the law of love."

Early in the lecture, Cayce states that, not only has he been guided to this subject today, but the source of the guidance is standing with him. One wonders how the casual visitor in the audience reacts to such information.

What Is the Holy Spirit?

Sunday, September 15, 1929
Cayce Hospital

I'm sure most of you have heard a great many sermons on the Holy Spirit or Holy Ghost, and many of you perhaps are wondering what that would have to do with—or why it would have *anything* to do with—the character of work that is to be conducted here at this place. What has the Holy Spirit to do with sick people? What has the Holy Ghost to do with the affairs of everyday life?

I don't expect to talk to you so much along the lines of theology, yet I'm going to quote from several places in the Scripture. But I am sure I will approach it from a little different viewpoint from those you have ever heard.

I wish I felt free to tell you *why* I am going to speak to you on this subject. Many of you may perhaps guess, from the little I have said to a few of you. For I believe, truly, if there are any of you present who have the psychic vision, you will be able to see who will stand with me this afternoon. Possibly that is far-fetched to many of you, but—to any of you who understand anything at all about the operation of the Holy Spirit—it is truly in keeping with that.

The first thing I am going to read to you is spoken by the Master Himself: "And whosoever shall speak a word against the Son of man, it shall be forgiven him: but unto him that blasphemeth against the Holy Ghost it shall not be forgiven." (*Luke 12:10*) Also "And when they bring you unto the synagogues, and *unto* magistrates, and powers, take ye no thought how or what thing ye shall answer, or what ye shall say: For the Holy Ghost shall teach you in the same hour what ye ought to say." (*Luke 12:11-12*) Then, in another place, He said: "And I will pray the Father, and he shall give you another Comforter, that he may abide with you for ever." (*John 14:16*) In the beginning, as we read in Genesis—possibly the best account that we have of creation—we find that it says, " . . . And the Spirit of God moved upon the face of the waters." (*Gen. 1:2*)

1

In and throughout the whole of the patriarchal age, we find there are a great many of these patriarchs, these prophets, and various teachers attempting time and time again to give the people something of a vision of *what* was operating in the lives and hearts of men that moved them to *do* certain things, or do things that were out of the ordinary, or that led them to give messages that were entirely different to the peoples. Down through the ages, as they went along—as they began to multiply in the earth—people began to forget about those sorts of things. They began to think more about the material side of life—about those things that were concrete, things that they could see with their own eyes and that they could use and be like the nations around them.

We have a beautiful illustration from the time when the chosen people were given a leader—a man who had been reared in the house of Pharaoh, who was then trained for forty years in the wilderness—by nature, by being close to God. When Moses was called, the first time God spoke to him and the Spirit or the Holy Ghost manifested itself in such a way that he could recognize he was called, the Holy Spirit told him the ground whereon he stood was holy ground and he must remove his shoes from his feet. (*see Exod. 3:2-5*)

When Moses asked Him what he was called for, and what was the purpose of this, God told him through the Holy Spirit that He had heard the call of Moses' people. (*see Exod. 3:7*) He knew of their oppressions that had been going on for forty years, and He knew the constant cry of the inner man seeking consolation, seeking help from a higher source. This call of Holy Spirit was constantly going out, but not always being heard.

Now, if you don't find out what the Holy Ghost is today, I'll be badly mistaken. Pardon me while I stop right here one minute and say, don't *think* that the Holy Spirit is something that you can put your hands on, or something that you can possibly call by name, or something that you can possibly *feel*. You have knowledge *of* it and knowledge *concerning* it, by the way it makes people *act*.

When this call came, Moses' cry was, "What shall I do? What am I to do? I am a man of slow speech—I can't even speak, or I stutter when I speak" God told him to *use what he had in his hand. (see Exod. 4:1-2)* Now Moses was a shepherd, yet a man raised to be a prince, to be a king, but he fled before his own people. Immediately upon his speaking, his own people rose up and said something against him. He was ready to flee from the face of these people, so he had his education here in the wilderness, here close to God. He appeared first in the burning bush. It was His Spirit that he saw.

Now in this material age, I remember reading an account not very long ago where someone said that, in this land, there is a bush that appears to be on fire at certain times of the year, and this was what Moses saw. Now I don't believe that, but even if we admit that it was all that he saw, he heard and felt something *from within.*

I want to state all of this with one text as to how we may know when we are being guided by the Holy Spirit—that which is ever present in this world. For "Thy Spirit—the spirit of man—will answer to *my* spirit, whether ye be the sons of God or not." *(see Rom. 8:16)*

Now what Moses heard, he harkened unto. Although at first he attempted to delay the game, as it were, or to delay the whole matter, he was persuaded that he should leave, even though his wife objected to his leaving. (Did any of you ever stop to consider what a hard time Moses had with his wife? He had an awfully hard time. She disagreed with him in practically everything he attempted to do.)

Now how do we explain these statements: The Son of Man speaks and says: "Suppose ye that I am come to give peace on earth?" Then He says, "The father shall be divided against the son, and the son against the father; the mother against the daughter, and the daughter against the mother . . ." *(Luke 12: 51, 53)* Why? Because one or the other does not harken to the Voice that comes from within—the Holy Spirit.

Throughout this whole age, from the time of this call to Moses—or even from the call to Abraham—we find this same force moving among men. We find this same thing when we come to their establishing themselves in the promised land. They were to be governed by the law as had been given to the servant on Mt. Sinai. There was set out for them the rules, the rituals they were to be guided by. Every so often they were to appear at the places prophesied, and they were to bring certain offerings at certain periods of the year, and they were to come and place their sins on the goat. Their sins would be rolled back for another year—and again and again this kept on. But they didn't get the idea of *what this spirit of God in the inner man meant.*

They lived in this land for a while, and the cry came out, "We want a king, like the peoples round about," and there was chosen for them a king, Saul, one who was really a kingly man—beautiful of countenance, and head and shoulders above any man in the whole group gathered together, or among all of the people. Yet when he came to follow those very same lines that had been given—as to how he should conduct himself—he too fell away. *(see 1 Sam. 8-15)*

Then it was necessary to choose another man. This man was chosen, as we know, from the flocks. He was a herder and a musician. David was the psalmist, and the only one we find about whom God repeatedly said, "I will *do* this for my servant David's sake"—a *man after God's own heart. (see 2 Sam.)*

I often wonder about this man David. From the moral standpoint of today, this man was possibly guilty of every sin you could think of, yet God said of this man, "He is a man after my own heart." *(see Acts 13:22)* What was it about this man that it could be said of him—even in his old age and even in generations and generations after, when there is a call to a man, it is continually repeated "I will do this for my servant David's sake." *(e.g.,1 Kings 11:32; 1 Kings 15:4; 2 Kings 19:34)*

This is about the only explanation I can find: David continued to harken to Spirit whenever he heard (even though he was a busy, busy man). He continued to fall, but he continued to get up, and you don't find him guilty of the same sin twice! Now that, I think, is a noteworthy point: *You don't find him guilty of the same thing twice.* But he hears the call each time, this same Spirit that God has sent—the Spirit that moved over the face of waters, that separated the firmaments below from the firmaments above—this same Spirit that moved over the earth, that brought into being all the things we have—this same Spirit that is in a blade of grass the same as it is in you, only in a different *form*—as has been told you by Mr. Blumenthal. But every living thing is a manifestation of the Spirit abroad in the earth and moves in its various forms and various spheres.

Only as *man* gives or changes it does it become good or evil. Some people say there is no such thing as evil. There is only good. It is good unless you are going away from God—and I don't know how you could call that good—going away from God.

But to get back to the same thing, and the first thing that God says: "Thou shalt have no other gods before *me.*" *(Exod. 20:3)* Now, whenever you turn your face on that, whether it is for your own self, your own selfish motives, your own selfish interests, your own selfish desires, then you are setting up something else, and you are worshipping something else. Whether it be a new hat, a new dress, or a seat on the New York Stock Exchange, it is all the same thing—it is *Money*—"and thou shalt not make unto thee any graven image," *(Exod. 20:4)* which is, in this day and age, the *specie*, or this new *coupon*, as some people call our new money.

But there came a time, as there was promised throughout all of the ages—from the time of the first in the Garden of Eden as given in the record—as to how this promise was made that there was a new day coming. (I'm stepping pretty close to next Sunday's Sunday school lesson.)

Now when the Son of Man comes—in fact, we find He is continually speaking of this Holy Spirit—I don't know how you will think of this, many of you who are very close in the churches. But to my mind, when the Master came into the earth—the first time He was acknowledged—the Holy Spirit departed from the earth. For peace remained in the earth during that whole time. For if it had *not* departed, how could He say, "I go to the Father, and He will send the Comforter to you, and He will guide you in all things, whatsoever I have commanded you. Take no thought, when you are brought before people, as to what you will say, but in the selfsame hour will the Spirit guide as to what you shall say or what you shall do." *(see John 14:16; 15:26; 16:13; Luke 12:11-12)*

As He came into the earth, so that the Spirit departs, so that the whole of flesh is one, He became flesh to be in an estate even as you and I are, that He might *know* all the environments of the flesh, all the earthly conditions that man goes through. And yet, being continually in communication with the same Father that had brought all into being, He was able to overcome the flesh and to take up His life anew.

Now, what *is* the Holy Spirit? How does it operate? How does it act? Is it abroad in the earth today? Is it different today from the time that it was guided in the creation of the earth? Is creation going on now? Is it?

It *is*—going on now just as it was then. Not as we may see it. Yet we see it every day before us and don't recognize it, because it has become commonplace.

When we see the Spring of the year come and we see everything begin to put forth new life, and when we see the dawn of a new day, we know that creation is taking place before our eyes. And yet we say: "Well, that's just Nature—that isn't anything unusual—that's been happening for years and years." It has! But how does it take place? What *is* it that is operating? What is *keeping* it going on? What is taking care of the flowers that bloom or *anything* that may come about? The same Spirit that brought it into being!

How does it operate among men? As we have seen of old, when God chose to make for himself a "peculiar people"—one to whom the promise was given, one to whom the promise is still given—we find that the Spirit moved in this man Jacob. He was called to separate himself from among the other peoples, and he was to make of himself a "peculiar people." He was to make of himself so that his seed—his descendants—would be as the sands of the sea, or as the stars of the heavens. They would be numerous among all peoples. *(see Gen. 32:12)* But for a special purpose were they called, that His name might be kept alive in the earth. That is the thing for which they were called.

I think I can say this truthfully: There has *never* been a religious movement unless it was fostered by those people that were called. There will *never* be a movement for good unless fostered by those people in some manner or form. Now, that is making a broad statement—a very broad statement—but if anyone will show me where there has been any movement for the uplift of man or for the call of man to understand his relationship to his Maker, except by these very same people called by His Spirit, then I'll take everything back that I have said. That's what His book says will happen, and that's what has been to this good day! What does it have to do with man today?

As it was given, we know when the disciples were scattered abroad. We find that on the day of Pentecost they were gathered together in one place, and they were all of one mind, and there appeared tongues of fire on all these people gathered there. *(see Acts 2:1-4)* Now, I have heard people say, that's the manifestation of the Holy Spirit. That's *one* manifestation, to my mind, of the Holy Spirit.

Now, if God is the same yesterday, today, and forever, then it will always be that whatever force is manifested in this world comes from God, and it must come *through* some manner that manifests His force within our own sphere. It comes through the knowledge of the Holy Spirit, or is directed *by* the Holy Spirit. Or, as He said, "If I go not away, the Comforter will not come; but if I go away he will come and abide with you always, and he will bring to you the remembrance of *all things* whatsoever I have told you." *(see John 16:7; 14:26)*

How long does that "always" last? From the very beginning to the very end. We find in another place it is said, "In the beginning was the Word, and the Word was with God, and the Word was God. There was not anything made that was made in the beginning without the Word. The Word came and dwelt among men, and the world knew Him not." *(see John 1:1, 3, 10)*

When that Word went away, He left the Holy Spirit—or the Holy Spirit came again into the world to abide with men forever. "If ye abide in me," or "if you will but abide in me," or if man will come just to the same place as he has always been commanded to: "Put nothing else before *me* and I will abide with *you*." *(see John 15:4-7)* Now you know how to get close to God. You know how to have the power of the Spirit in you: Put everything out of your life and mind, and seek God. He will come and abide with you, for that is His promise from the beginning, from the first time man was ever called and put into the Garden.

What happens when there is an outpouring of the Holy Spirit today, as there was on that day of Pentecost? Are men called today as Abraham was called in his day? Are men called to service today as they were called in and throughout all the ages? How may you *know* it when you see it? How may you be cognizant of it yourself in your own life, and what will it do to you? "Ye have seen the things that I have done," said the Master, "but when the Spirit of Truth comes, greater things than these shall *ye* do." *(see John 14:12-18)* Now that "ye" didn't mean just the little twelve gathered in front of Him. For if He was to abide *always*, that's a mighty long time, and that includes you and me. Now because it is an outpouring of the Holy Spirit at one time, they all spoke with tongues of fire, and each man heard in his own tongue. Is the same outpouring possible today? It is. And how does this happen?

Jesus prayed constantly. He had made it a rule of his life that at least three times every day he would go apart to pray. And Cornelius, a centurion, also prayed, and when he had fasted for four days, the Spirit appeared to him one day and said, "Send down to Joppa for one in the house of Simon the Tanner and call for Peter. He will come and tell you what you must do." *(see Acts 10:1-6)* Is it the *spirit* or is it the *operation of the spirit* that tells you? Let's follow it closely to see just how it operates in this particular case:

The Spirit appeared to Peter while he was asleep, and a great sheet went down from heaven containing all manner of beasts. And Peter was hungry, and the Spirit said, "Arise, wash, and eat." Peter said, "They are unclean." The Spirit said, "What I have called clean, call thou not unclean. Arise, for there are three men waiting for you." He goes out, and these men tell him their master Cornelius had sent them to ask that he come with them. He went down to the house and began to prophesy. Then he said, "Let who would partake of the water and not forbid that these should be baptized, for the Holy Spirit has descended on them, as well as on us." *(see Acts 10:47)* Now that's another operation of the Holy Spirit.

We find when Paul was speaking down at Corinth, he said that all Spirit comes from God, but "try ye the Spirit." *(see 2 Cor. 13:5)* To some is given teaching, to some exaltation, to some speaking in tongues, to some service. *(see 1 Cor. 12:4-11)* Not that one is better than another, but that they are *used*. Or it comes back to that first man (Moses) that was told, "Use that you already have in hand—then more will be given to you." *(see Exod. 4)* Just as it was when the Spirit Force parted the waters of the Red Sea before Moses and the Jews in the Exodus from Egypt. *(see Exod. 14:21-29)* What was that but the Holy Spirit? It can't be anything else!

That's the same thing that's about us—Creative Energy in the whole earth. What is Creative Energy? The Spirit of a thing that makes it alive! Just as it will be in the hearts of men and women if they will harken to the voice from within. Then we will be able to discern when and how we are called to service. If we are not so serving of our own selfish desires, we will be able to hear.

If we *are* so serving of our selfish interests, even blinded by selfish desires, we may be unable to hear Spirit. I have heard people say, "If I could just make so much money, then I'll be ready to serve the Lord." Whose is the money? Who does all the power in the earth belong to? Are you going to serve the devil that you might have money? The money doesn't belong to the devil, although it may appear so for the time, but it is only for the moment—and he will have his reward only in the moment. For as God has said, "The silver and the gold is *mine*, saith the Lord, and the cattle on a thousand hills. Seek ye first the Lord while He may be found, and *then* all these things will be added unto you." *(see Ps. 50:10; Luke 12:31)*

If we seek Him first, then we may be very sure that what we have need of will come to us, for, as He has said, "The Holy Spirit will guide you. It will guide you unto *all* things, and bring to you remembrance of all things whatsoever I have commanded." *(see John 14:26)* How long has that been possible? Since the very foundation of the world! How old is your own soul that you expect to carry back to God? Just as old as the foundation of the world—ever since you have been called into *being*. How long have you been called into being? "All things that were made were made by Him, and without Him there was nothing made that was made." *(see John 1:3)*

That's what the operation of the Holy Spirit is—how it moves among men today. How it moves is in the things you *do* for the other fellow. You can't render service to God. There's nothing in the world you can do that He has need of. Can you imagine a God that has need of anything that you could do and still call it God? Not a thing. So what can you do? The only way you can serve God is to serve your fellow man, who is also one with Him, or bring him back into that same oneness with God. Just as the Father, the Son, and the Holy Ghost are one, ye all may be one in Him, through the call of that spirit from within that answers to that Holy Spirit that is abroad, as to whether ye are children of God or not. Just as you are able to serve your fellow man in any capacity, the highest service that any blade of grass can do is to fulfill that purpose for which it was created.

The highest service man can do is to carry his soul back to God. He *can't* do it except by serving his fellow man. That's the only way. Man was called from time to time, just as Moses was called to answer the cry of the oppressed in Egypt. But did God come down and speak to all of these people? No. He spoke through one man to use this whole nation that was called out to service. Every man spoke to Him *through* one man who led the people in the way they should go. And *man*, acting or reacting to that that is presented to him, finds himself in whatsoever relation he has set before him when his Creator speaks with him through that Holy Spirit that is within each and every individual.

What is the greatest sin? To have so applied your own life and soul that you *can't hear!* That's the whole thing. Now, if you blaspheme against that—the hearing—if you have so blasphemed your own soul that it is incapable of hearing the Spirit abiding with it, how *can* it be forgiven? If you have shut yourself away from God, how *can* you get back? There is no approach.

But if one will harken to that voice from within, He has promised "I will come and abide with him, and I will guide him in all things whatsoever I have commanded." *(see John 14:16-23)* Also, "I, who go to the Father that ye may be in Him, as I am in Him," *(see John 16:16)*—that same voice speaks from within us, unless we have applied and blinded our own lives to such an extent that we are not able to listen to the voice from within, and we are blind and deaf to the Spirit of God. Whenever a man or a woman is not able to be touched by the love of a child, or by the beauty of a rose, or by nature as it spreads itself over the sky, he has gotten so far away that even the Holy Spirit can't awaken him from within, and *that* is when man has sinned against the Holy Ghost.

So finally, what is the Holy Ghost—the Holy Spirit? It is that Comforter that has been in the world since the foundation of the world, that the Master sent into the world that it might be a comforter to us. Do we have to die to enjoy it? No. I don't think very much of a religion that I've got to die to enjoy. I want a *living* religion. Did you ever have someone come to you and say, "I thank you," and you know that they meant it from the bottom of their heart? Didn't it start a little something tingling in you and you wonder what it is? Then you know what it is to be awakened first by the Holy Spirit that draws all men close together. Did you ever meet people you felt drawn to at once and loved them? What is love but a manifestation of that same Spirit? "For God is love." *(1 John 4:8)* Now, that may be abused, just as any other force that is manifest in the world. But when we allow those things and cultivate those things, we will know that He will abide with us forever.

During the Two Months Before the Lecture on "What Is the Soul?" (Nov. 17, 1929)...

Note: There are no records of Cayce lectures between September 15 and November 17. Morton Blumenthal lectured on "My Concept of God" (Sept. 29 and Oct. 6) and on "Heaven and Hell" (Oct. 27).

Around the world and in the U.S.: The major national and international event of this period is the U.S. stock market crash during the period from "Black Thursday," October 24, through "Black Tuesday," October 29—the day on which American common stocks lose 10 percent of their value. The market hits rock bottom on November 13. Within weeks, unemployment in the U.S. rises from 700,000 to over three million.

Europe, still struggling in its recovery from World War I, is also severely impacted—especially Germany, where added economic challenges provide fertile ground for the ideas and activities of the National Socialists and Adolf Hitler.

In Virginia Beach: As noted earlier, Cayce readings for the Blumenthal brothers—as early as March and April 1929—warned of "a great disturbance in financial circles" and "a break where it would be *panic* in the money centers." In a letter dated October 27 (the Sunday in the middle of the financial crisis), Edwin Blumenthal writes to Cayce, saying, "the market went to pieces." He goes on to say:

" . . . for the present I'll be unable to raise any cash. However, by hedging and trading we will, as given in the readings, be able to make some turns and once more be of service. It is nice to know that we are receiving guidance in these matters, and I am only sorry we had to take severe losses, but as I explained to Morton, it is merely a test for ourselves and we will either gain or lose, depending on how we accept that which we now find has been presented to us. [Edwin]" (from *The Work of Edgar Cayce As Seen Through His Letters*, p. 170)

Another major crisis for the Cayce Hospital begins in early September when Dr. Thomas B. House, hospital chief of staff, becomes critically ill. His readings over the years identified problems that needed careful treatment and monitoring. Cayce recommends specific spinal manipulation, and House leaves for Dayton to be put under the care of osteopath Dr. Lyman Lydic. Accompanying Dr. House is his wife, Carrie, who has been in charge of the nursing and housekeeping staff at the hospital. To help out, Cayce's father Leslie begins working at the hospital, and Cayce's sister Annie moves from Nashville to take over Carrie's responsibilities. Also, Gladys's cousin Mildred and friend Linden Shroyer both move to Virginia Beach to help with a variety of duties, including business affairs and records preservation. Dr. House receives additional readings through October 8, but he dies on October 12.

A new figure in the background is Mrs. Patricia Devlin, an employee of Morton Blumenthal in his New York office. According to Gladys Davis, Mrs. Devlin listened in to all conversations between the Blumenthals and Edgar Cayce or others in Virginia Beach. In early October, Mrs. Devlin reviews the correspondence regarding the plans for opening Atlantic University—a project close to Morton's heart and one that will receive substantial financial support from the Blumenthals. (Cayce has not been involved in the planning of the university, and the first reading regarding the university is still in the future.) Mrs. Devlin reports to Morton that Dr. William Moseley Brown, the intended president of the new university, is hiring more professors than Morton has agreed upon. Morton is irate. This is just the beginning of disagreements between Dr. Brown and Morton—a situation that will eventually contribute to problems at the hospital.

During the two-month period since the lecture on "The Holy Spirit," Cayce gives 106 readings, including twenty-nine for patients at the hospital and eight for the Blumenthals, which include cautions and warnings about the economy and guidance for one of Morton's Sunday lectures. On seven occasions, Cayce gave from five to seven readings during a single day.

About the lecture on "What Is the Soul?": This lecture was originally titled "What Is My Soul and What Am I Intended to Do With It?" In the lecture, reference is made to an earlier Cayce discussion of *truth*. It is possible that his lecture on "Truth," coming up in just one week, was given in whole or in part at an earlier time (perhaps July), but not as part of the Sunday afternoon series.

In his story near the end of the lecture, a patient calls Edgar Cayce "Judge," a nickname used by some of his close friends.

Following this lecture, Cayce responded to several questions from the audience. One question and its answer are appended at the end of the lecture. Two questions and answers about reincarnation are presented following the lecture on reincarnation.

What Is the Soul?

Sunday, November 17, 1929
Cayce Hospital

How many of you know what your soul is? How many of you are sure you *have* a soul? I am sure we all feel within ourselves that there is a "something" that we are unable to describe—a something that we feel will live on and on. None of us expects this purely material body, as we see it, to be raised. Do we expect the resurrection of the purely material body, or what body is it that we expect to be resurrected at the last day—at the time when the great change comes?

We know that change is constantly taking place, and—as explained to you by Mr. Blumenthal in a better way than I can—that is what is ordinarily termed *evolution* from the scientific standpoint. *Evolution* is constantly going on in the earth. But in man there is something entirely different. We reach a *decided* change in man, and when we reach that decided change, it is at that point where the *soul* comes into being.

When did the soul come into being in man? What is it that makes man different from the ordinary evolution of things in life? Man lives, born into the world just the same as all the rest of the kingdoms, whether we are speaking of the vegetable, the animal, or whatnot. Man lives and dies, passes through this earth's plane just in the same way as all the rest. Man changes—not by any *outward* condition in the pure physiognomy of the man, for there is possibly very little outward change except under environment and under varied conditions. But deep in the heart of each individual is a longing for the continuance of existence. What produces that? What *is* that? What *is* it that is *longing* for something else?

It isn't the purely material mind, for the purely material mind builds of material things. But it is that part of man that *longs* for the something that makes a continuity of his existence and makes him hope and wish for, long for, desire for a continuity of that existence.

Not an earthly existence. He doesn't hope for that. For when he stops

17

to think a minute, he *knows* that isn't possible. As commonly said, we know there are two things certain in man's life: taxes and death. Death must come to everyone, but it is only death of the material body.

That same thing that makes a man long for a home unseen—the home not built with hands—that produces something in the individual's life that has nothing to do with *material* things. You show me an individual who is hanging the hope of a future life on what he is doing today. It isn't building fine homes and things of that kind. It is making life—this material life certainly—more understandable, more worthwhile, more beautiful in every way possible. Those are the things that take hold of something else within the individual. They bespeak of a portion of man that has very little if anything to do with the material side of life, the material man.

What is it? It is the man's *soul*! We can read from the Bible, "And the Lord God formed man of the dust of the ground, and breathed into his nostrils the breath of life, and man became a living soul." *(Gen. 2:7)* Was man made and created a living body before he became a living soul? I am not going to try and discuss that with you. I want you to take that home and think it over—decide it for yourselves. There isn't but one place you can find it. You can find reference of it in the Book, and you can find the answer there. "My spirit will ever bear witness with *your* spirit as to whether ye be the children of God or not." *(see Rom. 8:16)*

We can take that home, think of it the rest of our lives. For as I said some time ago, that thing that you can hold before you that will develop your mind—whether your soul mind or your material mind—is *truth*. And "truth will make you free, and ye shall be free indeed, for ye *know* the truth and the truth abides with you. Then, indeed are ye my children." *(see John 8:31-32, 36)* All of that comes out of this Book. [*Mr. Cayce held up the Bible.*] If you will apply it in your life—*live* it. It isn't a thing just to be bragged about, it isn't a thing just to be heralded from the housetop, it isn't a thing you can send out any other way than to *live* it—simply *live* it! If you hold that in your mind, then the dwelling place of your soul within your body will grow and will be magnified, even in this earth.

Where in your physical body does your soul live? In your subconscious mind or in the mind of the soul? The mind of the soul is *not* the whole soul. It is the *mind* of the soul, as your *physical* mind, your conscious reasoning, which guides and controls your physical body in the application of that in your life that is called *will*.

What is the differentiation between will and mind, or soul and mind, or soul and body? Do they all live in one? Are they all parts of each other? How much are they *dependent* one upon the other?

All through the Bible, references are made to things in the mineral kingdom, the animal kingdom, things terrestrial, things celestial. There is the physical body. There is the spiritual body. The spiritual body dwells within this material body. It may or it may not control the physical body.

The physical body has physical attributes, known ordinarily as the common senses, the five senses. These things, as we know (described by many), are the things that, if harkened to, either build a man *toward* his creator or *away* from his creator. The desires of the flesh are carnal. "If ye be carnal-minded, ye are not my sons, saith Jehovah." *(see Rom. 8:6-9)* If we harken to the desires purely of the flesh, then we become carnal-minded, and we partake of those things which are not developing factors for the soul body—that portion of man given to him alone by the breath of his creator. When God made the rest of the world and worlds, and all that is in them, only to man did He become so personal that into *that* body breathed He the living soul!

Living soul means something that is so much a portion of the divine that it lives on forever. It doesn't mean that called the *spirit*—not the spirit, for the spirit of a thing is life-ever-after life, whether it be of the elements, of the fishes of the sea, or of *whatever* we may speak, and is of the Whole, and on the death of the body goes back into that very same Whole Being "in which we live and move and have our being," *(Acts 17:28)* which sustains physical life—the spirit of the thing.

But to *man alone* is given a living soul, that he either brings to his Creator, made one with that Creator, or separated entirely by the desires of the flesh and the reaping of those very things that *bring* separation. Then it becomes as other things about him, because he has lost his own soul! For, as said by the Master Himself, "What profiteth a man if he gain the whole world and lose his own soul? Or what will a man give in exchange for his soul?" *(Matt. 16:26)* That thing that's so individual that the Creator Himself sets it apart from everything else created in the whole universe—that's our soul.

Where does the soul dwell within us? It dwells just so far within us as we allow it to, so we make it a portion of our everyday existence. If we live carnal-minded, our soul has shriveled away. If we live spiritual-minded, ever hoping, working, desiring to do and to lift up and be lifted up, then our soul grows and becomes *broad*. As we often say, a body may be very poor in this world's goods and very rich in the spiritual life. Or, if we put it just a little differently, a body may live so that life is shriveled up, because it is so bound up by the material things of life that it cannot find peace. There *is* no peace if the soul has lost its way! If the soul within is seeking that which it can only be—the companion with the Creation, or the Giver of all that is good and perfect—if it has lost its way from that, can there be any peace?

"Why worry" (as the Master said in another place), "why take thought of what is going to be—this, that, or the other—if he knows that ye are one with the Father? Behold the lilies of the field and how they grow—they toil not, neither do they spin. Yet Solomon in all his glory was not arrayed like one of these." (*see Luke 12:25-27*) If ye know that the Father dwells in you and know that, if a man asks of you, you will give what you are able, then give (as they say) until it hurts, and *keep on giving until it doesn't hurt.*

That doesn't mean purely of this world's goods. It doesn't mean that, but we are so material-minded, we *judge* the world by those material things, and we do *not* judge the world by those things that have to do with the building up of the soul.

I have often been asked: What is the greatest experience that ever came to you in this work and in this phenomenon? It came to me last week, the greatest experience of the whole work that I have been trying to do. An individual came to me (he had been a patient in the hospital), took me into his room, and said, "Judge, sit down just a minute. I want to ask a favor of you. I've never asked a man for anything before in my life, but I want to ask you for something. You can grant it to me, and no one else could grant it to me, and I want you to do it. When I came in this place, I found one of those Books" (he had a Bible in his hand). "I'd never read it but very little. I could possibly buy more beautiful ones than this, but there is not a one that will ever read just as this one will. May I have this Book? Will you write your name in this Book? This will mean more to me than anything I've ever had in my life."

I can't help but feel that—even if this place cost a million dollars, even if that was *my* boy (and he's *some* mother's boy)—the way I feel about it, millions would be a very small price for that to have gotten into the *soul* of that individual. Don't you all agree with me? That's the greatest experience that has come to me—to have been able to—in some way or another, through the things that individuals have seen about this place —cause him to come to love this Book and the things it speaks of. For only in this Book do you find where you got your soul, or where that soul is seeking to reside—and your soul is all that is everlasting within you.

Thank you.

* * *

Question from audience: What is death?
Answer by Mr. Cayce:: By one man, death came into the world, and that was sin. It answers—that's death. It's sin. By one man came life, and that is to the soul. Death is produced by sin, to man. Sin brought death into this world. Death is the separation of the physical body from the soul body. That's what it means to man. Separation of the physical body and the soul body. You may be very sure the spirit always finds its home, but does it carry you back with it to God? That's the question with you. Will your spirit carry you back to your God? If you have made money your god—or power or place or position—that's the only place it'll carry you. It can't carry your soul anywhere else. If your soul has so ex-pressed your experience through life, your spirit will carry you back to your God. If your soul has been so earthly minded, it can't carry you anywhere except back to earth. The spirit will go to where it belongs.

During the Week Before the Lecture on "What Is Truth?" (Nov. 24, 1929) . . .

Around the world and in the U.S.: The attention of the country and the world continues to be focused on the immediate effects of the stock market crash a month ago. While the bottom of the market appears to have been passed in the U.S., no one sees signs of recovery any time soon.

In Virginia Beach: During this one week, Cayce gives eighteen readings, six of them on Monday, including one for Morton Blumenthal and three for patients at the Cayce Hospital.

A notable reading this week is for friend and major supporter of the work, Tim Brown, a Dayton manufacturer of auto parts and a creative thinker about concepts in the readings such as connectedness, energy, and technology. This reading (Tim's 67th) and part of Morton's reading (his 460th) this week are two of many concerning the development of a motor first envisioned by an Alabama engine mechanic, Marion Stansell. During a near-death experience in World War I, Stansell reports he was told by Jesus that he would be given information for a device that would eventually save the planet from environmental decline. (Once started, the engine would create its own continuing energy supply.) A Cayce reading for Stansell said that DeWitt Clinton, governor of New York in the early 1800s and sponsor of the Erie Canal, "gave" information to Stansell for the motor. Eventually, Tim and Stansell began working together trying to develop a prototype of the motor, with the support and enthusiasm of Morton. The motor readings this week respond to specific technical questions about tolerances and ratios among elements in the motor, motor ducts, and fluids. Of particular interest: Castor oil is recommended as a balance to mercury used in the motor ducts.

About the lecture on "Truth": The date of July 18, 1929, has also been associated with this lecture. That was not a Sunday and pre-dates several references to the August 1929 start of the lecture series. From his comments in the preceding lecture, he apparently addressed ideas about "truth" to an audience sometime before this Sunday lecture.

As Cayce and the spiritual principles in his readings became more widely known—partly through these lectures—it would be natural for some people to assume that Cayce and his organization would use this "new" and hopeful information as the focus of a new religious or spiritual movement, perhaps with himself at the center. However, as quoted earlier, Cayce himself wrote: " . . . I made no attempt to found a new sect, or an ism, or a body of thought, or to have a following of any kind." This lecture may have been in response to—or in anticipation of—questions about such a movement and, ultimately, about which sect or spiritual movement really has "the truth."

Readers familiar with the spiritual philosophy in the readings will recognize the concept of the "spiritual ideal," although that term is not actually used in this lecture.

What Is Truth?

Sunday, November 24, 1929
Cayce Hospital

We have spoken on various subjects from Sunday to Sunday. From time to time, I have been speaking of the things that have had to do principally with the material things of life—or have to do with the material—putting them in such a way and manner that we may be able to use them in our everyday life.

As I have said, I am going to try to talk to you this afternoon about Truth—or "What Is Truth?" I realize I am assuming a big job. I've read very little of the philosophers of the ages. Yet we know that throughout the ages there has been the continual cry of *"What is Truth?"*

We often hear it said that Truth is evasive, Truth is naked, Truth will not be downed. But what is Truth?

If we turn to the books of the New Testament, we remember that possibly the greatest moment in history was when Pilate asked of the Master "What is truth?" *(see John 18:38)* Possibly that was the only time it could have been answered in one or two words that would have at least satisfied the greater portion of the thinking world today. But Pilate did not wait for the answer. Yet we know that the Master said He came that He might show the way unto Truth. All right. Then we know Truth is something that we may be shown.

When we speak of *a* truth, or *the* truth, or *Truth*, possibly we mean different things. You will remember, those of you who have read the little story of the three men of Hindustan who went to see the elephant, but all three men were blind. Now that's us—we are all blind! Yet we are seeking the truth, and we are very much in the same position as those three men who went to see the elephant. One of these stumbled against the side of the elephant and he said, "I perceive, without a doubt, the elephant is very like a wall." Wasn't that the truth to him? Another one, as he stumbled about, found the elephant's trunk and said, "I perceive with a certainty that the elephant is very like a tree." The third man, as he stumbled about, got hold of the tail and he said, "I perceive the elephant is very much like a rope."

Now were they in error? Did they have *the* truth? Or did they have only a portion of the truth? Did they have *any* of the truth?

We often say that any movement of any kind succeeds insofar as it has a portion of the truth. We may be sure *that's* truth. Then don't worry because you disagree with any individual as to what your conception of any movement may be. Don't think anyone is going to hell because he doesn't think as you do! Remember the three blind men who went to see the elephant! Just know that people may be right, but wrong as *you* would see it with your eyes wide open.

Life in its projection into this material plane has been a constant growth. Then if we are to believe the things that have been presented to us—and *as* they are presented to us—we know that even Truth itself may be a *growth into* that understanding which we will be able to apply in our everyday life.

I am sure we believe God is Love. Our love for a person, then, is an expression of the force—the manifested force—that we define as Love. Here was an experience that came to a man: He was very much in love with his wife. He thought more of her than anything in the world, but God saw fit to take her home. When the man erected a monument in the cemetery, he had this inscribed on it: *"The light of my life has gone out."* He couldn't find anything that could reconcile him about his separation.

After a while, he met a young lady he fell very much in love with. Then he found that he was altogether mistaken about his first love being able to satisfy everything in his life! There was something else that had been added—he had gained the knowledge of someone else being able to fill up a portion of his life. The young lady, knowing about this inscription, said to him, "I might consent to be your wife, but I don't think I could ever do that as long as the inscription remains as it is." So he went about to find a man who could correct this for him. When the man who had charge of such things told him he saw how he could rectify this inscription, the man went ahead with the wedding. When they came back from their honeymoon, they went out to see how the inscription read. This is what they found: *"The light of my life has gone out—*

but I've struck another match."

So you see there are individual experiences of truth. When we read or get an idea of some particular thought or some particular rule, we gradually build into our own selves an idea that we have gotten the *whole thing!*

Now is Truth such a thing that those who have been followers of Mohammed have *all of* the truth? Have those who have been the followers of Moses, the Lawgiver, all of the truth? Or hasn't it been, rather, a growth in our individual lives. And what may be truth for one individual may not, in the experience of another individual, answer at all? Does that make the other any less true for the other individual? Did this man love the second woman any less, from his experience of being in love before?

Then if this be true, it is possible that truth is a changeable thing, a growth. Will it be possible for us to find something of which we can say *"This is Truth"* and know that it will answer in everything or in every way that life may present itself to us?

I believe that we can. You may differ with me. I don't think, however, that you will be able to refute what will be my definition, or what I will be able to say is *Truth*. Many of you will say, "Well, have you been given some peculiar power that you have knowledge of what Truth is?" Let's see if this will not answer the whole question in our lives:

First, we must know that if we are to accept any word of any follower as a truth—or *the* truth, or *Truth*—we must be sure of the *authority* that we quote. We must be very sure of our foundation or platform for what we have assumed. Where would we begin, as we would say, in assuming something as being true?

We must recognize these facts in our lives: There is a physical body and there is a spiritual body. We know the physical body is dependent upon its physical attributes for its development. It is also the temple or the dwelling place of the spiritual body. The spiritual body, we know, is of the Creator—whatever we may call the Creator. It comes from the same thing, even if we go back to scientific reasoning and say it begins from the lowest form of life. Wherever we begin, we have to say there is something beyond that, where it has developed—whether you believe in evolution, creative evolution, or what not. All reasoning has to go back to the very same thing, and if I can answer this at all, I don't believe I'm wrong in saying that you can reason from any standpoint you want to take—but *this is Truth: that which, when kept before your mental mind and your spiritual mind, will continue to develop you upward!*

Now, let's see if this applies to any of the phases that may present themselves, and if it answers any of the questions you would want to ask: That which, held before your mental vision, will *continue* to develop you upward! Not that which satisfies selfish purpose, no! Not that which tells you whether it is wrong to go fishing on Sunday or not, or to play baseball on Sunday. Not that which answers such questions. It furnishes answers, yes—but that which will continue to develop you upward.

All right, then: What do we mean by developing upward? That which will enable you to hold the vision of what *you* worship as *your* God.

Every man, every individual, every object has its conception of its superior position. We would ask then, "Well, would it answer the Indian who is looking for his Happy Hunting Ground?" Why wouldn't it answer? That which will enable him to hold before him what *he* worships as *his* God is Truth to him.

Now, what have we assumed or taken for granted? We have taken for granted that man has a mind, that man has a body—a physical body and a spiritual body. He has a soul, if you please! His soul, or his spiritual body, is controlled by his subconscious or his spiritual mind. Whatever continues to hold before the individual that which he worships as his God will continue, then, to develop the individual *towards* that which he worships. Then you will say, "What would have been the Master's answer to Pilate's question?" Would it not be, "I came into the world to do no other than conduct you into that which is Truth."

Truth, then, is *not* a thing that we can see or perceive with the ears or body senses. But Truth is the *essence* with which an individual builds *faith, hope,* and *trust.* That is Truth, that essence which we are enabled to hold before our mental vision.

Will it build your body? *It will!* Will it heal the sick? *It will!*

A few days ago I was talking to some people who told me about a book that had been written by some of the masters from the Far East. [*May refer to a volume of Baird T. Spalding's series,* Life and Teachings of the Masters of the Far East, *reporting Spalding's travels to the Far East in 1894; first two volumes published in 1924 and 1927.]* I had never seen the book before, but when I opened it to read it, I knew what was in it before I read it. I don't know how nor why, but I knew the experiences I was going to encounter. Within the first four or five pages, I found that in this book one thought was stressed: What you hold before yourself—to create that image you worship—that is what will develop you always upward and will continue to enable you to know truth.

Truth then, being a growing thing—truth being a thing that will develop you—is a something that is *entirely in action!* That's what God is! For in every *movement* that has ever been, there has been a continual upward development—upward toward that which is Truth.

If you hold malice, you can become one of the meanest persons in the world. You know that if you continue to send out thought (which may become a miracle or a crime), you create those very same cross-currents in your own mind. What is prayer but simply attuning yourself to that through which you are seeking assistance? That's all prayer is—the attunement to that very same thing, and *that becomes Truth when it becomes an action.* When it goes into action, to you it becomes Truth. It's your own conception of what your God is. If it makes you better in relationship to the very thing you worship—if it makes you more in accord with what you worship—then that is what you become, whether it's downward or upward. You go whichever way your standard is set.

Now as to who is to say whether you are building up, or how near it brings you to what you worship as your God (because *God is Truth*): Whatever you continue to hold, you develop toward. Someone else whose God might be something else, wouldn't find this to be his Truth.

I've been studying a long while, trying to understand what is meant by the second commandment, and, until the other night, I never did understand what it meant—that is, satisfactorily, in my own mind. The first commandment, as we know, is "Thou shalt love the Lord thy God with all thy heart and thy mind." *(see Deut. 10:12; Matt. 22:37)* The second is "Thou shalt not make unto thee any graven image." *(see Exod. 20:4)*

Why not? Because if you make an image, it becomes your God. But if you have for your God that which is within your own individual self—you yourself being a portion of the Creator—you will continue to build upward to it!

During the Four Weeks Before the Lecture on "Man's Relationship to God" (Dec. 22, 1929) . . .

Around the world: The economic crisis and associated unemployment affect even more nations around the globe.

On December 20, Pope Pius XI issues an encyclical on the "Promotion of Spiritual Exercises." The message urges not only priests and lay leaders, but also the laity, to give personal spiritual practice a greater role in their lives. It emphasizes the need to "come apart from the world for a time" and "to make a retreat," reawakening the "spiritual exercises" first outlined by St. Francis of Loyola.

In the U.S.: Since its high on September 3, the stock market has lost 26 billion dollars in value.

In Virginia Beach: The Association of National Investigators (ANI) publishes the first issue of *The New Tomorrow* with Tom Sugrue's inspiring article on the history of the Cayce Hospital.

Following Dr. House's death in October, the Dayton osteopath treating him—Dr. Lyman Lydic—is persuaded to become head of the hospital in December. To their dismay, Cayce and Morton discover that Lydic does not appreciate or accept the information in Cayce's readings unless it agrees with his own professional recommendations. (He will be dismissed about nine months later.)

Patricia Devlin's role and presence increase: Reflecting Morton's concerns about hospital management, he brings her from his New York office to keep an eye on activities and finances at the hospital. She also helps Morton prepare his lectures at the hospital and, in fact, gives a lecture of her own in December 1929. She gives readings to the Blumenthal brothers, claiming the same source as Cayce. (She says she remembers the content of her readings.) In a reading from Cayce, Morton asks about the phenomenon apparently manifesting through her for them and receives a non-evaluative response from Cayce's Source.

In the meantime, Cayce's fundamental "work" continues. During the four weeks between these lectures, Cayce gives thirty-six readings—nine of them on December 2. The month's readings include: seven for patients at the Cayce Hospital; two for the Blumenthal brothers (mostly about their upcoming travel abroad and about Mrs. Devlin's "phenomena"); a physical reading for Cayce himself on stomach and abdominal concerns; a first reading on Atlantic University (regarding Dr. Brown as the proposed head); and a life reading for renowned musician Vincent Lopez (for whom Cayce reports incarnations in Atlantis, Egypt, and Greece).

About the lecture on "Man's Relationship to God": Cayce draws upon Old Testament figures like Noah, Abraham, and David to illustrate his understanding that man's relationship to God is a *personal* relationship. There is no indication that Cayce knew about the Pope's encyclical on spiritual practices, noted above. However, his emphasis on the *direct connection* we have with God contrasts with other views of our relationship with God through the *mediation* of Christ and his priests, and with *intercession* through Mary and the saints.

Man's Relationship to God

Sunday, December 22, 1929
Cayce Hospital

I am not going to try to explain your relationship to God. I am only hoping that I will be able to tell you something that will stimulate you to thought.

First, it is necessary that we review man's experience in the earth's plane—as far as we have a history of it. The broadest understanding that we can get is from the Scripture itself. I don't mean that I am going to preach any special theology, or even give you an idea of what I believe in the theology of the day or the theology of the past.

It doesn't matter what we may claim to believe. What is really worthwhile is what difference does what we believe make in our lives? What change or difference does a belief make when it comes into your life? That's the thing people are really interested in. The world doesn't care whether you believe the whale swallowed Jonah, or whether Noah was in the Ark a whole year or only forty days. What is an individual's belief in those things that have come into his life—those things that have changed his attitude toward his fellow man or towards his God? This is what is important.

If we take the history given in the Bible, we would begin with the first individual who we find had a concept of his relationship to God. Who would this first man be?

No, *not* Adam. For Adam's concept at first was his relationship to his mate—if we consider him just as an individual.

It is the seventh from Adam who we find had a different concept entirely. "Now Enoch walked with God and he was not, for God took him." (*Deut. 5:24*) *Enoch* was considered by the people of that day as a man with an *individuality*. Enoch was one who began to consider his relationship to his Creator—call Him what you will, whether the God of the First Cause, the God of nature, or the God of the divine. It changed that man's life.

The next man we find who comes down through history as one who had a definite religious experience is *Noah*. Now, Noah was a *just* man. He was a perfect man in his day and generation, but his experience changed his attitude—not only as to his relationship to what he worshipped as his God, but also as to his relationship to individuals around him—and it brought a different activity in his life.

Abraham is the next. His experience brought to the world a great change. He was called out to make of his seed and of his generation "a peculiar people"—a separate and distinct nation. He was an elderly man without offspring, yet God spoke to him and made him a great promise: "Now separate yourself from among these people and go out to a strange land which I will give to your seed forever as a heritage. I will make of you a peculiar people, and through your seed will all the nations of the earth be blessed." *(see Gen. 12:3; Acts 3:25)* Abraham harkened to that call.

In this very matter, there lies for most of us a great fault. Have any of us so lived that we were called to do a special thing? Have any of us so lived that we may be guided by that something from within that will direct us if we would but stop to harken to "the Voice"? We notice that when this call came to Abraham, he heard the call and knew it was not in him that the people were to be blessed, but in the way that he was to act towards his brethren. He was to separate himself from these for a peculiar service.

This idea has grown to seed. This is held against those very people. They separated themselves from others as a chosen people of God. It was to make a nation that Abraham was called, and through Abraham all nations should be blessed. Through the acts of this individual, through his understanding and response to the call, all people were to find happiness. But when these people began to make this promise an individual thing—that "I can sin because I am chosen"—they began to fall by the way.

Next we come to *Jacob*. When the day came for him to be taken to his fathers, he called about him his twelve sons and explained to each his faults and virtues. He showed them what each, through his concept of his relationship to Jehovah, had built and was building—and what it would come to in their lives. All that he told them came to pass.

The next in line is *Moses*, who was raised up to be a deliverer of his people. Abraham had been told that his seed would be in bondage for four hundred years, and then one would be raised up who would lead them back to this promised land which he himself was not allowed to possess, but which would become the land of his people. For He would remain to them a God if they would remain to Him a people. There is something that man must do, as well as something that the Creator must do. There is a purpose in life—it is not a haphazard thing.

Now we come down to the days when the Jews went out to the promised land. As they wandered through the wilderness, they began to think about their own personal relationship to God. They forgot all the hardships through which they had passed in Egypt. Human nature has always been—and will always be—just the same. As we pass through life, we feel that the present is about the hardest time we have ever had, but after a few years have passed, we begin to look back on those things and see only what has come out of this. Why does this happen? There *is* a reason.

When the people murmured and asked that they might have a physical God, that they might see something that was tangible, they cried to Moses: "You speak of the spirit and you are able to go up on the mountain and bring us wonderful messages, but we don't see Him—we don't hear Him. We hear only those things that you come back and tell us. We have seen the pillar of fire by night and the cloud by day—but these have become everyday matters. We expect these. Now we want to do things that other people do. We want a God like they have." They had forgotten they were called out to be a separate and distinct nation. They had forgotten the call that had come to their forefathers, and the heritage they were about to claim.

Throughout all of this, Moses maintained his faith and upheld the God he had come to know through personal experience. He had heard the call from within. God to him had become a personal God For the people who fought among themselves at the foot of the mountains, God was still the God of war—the God with the big stick who beat off their enemies, but would turn on *them* if they went too far.

Can't we get his idea? *God is a personal God!* He is not a God of war or a God of plenty, nor even a God of an individual. *He is a God of all!* He is in all things, and our heritage is in Him. We may illustrate this: Just as the earthly parent feels in respect to his own children, so may we in our own selves conceive of *something* that God may feel—must feel—about His children, His people here in this world.

It is His purpose that we make ourselves a channel through which His spirit may manifest. He would use us.

We may be the channel through which the other fellow, less fortunate than we, may be aided in whatever is needed for him to gain a better conception of his relationship to His God.

It would be well if we could all remember the decision of the great Jewish leader who said, "Others may do as they may, but for me and my house, we will worship the living God." *(see Josh. 24:15)* Daily we are confronted with problems that require just such a definite stand. Let us remember His promise and be strong.

We may now trace the history of the Jews on down to the time when the first king was chosen. *Saul* was raised up to be their king and leader, yet he failed to understand that the time had come when the people had developed to the point where God did not desire a sacrifice of animals to His cause, but of individuals.

David was the next in line and, despite the fact that he did many things that we today call sins, we may learn many lessons from his attitude toward his God. Saul tried many times to kill him, yet always David said, "It is not meet that I should raise mine hand against an anointed of the Lord." *(see 1 Sam. 24:6)* It is not right that one individual should raise his voice against another individual who is doing his service in the manner he feels God has spoken to him.

Finally there comes the last rise to power. The Jewish nation came under *King Solomon*, David's son, one of the greatest of the time. After the beautiful temple had been built and prosperity came to the nation, the people began to forget their relationship to God; and led by the king, they turned to the worship of the physical pleasures of the world. Their fall is near. The period of the prophets follows. Individuals arose who had a vision of what the relationship to God should be, but the people would not listen to them, and the Jews were torn apart as a nation and scattered to the four winds.

This question has come down to every age, to every individual: *What is your relationship to your God?* It came to Enoch, to Noah, to Abraham, to

Jacob, to Moses, to Joshua, to Saul, to David, to Solomon—and it comes just the same to you today. What is your relationship to Him? Remember that He is the God of the Living, not of the dead. Remember that in serving Him you must serve your fellow man—that you must become a channel through which God may work His divine will here on earth.

When the burdens become hard to bear and you feel yourself beginning to slip away from the path you know is right, draw nearer to your God, and He will draw nearer to you. As a child will come and sit at the feet of its parents—seeking their guidance and advice, asking their help—just so must we, through prayer, approach the God who is our Father and Creator.

Now in coming to know Him, is it not evident that, as we consider and help our fellow man, so do we carry out God's work? Our relationship to our God then becomes our relationship to our brother. There is nothing that we can do for God, but there is much that we can do for His children, His created creatures, our brothers. As we go about our everyday work, let us remember to lend a helping hand wherever we may—and know that in so doing, we are fulfilling the Will of the Creator, and coming ever nearer to our God.

During the Fifty Weeks Before the Lecture "Astrology: Science or Myth" (Dec. 7, 1930). . .

Note: No records exist regarding lectures during this long period.

Around the world: Gandhi begins a civil disobedience campaign against British rule of India by leading a 165-mile march to the sea to extract salt (contrary to British law). He is arrested and imprisoned.

In accordance with the Peace Treaty of Versailles after World War I, the U.S. finally withdraws its troops from the German Rhineland and Saar. Meanwhile, Hitler's Nazi Party wins ninety-five seats in the German Reichstag. Delegates arrive in uniform, in violation of parliamentary rules. Hitler advocates scrapping the Versailles Treaty, and Italy's Premier, Benito Mussolini, demand revisions to the treaty. In the U.S.S.R., Joseph Stalin consolidates his supporters, justifying the exile and imprisonment of thousands of party members who have supported Trotsky.

In Great Britain, Sir Arthur Conan Doyle dies, having finally discontinued writing about Sherlock Holmes to give his full attention to spiritualism. (In 1926, he had published *The History of Spiritualism.*)

In the U.S.: Scientists in Arizona discover a ninth planet in our solar system and name it Pluto. Earlier, Edwin Powell Hubble discovered that distant galaxies are moving away from the Milky Way galaxy, implying that the universe is expanding—a fact many astronomers consider the most significant achievement of the twentieth century. A New York scientist predicts that man will reach the moon by the year 2050.

In August, police battle Communist protesters in Union Square in New York, and in early December, 500 Communist protesters are dispersed from the Capital with tear gas. The U.S. Marines are still trying to control protesters in Nicaragua. Douglas MacArthur is appointed Army Chief of Staff.

In Virginia Beach: Although they declare themselves financially stretched after the stock market crash, in April the Blumenthals commit to donating three thousand dollars a month for the hospital and five thousand a month for the university.

While the Blumenthals are away on an extensive European tour, Morton appoints Patricia Devlin as manager of the hospital. On their return, she reports to Morton that Cayce is taking them for a "financial ride." Cayce admits to not being much of a business manager.

In the meantime, Hugh Lynn Cayce graduates from college and approaches David Kahn for a job. Morton counters this with an offer to Hugh Lynn to become the librarian of the new Atlantic University, and Hugh Lynn accepts.

The Blumenthals both have their last readings from Cayce—physical readings—on July 4, 1930. They may now be getting readings regularly from Patricia Devlin.

Atlantic University opens in September in temporary quarters in two hotels, offering preparatory courses for a bachelor's degree in the arts or sciences. Edgar Cayce and others close to him felt the university should be started slowly, but since Morton was funding it, buying land for it, and planning it, "it was done as he thought best" (reports Cayce in his memoirs).

Conflict continues to escalate between the Blumenthals and David Kahn, with Edgar Cayce in the middle. Learning that Kahn made his contributions to the hospital operation directly to Cayce, Morton demands Cayce discontinue readings for Kahn, at which Cayce exhibits a rare show of anger toward Morton. Morton orders a reduction in the number of both staff and patients at the hospital. The interpersonal relationships among the key players in this drama are at their lowest point ever, a sign of even more of a crisis in the near future.

Noteworthy among Cayce's 778 readings over this fifty-week period:

- Cayce gives over two hundred readings for patients at the hospital. Every Monday, check readings are given for patients. In his memoirs, Cayce says the "Cayce Hospital of Research and Enlightenment" had ten patients in residence in October and eleven out-patients. At the end of one of the Monday check reading series is the spontaneous comment by the sleeping Cayce, "There's a lot of 'em wants 'em." In her notes, Gladys suggests: "Apparently EC was referring to appointments way in advance, or else people clamoring for appointments who had not yet been given a specific date." Nearly a hundred people were waiting for readings.

• Edgar Cayce's father, L.B. Cayce, who has come to work at the hospital, is told in a physical reading that he should become a patient in the hospital, and he takes that advice.

• As noted earlier, the Blumenthals have their last readings from Cayce in midyear. Between them, they have had exactly 600 readings from Cayce over the previous six years—and have requested many more on behalf of their families and friends.

• Tim Brown has another reading on his work on the Stansell motor, and one on his draft article on "Positive and Negative Force."

• Just before the September Board meeting called by Morton, a "work reading" is requested by Edgar, Hugh Lynn, and Gertrude Cayce; David and Lucille Kahn; and Gladys Davis, seeking information in preparation for the meeting. Cayce's Source identifies the "extravagant expenditure" by Edgar Cayce as the cause of the present discord. This is the subject of heated discussion in the subsequent meetings.

About the lecture on "Astrology: Science or Myth?": A significant portion of the lecture that follows is quoted directly from one of the 1923 "Lammers readings" on spiritual and metaphysical topics (the 3744 series). Early in the lecture, Cayce gives special mention to Claudius Ptolemaeus (often referred to as Ptolemy), a second century astronomer. He also mentions Galileo Galilei—renowned astronomer, mathematician, and physicist of the sixteenth and seventeenth centuries—and the lesser-known William Herschel—an eighteenth century British designer of telescopes, who discovered the planet Uranus with his home telescope (which discovery, by the way, helped double the known size of the solar system).

Astrology: Science or Myth?
Sunday, December 7, 1930
Cayce Hospital

The work in which I have been engaged for the last thirty years, or the information which has come through me, has touched on a great many phases of human experience. Astrology is one of them.

Astrology is one of the oldest sciences in existence. The ancient Egyptians and Persians were possibly better versed on the subject than any of our modern astrologers. Claudius Ptolemaeus, who wrote his treatise on astrology about two thousand years ago, is still considered an authority today. Although he and all his people at the time believed that the earth was flat, that the earth stood still, and that everything else moved around it, he set out the formulas for the study of the influence from the position of the stars. We practice every day many of the rules laid down by Ptolemaeus without recognizing the fact. We wouldn't know how to get along without him.

When Galileo, Herschel, and others began to know and teach that the earth was only one of the planets in our solar system, that the earth moved with the other planets about the sun, and that the earth was round, etc., naturally people began to question and to doubt. Many of the astrologers then were gradually cast into the discard, for they used such knowledge to tell fortunes and to obtain a little money here and there from individuals. We can understand, then, how astrological influences may be "evil spoken of." However, I am assured of the fact that we may gain much by the proper study of astrology.

In the first chapter of Genesis, it is said that the sun, the moon, and the stars were for the seasons and the years and "for signs" to the people. (*see Gen. 1:14*) When the children of Israel were being persecuted by the peoples roundabout after entering the Promised Land, Deborah—their prophetess and judge—in her song of praise for having been able to overcome the Canaanites, makes mention of this: "They fought from heaven; the stars in their courses fought against Sisera," the man who was subdued. *(Judges 5:20)*

In the book of Job, which must have been written thousands of years before the book of Genesis—and not even in the same part of the country—we find the first mention of the Pleiades, Orion, and Arcturus. It is given there, as God Himself speaking to Job, "Canst thou bind the sweet influences of Pleiades, or loose the bands of Orion? Canst thou bring forth Mazzaroth in his season? or canst thou guide Arcturus with his sons?" *(Job 38:31-32)*

I cannot help but feel that at least the people who wrote that book believed there was something to astrology. There is the same reference in Isaiah, Daniel, and Amos. *(see Amos 5:8, for example)* Also in the New Testament, we remember the story of the three wise men who came from the east to Jerusalem, saying "Where is he that is born King of the Jews? for we have seen his star in the east and are come to worship him." *(Matt. 2:1-2)*

Did those people of long ago understand more about these things than we do today? Or is it all just a myth? Did they understand that the earth was round, that it was just a portion of the whole great universe? Or were they as the people who put up the altar "To The Unknown God," and to whom Paul said, "Ye in your ignorance worship him that I declare unto you"? *(see Acts 17:23)*

In their seeking for God, and in their seeking for that of which the Psalmist spoke, "The heavens declare the glory of God; and the firmament sheweth his handywork" *(Ps. 19:1)*, did these people find that there were influences in our lives which we do not yet understand?

In 1923, I was asked by a group of individuals to present questions in readings (as we call them) on various subjects, and see just what would be given. I will give here some of the questions and the answers that were obtained regarding astrology *(see 3744-4 for complete reading)*:

(Question) Please give a definition of the word astrology.
(Answer) That position in space about our own earth that is under the control of the forces that are within the sphere of that control, and all other spheres without that control. That is astrology, the study of those conditions.

In the beginning, our own plane, the earth, was set in motion.

The planning of other planets began the ruling of the destiny of all matters as created, just as the division of waters was ruled and is ruled by the moon in its path about the earth; just so as the higher creation as it begun is ruled by its action in conjunction with the planets about the earth. The strongest force used in the destiny of man is the sun first, then the closer planets to the earth, or those that are coming to ascension at the time of the birth of the individual, but let it be understood here, no action of any planet or the phases of the sun, the moon or any of the heavenly bodies surpass the rule of man's will power, the power given by the Creator of man, in the beginning, when he became a living soul with the power of choosing for himself. The inclinations of man are ruled by the planets under which he is born, for the destiny of man lies within the sphere or scope of the planets.

(Q) Do the planets have an effect on the life of every individual born?

(A) They have. Just as this earth's forces were set in motion, and about it, those forces that govern the elements, elementary so, of the earth's sphere or plane, and as each comes under the influence of those conditions, the influence is to the individual without regards to the will, which is the developing factor of man, in which such is expressed through the breath of the Creator, and as one's plane of existence is lived out from one sphere to another they come under the influence of those to which it passes from time to time.

In the sphere of many of the planets within the same solar system, we find they are banished to certain conditions in developing about the spheres from which they pass, and again and again and again return from one to another until they are prepared to meet the everlasting Creator of our entire Universe, of which our system is only a very small part. (See 900-25, Par. 3-A)

Be not dismayed [deceived]; God is not mocked; "Whatsoever a man soweth that shall he also reap." (Gal. 6:7)

In the various spheres, then, through which he must pass to

attain that which will fit him for the conditions to enter in, and become a part of that Creator, just as an individual is a part of the creation now. In this manner we see there is the influence of the planets upon an individual, for all must come under that influence, though one may pass from one plane to another without going through all stages of the condition, for only upon the earth plane at present do we find man is flesh and blood, but upon others do we find those of his own making in the preparation of his own development.

As given, "The heavens declare the glory of God, and the firmament sheweth His handyworks. Day unto day uttereth speech, night unto night sheweth knowledge." This from the beginning and unto the end. (Ps. 19:1-2)

Just in that manner is the way shown how man may escape from all of the fiery darts of the wicked one, for it is self, and selfishness, that would damn the individual soul unto one or the other of those forces that bring about the change that must be in those that willfully wrong his Maker. It is not that which man does or leaves undone, but rather that indifference toward the creation that makes or loses for the individual entity. Then, let's be up and doing—doing—"be ye doers [of the word], and not hearers only." (Jas. 1:22) . . .

(Q) Is it proper for us to study the effects of the planets on our lives in order to better understand our tendencies and inclinations, as influenced by the planets?

(A) When studied aright, very, very, very much so. How aright then? In that influence as is seen in the influence of the knowledge already obtained by mortal man. Give more of that into the lives, giving the understanding that the will must be the ever guiding factor to lead man on, ever upward.

(Q) In what way should astrology be used to help man live better in the present physical plane?

(A) In that which the position of the planets give the tendencies in a given life, without reference to the will. Then let man, the individual, understand how will may overcome, for we all must overcome, if we would, in any wise, enter in. Not that the position gives man the transport, but that that force as manifested in the creation of man wherein choice between the good and evil, exercising highest will force, may be manifested the greater in man. Do that.   3744-4

So, in pondering over these things, I have come to believe that through understanding ourselves as individuals, we are better able to understand our relationships to our fellow man and to our Creator. The application of any truth must be an experience in our individual lives, for God is not even God to us unless he is our personal God or personal Savior. It doesn't matter how many people He may have destroyed or saved: Unless we can become conscious of the indwelling of the Creative Energy within our own selves, we cannot know God or the Savior to be ours. I don't believe anyone can prove otherwise.

Let us take stock, then, of ourselves as to whether we—in our own little sphere—have anything to do with the great number of stars or planets. Have we a part in their ruling? Are we a part of this whole universe? If we carry within us the spirit of God, who is the Creator of all things, are we not part and parcel of the Whole?

Then, are we doing our bit to keep it running properly? That's what I would like for us to ask ourselves. Let's not any one of us think when we have one truth that we have all the truth, for the same God that made the atom also made Arcturus and all the suns. The same God that made the sparrow made man in the beginning—and we are one—our lives are one. No matter how we may conceive of the hereafter, it must be a continuity of life—take it however we will or may. If we can get an understanding of the relationship of all this into one—One Great Whole—it will be worth our while.

All power was given Christ when He overcame the world. How close are we to Christ? Then we know how close we are to the Creator.

During the Two Weeks Before the Lecture on "The Subconscious Mind" (Dec. 21, 1930) . . .

Around the world: The Nobel Peace Prize for 1930 is awarded to Sweden's Lars Olof Jonathan Söderblom, known as the "architect of the ecumenical movement of the twentieth century." Söderblom pursued the theme of the uniqueness of Christianity in the historical and personal character of Revelation, incorporating the study of non-Christian religions into the discipline of Christianity. He emphasized the need for reconciling the competing philosophies of subjective spirituality and objective social action, and sought to find such unity as a road to world peace.

Sinclair Lewis, whose books make him the "enemy of middle-class complacency," wins the 1930 Nobel Prize for Literature—the first American to win this prestigious award.

In Virginia Beach: The final crisis is reached between those supporting the views of the Blumenthals and those supporting the views of Edgar Cayce with regard to the hospital, the work, and the financial situation. In a meeting at the nurses' quarters across the street from the hospital, Morton reviews the $10,000 in current debts and asks that the ANI board turn over the hospital property and assets directly to him. He is voted down, loses his temper, and threatens to close the hospital. Edgar Cayce's voice of moderation speaks: "Morton has given the property and if he needs it, we should turn it back to him." A second vote gives Morton the property. Morton bars patients from returning again if they leave the hospital for the Christmas holiday. The end of the hospital is very near.

Of the sixteen readings given during these two weeks, five are life readings (a higher proportion than usual), and one is a check physical reading at the hospital.

Of special interest is the second reading in a series on "buried treasure" given during these two weeks: In March 1929, a reading was requested by A.C. Preston concerning "the information given through these sources some years ago regarding the money lost by the Federal Troops near Washington, D. C." [near Kelly's Ford in Culpepper County, Virginia]. The December 1930 reading supplements prior information and verifies the activities underway to locate the "treasure". (Hugh Lynn Cayce plays a major role in this activity, which will continue for some time.)

About the lecture on "Subconscious Mind": This lecture may have also been given earlier this year to a public audience at the Arlington Hotel in Washington, D.C. (January 12, 1930). Furthermore, on Friday, January 23, 1931, Cayce gives a similar lecture to another audience on levels and aspects of the mind. The records are not clear about the place or the audience. In that later version, Cayce attempts to clarify the levels of consciousness by using a new term, apparently of his own creation: *the inter-conscious mind.* At the end of the transcript of the following lecture is a brief segment of the version using the new term.

The Subconscious Mind

Sunday, December 21, 1930
Cayce Hospital

In stating the premise on which I shall base this discussion, let me draw from the psychic data we have on this subject. "The subconscious mind is the mind of the soul." (*see reading 900-147*) It partakes of both the spiritual and physical consciousness.

What is *mind*? In our physical consciousness, we define it as that "something" with which we reason. We would divide the mind into three phases: the physical or *conscious* mind, the mental or *subconscious* mind, and the spiritual or *superconscious* mind. Our question, then, must be, "Where does one end and the next begin? How do these various parts of the mind function in an individual?"

We must not confuse the terms *unconscious* and *subconscious*. The *unconscious* mind is but a deeper portion of our *conscious* thinking through which the *subconscious* operates in the physical, and acts upon and affects the *conscious* mind.

This may be understood by considering how *habit* is formed. Habit is the arousing of something within our individual being that becomes conscious of a desire to satisfy that which has been building in the physical body. Every cell in our bodies is endowed with all the consciousness with which our physical body is endowed or with which the mind is endowed. In forming a habit, we create within each cell a desire that must be gratified, or the whole body suffers. While the expression of this desire becomes apparent in the physical, it has its beginning in the subconscious forces. The subconscious mind takes hold of everything that comes into the body and, wherever one of the senses is able to magnify it, it gathers in and feeds into every atom of our system, finding lodgment in various portions of the system, governed by that part from which it entered. *Mind is ever the builder.*

The *conscious* mind may be more clearly understood if considered in this manner: We are conscious of being here—being present. We know just what we see about us. We are conscious of conditions that existed in the past about us. How? By *comparison sense*—by the manner in which knowledge of these things reached our physical consciousness through the five senses. As long as we become conscious of any condition by sense comparison, it is our physical consciousness.

Thus with our physical bodies, we have physical consciousness. We know that, by cutting off certain portions of the body containing nerve centers, we can deaden or relieve other portions of the body of any sense of pain. The nerve is the contact between these parts. The action of drugs on a physical body is slightly different. Here again some part of the body may be desensitized, but the activity of the mind is increased. An individual under the influence of morphine, for example, may have the most beautiful visions, and the most fanciful experiences can be imagined. Many great artists in various fields have worked under such influences. In attempting to awaken something within themselves, through escaping from the surroundings of the physical, they arouse a portion of that something that is akin to the Creative Forces. That is, they awaken the subconscious mind upon which is registered the activities of the soul just as there is impressed upon the physical mind the activities of the physical body. As these impressions flow into the conscious mind, they at times become distorted and twisted by their contact with the crude physical operations of the conscious mind. Remember that conscious reasoning must *compare*—it must compare a thing with something it can feel, taste, touch, see, or hear. It must bring a given condition into its own surroundings where it can measure it, and where its various dimensions may be taken.

Did you ever see a sorter for pecans? Nuts of different sizes fall into different places. The physical mind operates in something of the same manner. Certain objects with which it comes in contact continually fall into established channels of associations, and thus habits are formed.

Perhaps you think that, if you do anything *un*consciously, you do it *sub*consciously. This isn't always true. We can fool our conscious mind. We can also fool ourselves into believing that we are reasoning from a *sub*conscious standpoint. Our physical consciousness can know nothing save by comparing it with something else. Once out of this realm, it loses its hold, and we say any given condition becomes unreasonable.

In bringing the physical consciousness and the subconscious mind into closer relationship, let us consider the difference in the consciousness of a flower, an animal, and a man:

The *flower* has all the spirit force man has, for it is made by nature—by the activity of the Creative Forces in the material world—by God. It is capable of doing that which man cannot do—stand still and take from the soil and from the air about it that which it requires to manifest its consciousness and fulfill its purpose. This performance of its duty is its highest consciousness, and it always does the very best it can with what it is given to work with by man or by God.

An *animal* is endowed with many of the physical attributes of man. It can move from place to place in order to seek that which will sustain its physical organism. There is developed a certain amount of ability to select and choose its surroundings, but there is only evidence of a physical consciousness seeking to express itself as itself.

Man alone is given a soul, with an attribute of a *sub*conscious mind that may enable him to know himself to be a portion of the whole, with the ability to make himself *one* with the whole, yet not the whole. (*see, e.g., Cayce reading 900-233*) Man alone has the *will* to choose for himself that activity that will either take him *toward* or *away from* his Creator. This *will* becomes active in the conscious and subconscious minds. In one, it brings the ability to reason both inductively and deductively, and in the other, the ability to transcend reason and know, even as it is known. It is through *mind* that the Creative Forces seek activity, whether in a lowly organism seeking to express itself, or in man seeking God or making a kingdom of his own.

Just what happens when illness comes in a physical body? When a cold germ enters a body in the manifestation of its consciousness, it becomes destructive to the welfare of a more highly organized body. If man will hold that consciousness which prevents the germ taking hold, it cannot harm him. Does a germ take hold first on the physical consciousness or the subconscious? As it is the consciousness of the germ that drives it to its activity, so with man it is the mind—the conscious and subconscious activity—that can protect. At times, the mind can work wonders—at other times it is necessary for us, in our state of weakened activity of the mind, to resort to another consciousness from without, which we call medicine.

If you believe that you have only a physical consciousness—that you must see, hear, feel, taste, or touch in order to understand—and if you refuse to accept any result not obtained through those senses, then you have lost the power to realize that there is another consciousness, which is of the soul and therefore much higher in development. That is the very thing that the Master promised He would make possible within human experience, by passing through the world and yet being present with God Himself. That He would bring to our consciousness that necessary to meet the needs of whatever might arise in our lives, if we would raise our consciousness to be *one* with that same power which is within and a portion of our own selves.

As we return to the relation of the subconscious mind and the superconscious, let us ask ourselves these questions: "Which are the most powerful influences in our lives—the physical or the spiritual? Which is building our bodies—the physical consciousness that must be gratified by the things of the world from without, or the subconscious which is endowed with all that we have developed through the ages?" We must remember that the subconscious is subject to both the action of the spiritual forces through the superconscious mind, as well as the action of the physical mind. The superconscious mind may well be called that part of the God-Mind that is in each and every entity that seeks, to make it desire to become fully conscious of its higher activity, its highest consciousness that brings a oneness with God.

The spirit is ever present and ever willing that we be able to meet every condition in our lives. It is the flesh that is weak! Let us be careful that we do not build into our consciousness those impressions that will hinder and limit the action of the superconscious forces. We may come to depend so wholly upon that which has been built from without that we become conscious that we enjoy poor health! As we become so closed that we seek only the gratification of the physical desires and habits we have built, we draw the soul away from the Creator.

As the subconscious mind is the mind of the soul, those who have passed into the Beyond certainly have not lost their consciousness. They have lost their *physical* consciousness, but not their *sub*consciousness. We can therefore readily understand by reasoning how one might truly be in torment if he had lived to gratify the desires of a physical consciousness that partook wholly of the carnal forces of earth and found nothing with which to satisfy those desires.

That which one contemplates, that one builds within self. If we have allowed something to interfere with our spiritual consciousness—or to put it another way, if we have over-emphasized the physical consciousness and have neglected the spiritual development—we prepare the way for pain and suffering in the physical. It is through the *sub*conscious activity in cooperation with the *super*conscious forces that one may be able to overcome the physical ills in the body and, yes, prevent disease. When we can put our whole trust in the Source from which all help comes, we can say as did the Master, "Is it easier to say to the sick of the palsy, 'Thy sins be forgiven thee', or to say, 'Arise, and take up thy bed and walk'?" (*Mark 2:9*) It is a sin for a man to be sick. It is a sin.

Let us consider just a few simple examples of the working of the subconscious mind. Were you ever in the position where your home was burning down, where everything of this world's goods you possessed was being destroyed before your eyes, where you had to do some physical deed which seemed impossible for you to do, and the strength and power was given you to do it? That is from the subconscious, the inner self, following the law of self-preservation. Many a man has risen to an occasion that required more strength than he possessed, more than thought of self. What was it? The subconscious self rising to meet the needs to that built within self.

A hypnotized man may be able to do all sorts of ridiculous things, yet he cannot be made to do that which is against his moral code. Why? His subconscious self rebels against doing that which it has been trained not to do and that upon which the action of the superconscious forces have been brought to bear. This is purely an action of the subconscious mind. Though his will is controlled, and he is not even conscious of what he is doing, the superconscious mind protects him through the action which it has had upon the subconscious.

We often have what we call hunches, intuitions, premonitions. They are indescribable, unexplainable, as to why we have them or from whence they come. If we believe in reincarnation, we might say they come from one of our former selves. If we study along other lines, we might say our guardian angel is behind us and directing us. It is a force within our own inner self that guards and protects us. This premonition, however, may be wrong. How? When we have fooled our subconscious—when there is too much of the conscious mind mixed with it. More often it is right, for it marks a flash in the thinking of the inner self.

This is especially true among women. And why women more than men? Because men think such hunches are effeminate, that's why. Is it any more effeminate for a man to be close to God than it is for a woman? It has been a consciousness—a portion of self that has been built—to think of such things as being old women's fancies, or something of which to be ashamed. Man builds the barrier himself that prevents him from receiving guidance from within.

We all remember the story of the first king of Israel who was "a choice young man" and "there was not among the children of Israel a goodlier person than he, from his shoulders and upward he was higher than any of the people." (see 1 Sam. 9:2) When Saul was anointed it was said that God spoke to him often through vision or through Urim and Thummin, and Saul harkened unto these visions. (see 1 Sam. 28:6) As long as he listened to that consciousness from within, he was guided by the Divine. But there came a time in Saul's life when God no longer spoke to him, either through dreams, through vision, or through Urim or Thummin. He was at a loss to know what to do with his life. What had come about? He had been told to go down and utterly destroy a certain people. It was a period when there was a required sacrifice of certain animals and the choicest were always given. In this land which Saul was to destroy, he found the most beautiful cattle, sheep, oxen. These he saved, but destroyed all that was vile and ugly. He stilled his conscience by saying that God should have the best for the sacrifice. But God spoke through Samuel, saying, "It repenteth me that I have set up Saul to be king, for he is turned back from following me, and hath not performed my commandments." (1 Sam. 15:11)

When Saul returned, he said to Samuel, "Blessed be thou of the Lord, I have performed the commandment of the Lord." Samuel answered, "What meaneth then this bleating of sheep in mine ears, and the lowing of the oxen which I hear?" Then Saul replied, "The people spared the best of the sheep and of the oxen to sacrifice unto the Lord thy God; and the rest we have utterly destroyed." Thereupon Samuel said, "Hath the Lord as great delight in burnt offerings and sacrifices, as in obeying the voice of the Lord? Behold, to obey is better than sacrifice, and to hearken than the fat of rams. For rebellion is as the sin of witchcraft, and stubbornness is as iniquity and idolatry. Because thou hast rejected the word of the Lord, He hath rejected thee from being king." (see 1 Sam. 15:13-15; 22-23)

If we are going to tell God how to do His work, instead of carrying out His command, we may know that we are using our physical consciousness, that we are not listening to the spirit from within. Saul was forced from this time on to rely on his poor weak self. Yet when he was first called, he was a man not of an exalted position, but just one among his brethren who was willing to be led by the spirit from within, who relied upon those voices from within—call them intuitive forces, visions, spirits, or whatever you may. They really mean the same thing.

It is that something within us endowed with power from on High that really gives us being, that makes us above every other creature in this world. It is a soul that is seeking its way back to its Maker. Whether we carry it back or not, that is up to us. Our soul is ours and our will is ours.

God is ever willing. As he has said, "If ye will be my people, I will be your God, but if you have turned your back on me, I have turned my back upon you." (see Levit. 26:12ff) "For this commandment which I command thee this day is not hidden from thee, neither is it far off. It is not in heaven, that thou shouldst say, 'Who shall go for us to heaven and bring it unto us, that we may hear it, and do it?' Neither is it beyond the sea, that thou shouldst say, 'Who shall go over the sea for us and bring it unto us, that we may hear it, and do it?' But the word is very nigh unto thee, in thy mouth, and in thy heart, that thou mayest do it." (see Deut. 30:11-14)

Can it be within our physical consciousness? No, for that partakes of the material things, such as "What will tomorrow bring forth? What will so-and-so think about this or that?" It is that portion of us which partakes of God Himself, for His Spirit beareth witness with our spirit, and our soul's companion is the Spirit of God Himself. It is that gift from

God which makes us master over all, if we will but allow it to guide and direct and mold our subconscious. Simon said to Peter, "Give me also this power, that on whomsoever I lay my hands, he may receive the Holy Ghost," but Peter answered him, "Thy money perish with thee because thou hast thought that the gift of God may be purchased with money." (see Acts 8:19-20) It is something that cannot be bought, for "The silver is mine and the gold is mine, saith the Lord of hosts." (see Haggai 2:8)

Peter later says for himself, "Silver and gold have I none, but such as I have give I thee." (see Acts 3:6) How fine it would be if we could all take this attitude, if we could but learn to allow the subconscious forces to guide us and direct us through the subconscious to make ourselves one with the Divine Will! It is the heritage of each soul—not only the *right*, but the *will*—to accomplish the Divine purpose. The way lies through understanding and using the guidance that comes through the subconscious from the superconscious forces.

To every one of you comes the question, "How may I develop this? How may I know and understand the guidance of the higher forces?" The following question was asked in a reading:

Question: How can we best develop our subconscious minds to be of the most benefit to our fellow men while in the physical plane of living?

The answer might be summarized in this: "Use what thou hast in hand." It came in this form:

Answer: By developing the mental or physical mind toward the uplift of mankind toward the Maker, leaving those things behind that so easily beset the physical body. By the training of the mental, through physical force, the subconscious urge, as we have given, the faculty of doing in the right or direct way, and lending assistance to the uplift of all.

The thought held against an individual directs the mind either of masses or classes, whether toward good or bad. Thought is reached through the physical forces, and by becoming a part of the physical or conscious mind either lends the strength of subconscious forces or allows the subconscious to direct. Not that the physical mind gives strength, but by allowing the subconscious to direct, and not building the barrier between to be overcome.

That to be overcome might as well be met in this plane, for it will have to be met before we can gain the entrance to the Holy of Holies. This is the manner in which to train or conduct the physical to lend the assistance to the subconscious forces to direct and give the help the world or populace needs.   3744-2

In attempting to develop our subconscious faculties, let us remember this: The forces of the superconscious mind are ever trying to assist through the subconscious. It is not that we must seek with our physical minds (which are so limited and incapable) the entrance to the subconscious, but that we so think that we do not build a barrier of material desires against which the subconscious will have to fight.

In plainer terms, "The kingdom of God is within you." Do not seek it outside of yourself.

[Below is a segment of the subsequent lecture introducing the new term, *inter-conscious mind*:]

There is nothing so confusing as tangled concepts resulting from misunderstood terms. When I use the word "subconscious," you turn back to certain explanations you have read, lectures you have heard, or studies you have made, and then you formulate a basis upon which you judge all further remarks on this subject. If in the course of my discussion I use expressions that do not coincide with your preconceived ideas, a conflict ensues regardless of how hard you may desire to understand.

Mind is the creative, building force of the universe. It is a stream, not a series of lakes. It is a moving, vital force which at one and the same time comes from and is the Creator. As we break this force up into *conscious, subconscious, unconscious,* and *superconscious,* we are like men standing at different points on the bank of the same river. We observe

the same stream, but in a different setting and having to do with different activities.

In order to avoid confusion, I have selected a term for this discourse
which may be explained without becoming too greatly entangled in
the more common ideas of various phases of the mind. Let us consider
the *inter-conscious mind* as the mind of the soul–entity, partaking of both
physical and spiritual consciousness, existing in both the physical and
spiritual realm. This is the mind that gathers the bits of experience that
constitute the complete entity. It is the core about which the thread of
the soul–entity is being wound. While the soul–entity inhabits a physical body, this mind finds expression at times through what we call the
conscious (physical) mind. As it evolves in other realms, it gives way to
the activity of the *superconscious* (spiritual) mind . . .

[Note: The reader can probably see what Cayce was trying to do to
clarify the language. The term "inter-conscious" never appears in the
readings themselves, and no other use of the term has been identified
in the files except in a background note for one of the Lammers metaphysical readings (3744-2). There "interconscious" is explained as "EC's
contacts with the universal forces"–a meaning different from Cayce's
use in this lecture.]

During the Four Weeks Before the Lecture on "Dreams" (Jan. 18, 1931)...

Around the world and in the U.S.: As of the end of 1930, there are four million unemployed in the U.S. and millions more in Europe and around the world. Five hundred Arkansas farmers storm a small town demanding food for themselves and their families.

Pope Pius XI issues an encyclical denouncing "trial marriage," birth control, and divorce.

Eight U.S. Marines are killed in an ambush in Nicaragua while helping the government "enforce peace." Official American intervention, which began in 1910, will finally come to an end in 1933.

In Virginia Beach: Cayce gives thirty-one readings during this period (none between Christmas Eve and New Years Eve). No readings are given for hospital patients. Of special interest:

In mid-January, he gives the one and only reading for Mrs. Patricia Devlin—a physical reading requested by Morton Blumenthal, who discontinued his own readings from Cayce six months ago.

Three more readings are given about the "buried treasure" in Virginia. In one of these is the following commitment: "It is the desire of [Edgar Cayce, Thomas B. House, Jr., Gray Salter, and Hugh Lynn Cayce] to aid mankind through the carrying out of the work of Edgar Cayce in absolute accordance with information obtained through his readings. These four pledge themselves to carry out in detail and in accord with the ideal of this group to help mankind [by means of] any advice and information which may be obtained through these forces that lead to the finding of buried treasures." (3812-4) It goes on to specify how any found treasure will be divided.

About the lecture on "Dreams": Over the years, Edgar Cayce gave hundreds of readings interpreting dreams. A portion of this lecture describes one of Cayce's own dreams with a brief interpretative statement. Another portion is quoted from one of the 1923 Lammers readings on a variety of metaphysical and spiritual topics (3744-5).

Cayce's reference in the lecture to Captain Kidd and his buried treasure may not be coincidental, given that this follows three readings on the Virginia treasure.

As a preamble to the lecture, Cayce says: "I feel very much as Seth Parker expresses himself in his radio programs each Sunday night: 'Friends, we are gathered here to get better acquainted with the Lord, and to feel that He is one of us.'" This may refer to a radio personality named Seth Parker, created by Philip Lord in the 1920s and the subject of a 1930 book called *Seth Parker's Album*.

Dreams

Sunday, January 18, 1931
Cayce Hospital

In my approach to the subject of *dreams*, I hope to give you something that will be worthwhile in your own life. If I fail to give you something that you may use tomorrow, or in your everyday life, I have failed entirely in the whole purpose.

It is really the dream of everyone that they may gather something from their experiences through life which will make life more interesting, more worthwhile, a life more purposeful, a life more definite, with a definite aim, a definite purpose. They are trying to carry out that which they will not be ashamed to present to their Maker or God. That is the purpose of life, as I understand it.

But the phase of *dream* I want to speak about is that something we experience in what is sometimes called a passing fancy, or that something which passes through our experience while asleep. That we call a *dream*.

The information we have gathered through the years treats the subject in this manner, when the question was asked, "What is a dream?"

> Answer: There are many various kinds of manifestations that come to an animate object, or being; that is, in the physical plane of man, which the human family term a dream.
>
> Some are produced by suggestions as reach the consciousness of the physical, through various forms and manners as these.
>
> When the physical has laid aside the conscious in that region called sleep, or slumber, when those forces through which the spirit and soul has manifested itself come, and are reenacted before or through or by this soul and spirit force, when such an action is of such a nature as to make or bring back impressions to the conscious mind in the earth or material plane, it is termed a dream.

This may be enacted by those forces that are taken into the system, and in the action of digestion that takes place under the guidance of subconscious forces, become a part of that force through which the spirit and soul of that entity passed at such time. Such manifestations are termed or called nightmares, or the abnormal manifestations on the physical plane of these forces.

In the normal force of dreams are enacted those forces that may be the fore-shadow of condition, with the comparison by soul and spirit forces of the condition in various spheres through which this soul and spirit of the given entity has passed in its evolution to the present sphere. In this age, at present . . . there is not sufficient credence given dreams; for the best development of the human family is to give the greater increase in knowledge of the subconscious, soul or spirit world. This is a *dream*.

Question: How should dreams be interpreted?
Answer: Depending upon the physical condition of the entity and that which produces or brings the dream to that body's forces.

The better definition of how the interpretation may be best is this: Correlate those Truths that are enacted in each and every dream that becomes a part of this, or the entity of the individual, and use such to the better developing, ever remembering develop means going toward the higher forces, or the Creator.

3744-5

You will see how all these various subjects link together with the *subconscious mind* [that we talked about a month ago]. I think the most vital words ever given to man were, "Hear, O Israel, the Lord our God is one Lord" (*Deut. 6:4; Matt. 12:29*) and "God is one." (*Gal. 3:20*) So, every phase of our lives is so linked one with another that it is all one. The various experiences that we are able to have in our sleeping state are, in many instances, the most real. Have you ever dreamed of kissing an individual? Which has been the most lasting, when you have met an individual and embraced them in everyday life or when it has been a portion of your subconscious or your soul's experience? I know from my own experience that the dream is certainly the most lasting. Why? Now, if we could answer that, possibly we could realize what dreams are, and how we may use them in our lives from day to day.

When we lay aside our physical consciousness in sleep, it is the nearest state akin to death that man knows anything about—except when he is etherized or put into such a state that brings about the loss of consciousness. In ordinary terms of life, we speak of sleep as being the nearest state akin to death. Now, what is it that takes care of us while we are in dreamland, or in sleep? Our organs function properly, our heart beats on just the same, and we are able to wake up feeling refreshed.

Our physical organism has been built up by what? The stored energy takes hold and builds up the organism, or the reverse happens—and what has done this? A something we have never been able to put our fingers on or to definitely say just what it is. We call it mind, or the natural order of things, or nature, or anything we like. We say it is the natural thing. What do we mean by that? What is it that is natural about it? Because it happens over and over again, is that why? Have we ever stopped to consider that almost half of our existence is spent in the unknown, where we are not even able to follow with our consciousness that which cares for our bodies during that time? This is the *subconscious* mind, the soul mind, that lies in between the physical body mind and that gift of God to every human being that they may carry back to Him or that they may separate from Him. That is our real self, the self that lives on and on just as it is able to live through such an experience as we call sleep and build up the whole organism during that time. Just so in death. If we have lived properly, if the soul has been fed properly, it may have that necessary to sustain itself.

Mind is ever the builder, whether it be of the physical mind, the mental mind, or the soul mind—or the physical consciousness, the subconsciousness, or the superconsciousness. The dreams partake of those three phases.

Many of us have gone to sleep after a hearty meal and had a nightmare. What has taken place? That taken into the system has an objective in itself. It begins to move and have its own activity within the system. It arouses within all the vitality and energy of the body which brings about those awful visions that we experience under such conditions. If our lives have been such, those visions may take on pleasant conditions, or they may be the demons themselves. Some of them take the experience of being suddenly cast into the street only partially clad, or with something after us. Most of these arise from improper conduct of our appetites, whether from eating too much mincemeat pie, too much pickle, or the like—or too much *spirits fermenti*, which may eventually bring those experiences of seeing horrible things. Those are visions of what? That which we have builded in our own selves. If there is a misuse of that which is set before us, then we suffer the consequences.

Then there is the vision that might be the activity of the subconscious mind itself. This phase is held by some people to be very scientific, especially in psychoanalyzing peoples' ills. They claim that the suppression of emotions in the body during the developing periods builds that which comes to the surface when the physical consciousness is laid aside. There are those who say this is a lot of "bunk," while there are others who have spent thousands of dollars following out this theory: that the suppression of desire in a developing child, or in the developing minds of individuals, indicates—through the visions they may have—that which may change the whole outlook on life for the individual. These are called the *hallucinations* of the *subconscious* mind.

There are people in the large centers of our country who make it their business to study this theory, and there are recognized authorities on certain kinds of diseases. There are some who claim they can make a person dream whatever they wish, by making certain things happen while they are in that state. That is possible, but it doesn't change the character of the presentation nor what is presented. For we must pass into that consciousness that is *taking care of us* while we are in the normal sleeping state, or even while we are in an induced state there is another consciousness controlling the activities of the whole body. Remember, every organ—every atom of your body—is a universe in itself, and it has its own consciousness to be dealt with. The things we experience through such dreams may be worthwhile or they may not. Where is the differentiation?

Let me tell you a dream that has come to me more often in my whole experience than any other. Every time I have this dream, I gain a little more of the interpretation. It has come to me possibly fifty times during this life. Possibly I have actually experienced it. I don't know.

I am walking down a little slope, and a young lady has her hand on my arm. The ground is covered with vines, and the vines are in blossom—they are little star flowers. The trees we are passing under are not large, but seem to be cone-shaped at the top. We come to a stream of water. It is just a narrow stream, the water is very clear, and I notice there are white pebbles. As we step over the stream and start up the other side, we meet an individual who seems to be one of the Grecian gods, or a messenger with wings on his feet and on his shoulders. In his hand he has a braided piece of cloth that we realize is made of gold, about thirty inches long. He asks us to join our hands and he lays this strip of cloth over our hands, saying, "Together you can do anything, separate you can do nothing." Then immediately he disappears. In going up the hill, we come to a very muddy road, and he appears suddenly again as we are trying to find our way across. He says, "Just think it," and as we clasp the cloth, the road dries up. Passing over it, we come to a very high cliff. As we attempt to climb it, I cut niches in the side of the rock. We keep slipping every now and then. Only once in this dream have I reached the top of the cliff and been able to look over the wall." (see 294-62 for reading on this dream)

Now this, according to our information, is an emblematical dream. It partakes of conditions pertaining to the subconscious experience, correlating them with the mental experience. This kind of dream partakes of something that is almost a vision, and something that is very material in some of its aspects.

There are experiences when we have entirely separated ourselves of our consciousness from the physical being until we really have a vision. A vision may partake of a very material condition, either as an emblematical condition in our lives or something very real. We have heard of people who have dreamed of a pot of gold buried in such and such a place, and who when awake found it exactly that way. How does such a thing reach an individual? Being separated entirely from the material self, the subconscious is able to go out into that known as the universal, or the cosmic consciousness, and those on the other side—who see and know those conditions that surround us—may put within our own selves that which we may use to be helpful or detrimental, dependent upon how we use it in our own experience.

So, there are three or four classes of dreams with which we have to deal. How can we apply them? How can we know the good from the bad?

To my mind, the answer is in the Good Book itself. We may apply it in our lives to our own undoing or to our own upbuilding. "There is this day" (meaning now, just as it meant yesterday and will mean tomorrow) "set before thee good and evil" in all of the various phases of experience we may have in our life. (see Deut. 30:15) We, throughout the eons of time, may apply those things we experience to our own good or to our own undoing. We want to know then, all of us, how we may bring only good. Very few, if any of us, want to have that which is evil. How may we bring these things to bear on our own lives and experiences?

An answer to this might be found in the study of the life of Saul. His life started out most beautifully, but it was a miserable failure. Why? He reached that period in his experience when—with the power, with the conditions that surrounded him—he was sufficient unto himself, and God no longer spoke to him in dream or in vision, for he had reached that place where he felt he did not need to be guided by the divine from within.

Why seek information from anyone who might be able to give it to us from the other side, when we may have it—as this man Saul was at first able to have it—from God Himself? Why seek it from anyone? Why seek to know from someone in the Beyond where Captain Kidd buried his treasure? Why not seek it from that builded from within—which, if builded in the proper manner, will bring about those conditions needed for our own development?

What was meant when it was said, "God is able to raise up unto Abraham children of these very stones?" (see Matt. 3:9) What does it mean, unless it means that builded in our own selves gives God the privilege to use us? For there is nothing in heaven or earth that can separate us from God but ourselves. Nothing! Why? Because we are a portion of Him. Through what? That soul which he has given us, which—with its mind—brings us a dream, brings us a vision. Whether it is of the promised land of our mother, our father, our sister, or our brother, it brings to our mind the consciousness that satisfies us of the continuity of life.

Many people have said, "If I could just speak with someone from the other side, I would be satisfied of the continuity of life." What did the Master say about that very thing? "If you will not listen to those that you have about you, you would not listen though one returned from the dead." (see Luke 16:30) Even when He came up from the grave Himself, for thousands of years we have been trying to preach to people. Some of us say we believe it, but do we act like it?

If we are right with God, then we know better how to interpret our dreams, because each individual can interpret his own dream better than anyone else can ever do for him. If God ever spoke to anyone (and we believe that He did), he will speak to us if we'll let Him. How is He going to do it? He aforetime spoke in dreams. Why wouldn't He do it now? Has He changed, so that He doesn't speak to us except through someone else? We don't want a secondhand God, do we? We can get our knowledge firsthand, if we will seek it, whether through dreams or what not. First know that we are right with God, and day by day we will be guided. For He has promised: "My Spirit beareth witness with thy spirit as to whether ye be the sons and daughters of God or not." (see Rom. 8:16) God is Spirit and seeks such to worship Him, in spirit and in truth. (see John 4:24)

When you have visions or dreams from day to day, put them down in black and white and see what they look like. Compare them with your experiences. No one passes into dream land, if they are sound asleep, without passing out of the physical body. The silver cord is not broken, that connection between the physical and the subconscious. We should study these experiences and judge for ourselves. Why ask someone else? We may know these things by applying them in our lives. Set them down, look at them, study them. Compare them. He who compares himself by himself, however, is not wise—but he who compares that experience he may have with his relationship to God is very wise, for he has taken God into partnership with him.

Has God seen fit to speak to us? Are we able to contain that which He may give us? Are we willing to do what He would have us do? He speaks to all of us, for He has not forsaken Israel. Neither has He forsaken those who seek after Him, for those that will seek Him shall in no wise be cast out. That has been the promise through all the ages. That is the promise to us today.

We can make visions or dreams mean a great deal in our lives, if we conduct our lives in such a manner as to entitle us to receive such messages. For we are all heirs to the Kingdom through Christ, and we are sons and daughters of God.

If we keep a record of our dreams from day to day, we will soon learn to differentiate between those that are worthwhile and those that are not. If we conduct our lives in such a manner as to make such possible, we may be warned by our loved ones as to impending danger, granted by God Himself. Compare such visions with your knowledge of God. Don't forget that it has been said from time to time, "Put away out of your midst all soothsayers and those that partake of familiar spirits." Why ? Because through such forces we are calling upon those forces that are loosed by the spirit departing from the body, that have been called earthbound, and have power in the dark side or the night side of life to be harmful, if we open ourselves to such. We can guard ourselves by knowing that we have surrounded ourselves with that bond which we may hold with God Himself. It has been given. "Where two or three are gathered together in my name, there am I in the midst of them." (Matt. 18:20) We say that and think it is beautiful, but how many of us really believe it?

If our relationship to God is such that it is necessary for Him to speak to us, He will do it—if we will ask for it and live it.

During the Two Weeks Before the Lecture on "Mind as Related to Healing" (Feb. 1, 1931) . . .

Around the world: Mahatma Gandhi is released from prison in India after his peaceful protest. His chief followers order civil disobedience to continue.

In Virginia Beach: The closing of the hospital has been announced for later in February. Edgar Cayce is at the most discouraging period of his life, seeing his dream of a hospital coming to an end in the midst of emotional upheavals involving many of those who have been his supporters for many years. In his memoirs, he writes, "No one can imagine how it hurt . . . I have gone over every detail of the happenings in my own mind many times, for no one, not even I, can ever put into words what that meant to me; but put it all down as a very miserable failure on my part, and certainly I blame no one else but myself for its failure." (from *Edgar Cayce—My Life As a Seer: The Lost Memoirs*, p. 228)

During these two weeks, he gives twenty-three readings, including the last two readings for patients at the hospital and seven life readings.

About the lecture on "Mind As Related to Healing": It must be with some feelings of incongruity as well as irony that Cayce talks about the healing treatments and facilities at the hospital—in light of his anticipation of the imminent closing of its doors. Also, while he talks about the healing properties of the digitalis, derived from a common plant, he does not mention the fact that digitalis can also be toxic in itself—another of nature's ironies.

He precedes the lecture with this preamble: "Many of you have possibly received an insight into this subject such that you will disagree with what I say. Please remember, I am speaking from my own experience. Though we may approach this subject from different angles, let us not be confused and fall out because we disagree." These words may reflect Cayce's ambivalence and lack of self-confidence at this time.

Mind as Related to Healing
Sunday, February 1, 1931
Cayce Hospital

Mental healing has been a portion of every new idea that has been presented to the world as a new religion. I do not mean to lead you to believe that I am attempting to found a new sect or ism, or body of thought, or to have a following of any kind. What I want to give is a better understanding of the Great Physician—that One who was able to heal by the touch of His hand.

Immediately you will say, "You're going to talk about religion," or about things that deal with cults or cisms or isms that have sprung up from Jesus the Christ, Jesus of Nazareth. I want to approach it rather from the questions in the minds of most people who have not come in touch with some phase of Christian living, and try to awaken another consciousness within their lives. I have often made this statement in respect to healing or the assistance that may be rendered through whatever source it is that manifests through me from time to time.

This is a very crude illustration, but I feel sure all of you will be able to understand it: If an individual has any form of disorder that is termed "malarial" in its nature and he has a "quinine consciousness," all the prayers in the world will not help that man! For he has been taught—he has had demonstrated to him to his own perfect satisfaction—that quinine will relieve that condition! He doesn't know about prayer.

Now if we are able to get hold of an understanding of the conditions that exist in our material plane, knowing all the things that have gone before—just how thought is operative in the lives of individuals—then we will understand how some individuals have a consciousness of this, that, or their other nature.

Some years ago, there was discovered growing in our gardens all over the country a plant the juice of which was good for a certain condition in the physical body, for that known as low blood pressure, or a disturbed circulation, or a slowed pulse. What has that to do with Mind and mental healing? Just this: All force (we come back to our same old routine) is of one force. Is that plant a representation of God's love to His people or not? Answer it yourself. Not only as a beautiful flower (known as Foxglove or Digitalis), but as something containing an element to awaken a consciousness in life-giving forces within the human body such as to aid in many conditions.

Some of you who have studied along certain lines would say, "If I raise my consciousness, I could be rid of all these things. Why is it necessary for medicine?" Let me read a quotation which I think answers this:

> *And he asked the father, "How long is it ago since this came unto him?" [This is the Master talking to a child's father.] And he said, "Of a child. And ofttimes it hath cast him into the fire, and into the waters, to destroy him: but if thou canst do any thing, have compassion on us, and help us."*
>
> *Jesus said unto him, "If thou canst believe, all things are possible to him that believeth."*
>
> *And straightway the father of the child cried out, and said with tears, "Lord, I believe; help thou mine unbelief." (Matt. 9:21-24)*

After the "foul spirit" left the child, the disciples asked, "Why could we not cast him out?" and He said unto them, "This kind can come forth by nothing but by prayer and fasting." (*Mark 9:29*) A variation, as it were.

These disciples had been able—with His permission, being sent by Him—to go to the lost sheep of the house of Israel to awaken within their consciousness their needs. And to cinch the matter, as it were, they would heal those that were sick, aid those who were lame, and cast out demons.

Now this healing ability—this mental attitude which they had to be in to receive this gift—had to answer or correspond to something from a higher source that was sent to them for their good—that they might be able to receive this within themselves. You may say, "What does that have to do with the work here—even that which you have been attempting in your hospital?"

Does faith and does mental attitude have anything to do with the treatments we have here? As you go about the place, you will find equipment to do practically any kind of work. All the treatments we are prepared to give here have been suggested from time to time for other individuals to apply in their lives and to help them gain that consciousness that will enable them to get hold of that which produces any healing that may come to an individual.

Man has been able to gather from nature's storehouse— from the many things found throughout the world in the form of drugs, mechanical appliances, various elements of nature itself—the combinations that may aid in various conditions. Does that lessen at all the ability of the individual to be able to gain a consciousness of the divine force from within? Or is it proof of it all being One? That's the great question we have to answer.

If we have a thing happen once, it may happen again, though we may call it chance, guesswork, or whatever. If these disciples—these companions of the Great Physician Himself—were capable individuals able to meet all the conditions they had contacted heretofore, why did they fail this once? The Master said, "This can only be met or cast out by fasting and prayer." (see Matt. 17:21) Hadn't He taught His disciples that they were to have periods of fasting? Hadn't He taught by example and by precept that periods of prayer were necessary for them to carry on, even in their everyday life—as well as to meet the contingencies arising from time to time?

We remember again when the Master said to His disciples, "Who do men say that I am?" They answered, "Some say John the Baptist; some say one thing, some another," "Whom do ye say that I am?" Peter answered, "Thou art the Christ, the Son of the Living God." "Flesh and blood," the Master said, "hath not revealed this unto thee, but My Father in Heaven." (see Matt. 16:13-17)

Then, in almost the next breath, He begins to tell them that it is necessary for Him to go up to Jerusalem and suffer many persecutions. Peter takes him aside and says, "This doesn't need to be. Look how many people are already your followers. Look at the abilities we have to call out these many things for the people. Look how you are able to feed your followers. Remember the loaves and fishes. It isn't necessary for you to go through all this." And the Master answered, "Get thee behind me, Satan, for thou savorest of the things of earth and not of the spiritual things." *(see Matt. 16:21-23)*

Just so, it is necessary in our lives to so set or center our minds on the kingdom in order to get hold of the kingdom. For, if there is any healing that ever comes to an individual, it comes from the divine within.

Then, what does the mind have to do with healing? It has to be awakened—either by those things from without or within—to that consciousness where the divine may heal. "Whether it be easier to say, 'Son, Thy sins be forgiven thee,' or to say, 'Arise, take up thy bed and walk?'" There had to be brought to the individual a consciousness that the healing is from within, not from without. Just as we have said about the kingdom of heaven itself, it isn't that we go to find who will come in and tell us, but it is within our own selves. *(see Deut. 30:11-14)* If an individual can be awakened sufficiently from within, all the medicines, all the appliances, or all the treatments that may be given mean nothing. Why? The Great Physician Himself is ever ready and willing that we should have that which is our heritage—if we will but open ourselves to that heritage. But if we are so earthly minded, if we have so turned our own mental vision or so trained our subconscious self that we are unable to get beyond those barriers, it is necessary that we be awakened by those things in God's own storehouse which He has allowed man to gather and put in such a shape as to assist in awakening that necessary for the healing to come.

Two weeks ago I received a request from a man for information concerning his physical condition. I will give you a portion of this reading [given four days ago], so that you may see if it is in keeping with that we have just discussed:

> Yes. Now, we find there are conditions that are of a hindrance in the physical, and there are conditions that are as destructive in construction of the physical organism of the body, affecting directly the sensory organism, especially as related to the eyes.
>
> In giving even assistance, much might be said as respecting the conditions that brought about this condition of destructive building, as to the mental, of life, of thought, of experience, in the entity's program; as to that necessary for the entity's experience to gain insight into the spiritual life, the differentiations

between those of constructive thought and those of destructive thought, those entering in from a material basis and finding lodgement in the mind of the soul, as to become a hindrance in a physical sense, with the abilities of awakening within the soul mind the continuity of forces—yet physically, hindrances.

The conditions, however, that face the body for that of material help to the physical forces of the body, enabling the body to again get hold of self, self's own physical construction, as to create or enliven the forces in system as to overcome or to meet the emergencies as they arise, to prepare self to meet the various contingencies that comes from the afflictions or the forces that manifest in the body.

In meeting these, there must be held and known that all healing, all resuscitating forces of a body must come from the divine from within, and to some this may come only to those who are enabled to gain such a consciousness from within that will make for constructive forces, doing away with passiveness in even the physical by holding to the divine, as to bring healing in the wings. These conditions, however, as we find, may be aided by the use of forces external; for all force, all power, emanates from one source. So, as has been given, that which makes up even the electronic energy—that man knows as electrons or energy in electricity, which may be used as a convenience, as a necessity for man's experience—is of God itself. In awakening dormant forces, then, those forces in nature—of whatever radiation necessary to awaken within a physical being that portion that will enable the individual to gain that vision, or to lay aside those things that so easily beset in a physical consciousness and gather a vision of that from over the way, from the Beyond, that that dwells within; for think not who will ascend to bring Him unto us, or who will go beyond the sea that we may know that He lives, but He is in thine own heart, within every atom of thine own being, and that awakening from within will enable the individual to gain that consciousness, knowing that that committed unto Him is safe, and He is able to keep that committed against every condition that may arise within our own experience.

In the physical forces, then, that have been builded in this
body, we find elements from the central nerve system have been
influenced by the pressures that exist in the 3rd and 4th dorsal,
3rd, 4th, 5th, and 1st and 2nd cervical, that prevent an even
flow of the nerve energy to the optic forces, and a constant dry-
ing of these forces is producing atrophy—as materially known—
to the optic forces themselves. Then to awaken same, to enliven
those forces from within, an application of that from without
which will bring a consciousness of the divine, of the *living* God,
of the *living* forces, able to keep all that may be committed in a
way that, while we ourselves may not understand, "Let thy yeas
be yea, and thy nays be nay"; and as we build, little by little, line
upon line, precept upon precept, know that the Redeemer liveth
in thee, and that thou sheddest abroad is as the light that is
gained by thee of that living force. If thine eye be single, if thine
heart be as one with Him, the issues of life may be brought to
such an understanding that will enable the individual to see,
know, understand those purposes for which the entity entered
into the world, that the world might be benefited by that the
entity itself is able to shed as to the light. That maketh the world.

[Then followed material suggestions for treatments. After that information . . .]

These will bring an understanding, and better cooperative forces.
Get a hold upon self. Read, study, to know by heart, that given,
"In my father's house are many mansions. Were it not so I would
have told you, for I go to prepare a place, that where I am ye may
be also, and I—if I be lifted up—will draw all men unto me."
Even as Moses lifted the serpent in the wilderness, and he that
looked was healed from within—he that looketh on me, as I am
lifted in that consciousness of the individual that the soul hangs
upon that clarifying of the life from all forces of the material
forces, may be lifted up and enlivened from within." Following
these on, as was given, "The way I go ye know," and when thou
hast attained the way into the inner consciousness, through the

> addition even of the forces from without to enable the individual
> to raise the consciousness in the various forces from oppression
> from without and from within, allowing the full force of life itself
> to emanate, that necessary of the light for thine development in
> the spiritual light is given. We are through.   4757-1

Now, what will be the outcome of this individual case I can't tell you.

In all my experience I have only seen one case of instantaneous re-
lief. About twelve years ago, a young man came to my office one day
and asked for a reading for his wife who was in Wisconsin. I asked him
to have his wife come to listen to the information. He said, "All right, if
you think that's best—but she can't hear it—she can't hear anything!
That's what's wrong with her!"

A few days later, they both came in the studio. As soon as I talked
with her, I could see that she was able to read one's lips. She said it had
been three years since she had been able to hear. The reading gave that
it was a case of suppression because of the treatment accorded her by
her husband, who made fun of her abilities. When I became conscious
again, the husband said to me, tears streaming down his face, "Old man,
God alone knows how true the things are that you have given. I don't
know how you knew them." He hadn't noticed his wife, and when we
looked around, she was almost hysterical, her hands going up and her
eyes wide open. "I have heard every word that man said, and I can hear
yet!" She has been able to hear ever since.

This was the story they told: He had met her on a Sunday afternoon,
and they had married on Wednesday. He didn't know anything about
her family, and she didn't know anything about his family. They decided to spend one day there and then go to meet the families. That
afternoon when they went to their hotel and were in their room, all of
a sudden she said, "Listen! Uncle John is talking." He answered, "What in
the name of God are you talking about?" He said, "I didn't know what
sort of a person I had married—I didn't know anything about such
stuff." She said nothing more. "We went out to dinner, and when we
came back we talked a little while, and just before I turned out the light,
she said, 'Listen, Uncle John is talking again.' I gave her a genteel good
cussing, and the next morning she couldn't hear anything I had to say,

and hasn't heard from that day to this.

"I haven't been able to stay away from her. Neither have I been able to stay with her. But what you have told has aroused within me a consciousness that I haven't understood what this is all about. I understand from what you have given that she has possessed some ability not given to ordinary human beings to understand—and many of us don't want to understand—for we have built something within our own selves that makes us afraid to understand anything about the unseen forces, or the things we can't feel, touch, hear, and taste, which pertain to the psychic or to the spiritual side of things. We want to hear about them, but to experience them—no!"

If we are willing to pay the price, mind is able to build within our own self that necessary to bring healing—that necessary for our own understanding of our relationship to our God. Now, if our god is fame, fortune, or what not, we can't expect that god ever to heal! Most of us are of the opinion that we are able to buy most anything we want, but health is one thing that's mighty hard to buy. For unless we can gain a consciousness of the divine from within, very little help can come to these poor weak bodies of ours.

Some years ago, I had an experience which came very close to home to me. An accident happened to my little son, and my wife and I didn't feel it was possible for any aid to help his suffering. The physician told us nothing could possibly be done. Yet when he told us that the child would never see any more and that his eyes must be taken out in order for him even to live, the child himself said, "No, 'cause my Daddy, when he's asleep, is the best doctor in the world, and Daddy will tell you what to do and you will do it, won't you?" He promised that he would. Did I do anything? Did the doctor do anything? You ask any physician who saw the condition happen (for I have talked to many of them through the years), and they will tell you as they did me, "It was just a miracle."

Mind is the builder, the healer—that is, mind at work—not passive, not concrete, but active with the forces God has given man to make himself one with the Law of God, which makes him free. "And ye shall know the truth, and the truth shall make you free . . . If the Son, therefore, shall make you free, ye shall be free indeed." (John 8:32, 36)

During the Two Weeks Before the Lecture "Mind Reading and Telepathy" (Feb. 15, 1931)...

In Virginia Beach: Final activities are underway for the closing of the Cayce Hospital and the dissolution of the Association of National Investigators, which will take place on February 28, 1931.

Cayce and those close to him want to continue the Sunday lectures, and arrangements must be made for another location. Cayce has been teaching a Bible class at the First Presbyterian Church in Virginia Beach, and its minister, Dr. Frank Scattergood, is a friend and supporter of Cayce's work. He will host subsequent Sunday afternoon lectures at his church.

Cayce gives sixteen readings during this period. A reading for Atlantic University reveals more about the schism with the Blumenthals. The opening instruction includes the words "working on the plans of rehabilitation" of the University, as well as the names of those involved in that planning, such as Linden Shroyer, Dr. William Moseley Brown, Dr. Scattergood, and David Kahn, as well as the Cayces. The reading explores how to get the Blumenthals to carry the university expenses through part of 1931, while also getting them to resign from the Atlantic University Board of Trustees. A follow-up reading in March reveals that the Blumenthals refuse to resign from the Board. They close the university later in the year, leaving students and faculty stranded.

About the lecture on "Mind Reading and Telepathy": The focus of this reading is our innate ability to influence another person's behavior through our minds, as well as the ethics of using that ability. Considering what Cayce was experiencing at this time with the Blumenthals, the lecture is an affirmation of his self-control of his own ability in this regard.

Mind Reading and Telepathy
Sunday, February 15, 1931
Cayce Hospital

Mind reading, or mental telepathy, does exist—we know that. We experience it ourselves every day. Many of us have had the experience of thinking about someone, and that person calls us on the phone. Again, we may have been speaking about certain people, and they walk in the door.

This kind of thing happened to me just a few days ago. We were discussing a subject. As far as I knew, there was no reason on earth for the person involved to come to my home. But as we were speaking of him and his abilities, it happened that he appeared right then.

What caused this? Was it chance? Just an everyday occurrence? Or was it that the *thought vibrations* between our minds and his mind brought about the conversation?

My experiences have taught me that practically every phase of phenomena may be explained by activities of the subconscious mind. First, let me tell you one of my own experiences along these lines—an experiment I have never repeated! In telling you why not, I can give you my ideas as to how mental telepathy should and should not be used.

While I was operating a photographic studio, a young lady was working in my studio who was really a musician. Yet she had become interested in photography and in the phenomena as manifested through me. We had many discussions about the various phases of these phenomena.

One day I said to her that I could force an individual to come to me. She said it was impossible, and I told her I would prove it to her. I said this because I had been thinking about the subject and studying it. I felt that I had an inkling of what this great force was—the subconscious mind—which we had been discussing. I believed that one should be able to hold mental images within one's self by deep concentration, and by seeing another person doing a thing, one could mentally force that person to do it.

The young lady said. "Well, I believe most of the things you've told me, but this is one thing I do not believe. You'll certainly have to show me that."

"All right," I said. "Who are two people you consider it would be impossible for me to influence?"

"You couldn't get my brother to come up here," she said, "and I know you couldn't get Mr. B—— to come here either, because he dislikes you."

I told her that before twelve o'clock the next day, her brother would not only come up to the studio, but he would ask me to do something for him. "And the next day before two o'clock," I told her, "Mr. B—— will come here."

She shook her head, and said that she couldn't believe anything of the kind.

Now our studio was so arranged that, from the second floor, we could look into a mirror and see what was going on in the street below. At ten o'clock the next day, I came in and sat down. I sat in meditation about thirty minutes, just thinking about the boy. Yet I wondered if perhaps I hadn't overstepped myself in saying he was going to ask me to do something for him, because his sister had told me that he didn't have any patience with the work I did.

After about half an hour of this concentrated thought, I saw the boy pass on the street below, then turn and come up on the steps. He stood there a few seconds, looking up the steps —then walked away. In a few minutes, he turned in again and came up the steps to the second floor.

His sister looked around and said, "What are you doing here?"

The boy sat on the edge of the table, turning his hat around in his hands. Then he said, "Well, I hardly know . . . but I had some trouble last night at the shop, and you've been talking so much about Mr. Cayce, I just wondered if he couldn't help me out." His sister almost fainted!

The next day, at eleven o'clock, I took my seat in the same chair. The girl said, "I guess you can work it on Mr. B—— if you worked it on my brother."

I told her I wouldn't be in when Mr. B—— came, because he disliked me so much. And he wouldn't know why he had come in. She told me afterwards that he *did* come in about twelve thirty, after I had gone out. She asked him if she could do anything for him. He said, "No. I don't know what I'm doing here—I just came up," and walked out.

Now, to my way of thinking these are examples of mental telepathy, or mind reading —but they show a forcing of yourself upon someone else. That's dangerous business! It pertains to the black arts. It's one of those things none of us has a right to do unless we are very sure of what we are doing and of our motives. Sometimes it might be used well—perhaps at times to control our children in that way. Yet even then it might be dangerous for, as our information says, anyone who would force another to submit to his will is a tyrant! Even God does not force His will upon us. Either we make our will one with His, or we are opposed to Him. Each person has an individual choice.

Then what part may mental telepathy play in our lives—that is the big question. For anything good can also be dangerous. I could mention nothing good but what it also has its misapplication, its misuse. How then may we use mind reading or mental telepathy constructively?

The best rule I can give is this: Don't ask another person to do something you would not do yourself. The Master never asked such a thing, and let us never ask it.

When the Master went down into Judea, He was asked by one of the noblemen of the district, a Pharisee, to have dinner with him. He accepted immediately. *(see Luke 7:36)* Did He ask who the man was, or why he had asked Him, or why this opportunity was being offered Him? We answer, "No, because He knew these things." Certainly, He knew! So should we, too, know things within our inmost selves. And why should we know things within? We should live right, within our inner selves, so that we know each contact we make is an opportunity to speak according to what we represent, from a spiritual standpoint.

So Jesus accepted this invitation to dinner, and His disciples went with Him. As they sat at the table, a woman of the street came in and washed His feet with tears and wiped them with the hair of her head. She also anointed His feet with precious ointment.

The nobleman thought to himself—as many of us would today— "What kind of man is this? Doesn't he *know* the kind of person she is?" Jesus, *knowing what was in his mind*, said, "Simon, I have somewhat to say unto thee . . . There was a certain creditor which had two debtors: the one owed five hundred pence, and the other fifty. And when they had nothing to pay, he frankly forgave them both. Tell me therefore, which of them will love him most?" Simon answered and said, "I suppose that one to whom he forgave the most." And He said unto him, "Thou hast rightly judged." (see Luke 7:36-50)

Note that Jesus did not say to Simon, "This is what you are thinking about," nor accuse him of being discourteous in that Simon did not provide water for His feet, nor oil to anoint His head. Jesus simply spoke in such a way as to awaken in Simon the realization that he should not find fault with another.

At times, then, we too are able to sense what people are thinking, and we may know the trend their thoughts are taking. At such times, our conversation and actions toward them can be such as to show— even as the Master showed Simon—that the inmost thoughts can be known to those who are closely associated with the Divine.

We hear a great deal about people acquiring mental powers. The advertisements say, "Be a strong man—control others by your powerful mind." But it's dangerous business trying to control any other person so that he will do your bidding. To influence someone mentally, just as we would in his presence, so that he does God's bidding and comes to know light and truth—that's different! Did you ever pray for a person? Did you ever get down on your knees and pray to God that someone's life might be changed? That is using mind-power, or telepathy, properly. For the force that changes must be from the Divine Source.

Since that first experience of mine in the studio, I have had others of the same kind. I have tried to demonstrate to people the power of mind. But as I studied these matters more and more, I decided never to do such a thing again. Anyone who wants to control another person can do it—but beware! The very thing you wish to control in the other person will be the thing that will destroy you—it will become your Frankenstein!

Many of you who have studied something of the history of Atlantis know that such mental forces were highly developed there. Numbers of people were able to think with such concentration that they could bring material things into existence by the very power of their thought. To use such forces for selfish purposes, as they used them, can result only in evil. The greatest sins in the world today are selfishness and the domination of one individual will by another will.

Few people have the desire to allow other individuals to live their own lives. We want to tell them how—we want to force them to live our way and see things as we see them. Most wives want to tell their husbands what they can do, and most husbands want to tell their wives what they can and cannot do. Have you ever stopped to think that no one else answers to God for you? Nor do you answer to God for them.

If a person will seek first to know himself, then the ability to know another's mind will come. Most of those who will practice it for just a little while can develop along this line. But be sure you don't attempt to do God's work! Do your own and you'll have your hands full. It is your business to make your own paths straight—not another's. The straight and narrow path leads directly to Him—by your own manner of living, not by trying to control.

The force of mind exists, just as it did in ancient Atlantis. What happened when the Atlanteans attempted to use that force selfishly? *Destruction*—for these may be destructive forces. We all have this mental ability; we can all train ourselves to use it to force others to our will. But we have no moral right to do this. We have the right to tell people our own personal experiences and let them decide for themselves, but not to force them. For God calls upon every man everywhere to look, to heed, to understand.

When we use the forces within to serve the Creative Forces and God, then we are using them correctly. If they are used for our own selfish interests, they are being abused. Then we become even as the son of perdition—call him whatever we will.

Part Two

Sunday Lectures After the Hospital Closing

1931

INTRODUCTION TO THE SUNDAY LECTURES AFTER THE HOSPITAL CLOSING

In the words of Mary Ellen Carter in her memoir about Gladys Davis, "The year [1931] was fraught with trouble for them all and brought with it some of the worst blows they had yet received, as well as some of the greatest insight and spiritual growth." (from *Miss Gladys and the Edgar Cayce Legacy*, p. 60). Yet through crisis after crisis, Cayce continued his lectures on Sunday afternoons at the First Presbyterian Church, at a local hotel, or at his home. Thirteen of these were recorded and preserved and are presented in this series.

Because these lectures are close together in time, there are fewer notes about what is happening in the world or in the U.S. The Great Depression and its consequences for many people are still in evidence everywhere. This adds to the challenge of seeking funds to help the Cayce work continue. The introductory notes remind us what is taking place in Virginia Beach and point out some interesting and significant readings during this period.

During the Two Weeks Before the Lecture "Fate" (Mar. 1, 1931) . . .

In Virginia Beach: The Cayce Hospital of Research and Enlightenment, the long-awaited realization of Edgar Cayce's dream, closes on February 28, 1931, two years after it opens. The last of the employees is paid at 5:00 p.m. that afternoon.

As planned and arranged, the Sunday afternoon lectures continue at the First Presbyterian Church in Virginia Beach, usually every other week.

Cayce gives fifteen readings during these two weeks. Seven of them are life readings, which seem to be requested more frequently these days. Three other readings are noted as "physical, mental, and spiritual" in their range of questions and answers, and one is primarily concerned with business matters in the requester's life. Only four purely physical readings are given.

About the lecture on "Fate": As you read this lecture, keep in mind what Cayce has just been through in his own life and career, wondering about the fate of his hospital and of his work: "How did this happen?" "What do we do now?" The very last paragraph is particularly poignant. "Most of us are inclined to feel that if we had other surroundings, if things had happened a little differently, we would be entirely changed. Would we?"

Fate

Throughout the ages, from time immemorial, man has studied and wondered about the idea of *fate*. It is one of the primary considerations of most great philosophies, and attempts to label and define it have brought into being the religions of the world. As the understanding of *fate* has changed time after time, man's whole process of thinking has changed. The study of certain universal laws which govern all forces and man's ability to control these forces has gone far in the present age and has opened new fields of vision. The *fate* of the dark ages of superstition, fear, and ignorance has become a clean-cut, definite, immutable system of law. But with all our material knowledge, do we really understand?

With the teachings of Jesus of Nazareth, followed by the Christian era, came a change in the whole concept of fate. One of the greatest differences between the teachings of Jesus and many of the other great teachers in the world is found in the concept of fate which he explained through His manner of living, more than by anything which He taught.

At this point, let me remind you that it is unwise for us to feel that we can blot from our lives the effects of the teachings of many great teachers who are not connected with the religion which we profess at this time. The effort expended in keeping away from such knowledge might well be devoted to far more constructive ends. Just as many avoid the study of religions other than their own, so do many avoid the study of the influences of the planets, of numbers, of the power of thought, and of other forgotten sciences. Remember that a few years ago and even recently, in certain sections of enlightened America, men refused to accept the idea of the influence of heredity and environment in their more basic meanings, and they even scoffed at the idea. We recognize that the forces which act upon and, in a measure, control man are many and varied.

Let us take the concept which was expressed through the life of Jesus and see if it does not answer many of our questions. In every individual lies a force which is a part of all the forces without. If we will understand this relation, if we will awaken this latent power, fate will come to mean a much different thing. "The Kingdom of God is within you." (*Luke 17:21*)

As the readings have given, when the worlds were set in motion, the forces which later were to become the directing and controlling tendencies in man's life came into being. For example, the moon became the directing force for the tides, and, as the tides affect man, the moon becomes an indirect force of control. Everything which exists in the world is bound up with and related to man—if not directly, then indirectly. In an even more concrete form, we may say that a portion of everything that exists is embodied within the living human organism. Not a dead one! Let's don't get that idea.

Just as when the human body passes through that condition which we call death and, in so doing, loses many of those elements of the earth and returns to the earth, so when an individual ceases to think and begins to drift with the stream, he becomes dead in a far more terrible sense. Someone else does his thinking. Like sheep, he is willing to be led this way or that, influenced and controlled by those individuals and those forces about him. A vital, living, thinking individual comes to know the true meaning of "your fate is in your hands." They are able not only to understand their own tendencies and control them, but are able to assist others in directing their lives into channels where the stream of life is flowing strong. Too many of us are attracted by the life of ease about the dead, stagnant pools along the way and turn aside for a prolonged rest. Look about you! Life is movement! It is virtually alive! Tear the layers of protective covering from that inner spark of the creative which lies within you. Realize your relation with the Creative Spirit which moves through all that is.

Your entity, your soul, takes on a physical form in this earth, a physical body which is subject to the laws, the directing tendencies in all things material. Your body is influenced by the laws of heredity and by environment. Planetary conditions have an influence. Numerological conditions affect you in a certain manner. Indeed all the laws governing matter influence you in a ratio proportional to your personal relation to any given condition. Now you may ask, can we control our lives? Are we not wholly subject to these various predetermined conditions?

Each of you has a will capable of choosing your path through life. By that I mean you are capable of choosing what you will do with that which you have in hand. As you use bit by bit that knowledge, that ability which you acquire day by day, you will direct the trend of your life. Do not think the soul and the will are one, any more than a husband and a wife are one. They are one in many things, but the manner or way of thinking may be controlled by the individual or physical man. Each of you has a soul which you are carrying back to its Maker. Would you dare to introspect for a moment and gaze upon that which you intend to present to that All-Creative Power? You believe, do you not, that the Creator wills that each return? In each of you there is a spark of that Creative Will. Arouse it and make your will one with it. In so doing, strength will be yours, and we all need that strength, for it is a long journey.

Our living day by day is important, for we are today what we did and thought yesterday. With each act, with each thought, you build into your being another part. You are today a total of these collected parts. We look about us at the results of the combination of these parts and say, "This was my fate." Day by day you have built this fate through the use of the forces which affect you.

We have a very good example in the life of Moses. You say he was raised up for a special purpose. Remember the long period of training in the house of Pharaoh and then the second long period of forty years in the wilderness. In one day, he changed his whole environment and entered on this second period which ended up in his coming to lead the people out of Egypt. Why was he raised up for that purpose? The needs of individuals, the needs of the people, called for such things—they builded such things.

If we cry out for a thing, and call on God for it, we get it—*provided* our lives are in accord, for prayers are answered from within. God is within us certainly, if He is everywhere else. As we pray, we awaken that within us and so build our lives for that desired. Do you not see that a man literally becomes that which he prays for within his heart?

We come then to *faith* as it influences *fate*. Moses again is a good example. After going into the wilderness, he determined within himself his work, and God was able to speak with him, saying, "Use that thou hast in hand." This is passed on to each and every one of us if we are to guide our own fate, if we would meet and understand the various conditions that arise in our lives. Don't forget that which was said even of Him, "Though He were the Son, when he came into the earth He learned obedience through the things which He suffered." *(see Heb. 5:8)*

What does that mean? If we believe in the orthodox teachings, we say "Why, He was the Son of God—He was raised to be the Son of God. He couldn't be anything else!" So are we! We can't be anything else! Perhaps not in the same manner, but if our soul is the gift of God and if, as He has said, we are no longer aliens—no longer cut off—then we are no longer in this position or that position because today we have a darkened day, or tomorrow the sun shines and we will have fair weather. We are no longer in that position, for we are *heirs—joint heirs* with the kingdom—*if* it has been awakened within our own selves to the *possibilities*, to the potential factors necessary for us to be one with that whole divine force. The ruler of the tendency, the ruler of worlds, lies within our own grasp.

Just what have you in hand? Do well what you know to do, now—today, tomorrow, each day as you go along—and, as God said, here a little, there a little, line upon line, line upon line. *(see Isaiah 28:10, 13)* As it all begins to accumulate, then work out those things that will make for your understanding, your own fate, the fate of those with whom you associate. If they themselves contact the same source of the activities, it must lie in just one direction.

Now, the very purpose of these talks is to try to awaken within ourselves our own abilities, because—as God has said—He calls on men everywhere to know themselves and to be one with Him, using our own abilities—not someone else's, but our individual selves. For our soul is our own, and nothing in this world can keep us from God, but ourselves! Whatever we may term *hell*, if we stumble into it, it will be over our own selves. It will be through either the misuses or the misunderstandings that we create within our own selves, so that our own fate, our own tendency, lies within the use of what we have today—not what we are going to have tomorrow. It's like the man who spends today what he's going to earn tomorrow. He will never have a great deal of money, will he? If a man spends his whole life in putting off what he is going to do, we already know what his fate or his tendency is to be. If he presents himself at all before the throne of grace, it will be rather a warped, withered result. How did the apostle put it? "If the righteous *scarcely* be saved, where will the sinner and the ungodly appear?" (*see 1 Peter 4:18*)

Most of us are inclined to feel that if we had other surroundings, if things had happened a little differently, we would be entirely changed. Would we? "If they hear not Moses and the prophets, neither will they be persuaded, though one rose from the dead." (*see Luke 16:31*) The greatest world teacher said that, and that is true! Let's don't say that if we could have this, that, or the other experience, our lives would be marvelous. If our lives are not a marvel already, no matter what happened, they *still* wouldn't be marvelous. It couldn't be! It all comes back to how we use them There has been set for us a way. We can use it, or abuse it. "Not every man that saith unto me, Lord, Lord, shall be saved, but he that doeth the will of my father." (*see Matt. 7:21*)

During the Two Weeks Before the Lecture on "Faith" (Mar. 15, 1931) . . .

Around the world: The Union of Soviet Socialist Republics officially bans the sale and importation of Bibles.

In the U.S.: President Hoover signs the bill making "The Star-Spangled Banner" the national anthem.

In Virginia Beach: This is a crucial period for Cayce and members of his inner circle to appraise what has happened and look toward the immediate future, both for the day-to-day work (e.g., readings for individuals) and for specific endeavors like Atlantic University. Cayce gives twenty readings during these two weeks, including three on the future of the work and one on Atlantic University.

In a work reading, those in the group around Edgar Cayce ask "what is the proper and correct method to proceed under the existing circumstances and conditions . . . ?" (254-52) Cayce's Source reminds them: "Many having lost sight of the purposes, the ideals, have presented strange fires upon the altars of truth." They are cautioned that "harsh words that stirreth up anger are in the minds and the hearts of many . . . Be not hasty either in word or deed," but instead rely on guidance from "as perfect a meditation from the heart and soul of each." And if each of them would ask for guidance and support, *believing*, "ye shall receive according to the faith that lies within each and every one of you . . . " How appropriate for Cayce to follow this with a lecture on his own beliefs about "faith"!

These work readings go on to give preliminary suggestions for creating a new organization for the work, marshalling those believing in the work, and choosing a new manager (other than Cayce). They are reminded that this work "here—in this place—now—may become as a shining light to many, or may become the laughingstock of many. Do not expect that evil days will not come upon each and every one." Those who want to go on with the work are asked to search themselves, to ask "whether they are willing to drink of the cup necessary." And if so, to ask within what their individual roles should be and to "*consecrate* their bodies, their minds, their souls—and all will be well!" *(254-52, -53)* The Source recommends a "gathering" within the next two weeks of those "wholeheartedly . . . in accord with the findings that may have been . . . through the channels." *(254-53)* (In correspondence following the review of these readings by several members, one member suggests as a title for the new organization, "The American Apostolic Association.")

The reading on Atlantic University first makes this broad request: "You will analyze the present status of affairs of the Atlantic University and further direct the necessary steps to be taken immediately in the rehabilitation of that institution." *(2087-6)* The first question to the Source is: "In view of the refusal of the Blumenthal brothers to retire or resign immediately from the Board of Trustees, and to make proper settlement suggested in previous reading, what should be done to obtain such resignations and settlement?" The Source directs them to "the Corporation Commission, or those channels that handle institutions or corporations organized under State charter for the operations of such institutions"—cautioning them not to take action without such authority. As in the work readings, questions are asked about several specific individuals and their potential roles in helping resolve the Atlantic University impasse. The suggestion is made that "The greater help and aid that may come to the situation will be the . . . combining of the efforts of the faculty in a body, as near as possible, to the situation." Again the counsel is for those directly involved to examine their motives, their dedication, and their abilities.

About the lecture on "Faith": As you read the lecture, consider Edgar Cayce's circumstances while he presents his views on "faith." These ideas will be confirmed and elaborated in a series of readings a year from now—March and April 1932—as part of the fourth lesson in *A Search for God,* the study group course on personal spirituality.

Faith

Sunday, March 15, 1931
First Presbyterian Church, Virginia Beach

The meaning of the word "Faith" is best expressed by the writer of the eleventh chapter of Hebrews, which begins: "Now faith is the substance of things hoped for, the evidence of things not seen." *(see Heb. 11:1-40)*

There are many who would tell us that these writings are fables, gathered by people who would have us believe as they believed. Yet there are many who believe that these writings are words of truth given to the writers by God Himself. This is for each individual to decide for himself. Irrespective of our beliefs, ideas, or ideals, we *live* by faith whether we choose to say we do or not. If we do not have faith in our fellow man, our life becomes a nothingness. When an individual finds life a turmoil, a strife, and not worthwhile, it is usually because he has lost faith in something or somebody. It is because of a misdirected faith.

We can tell what faith *does*, but as to what it *is*—that's harder to describe. We are unable to give it a form or shape or to give it a place, except in our own personal experience or the experience of another.

"Faith cometh by hearing." *(Rom. 10:17)* Thomas would not have faith in the report given by the other disciples, except when he could see with his eyes, hear with his ears, and touch with his hands the nail prints. *(see John 20:25)* To my mind, believing and hearing—or belief and faith—are not altogether the same. Faith is *believing* in a thing sufficiently to *act* accordingly.

Faith then comes to our physical understanding through one of the five senses. There are many things we have been taught for years to believe without question. I do not think that God has asked that of any man. How oft do we find it said in the word of God, "Try me—trust me—know in whom ye have believed!" In other words, He is telling us to find out whether these be true or not.

Jesus said, "Believest thou not that I am in the Father, and the Father in me? The words that I speak unto you, I speak not of myself; but the Father that dwelleth in me, He doeth the works. Believe me that I am in the Father, and the Father in me; or else believe me for the very works' sake." (John 14:10-11)

James said, "For as the body without the spirit is dead, so faith without works is dead also." (James 2:26)

There is one verse which, to my mind, has often been misinterpreted. The eleventh chapter of Hebrews begins, "Now faith is the substance of things hoped for, the evidence of things not seen. For by it the elders obtained a good report." (Heb. 11:1-2)

From whom did they obtain the report? Was it obtained because they were elders of the church, and was it obtained from the activities of the people in the church? To my mind, it was *not* from the people that the elders obtained the report. They obtained that which they gave back to the people they were leading. Then, from whom did they obtain the report?

The next verse reads, "Through faith we understand that the worlds were framed by the word of God, so that things which are seen were not made of things which do appear." (Heb. 11:3) It seems that God Himself *called* things into being by faith, knowing that He was able through the power within. Now if the power was within life, it must be within us.

"By faith Abel offered unto God a more excellent sacrifice than Cain, by which he obtained witness that he was righteous, God testifying of his gifts; and by it he being dead yet speaketh." (Heb. 11:4) If we believed orthodoxly, then we would say that there were only four people left in the world from whom a report might be obtained. If the report was obtained from the people, was it obtained from Cain or Adam, or was it obtained from God Himself? So the elders must have obtained their report from God, which they gave to the people they were leading, or from within themselves. And when we say "from within ourselves," we mean the spirit of God within us.

Now, if we lose faith in the world, who have we lost faith in first—ourselves or God?

We are all seekers after truth, not accepting anything we have been taught, but reasoning with ourselves in order that we may be able to answer for the faith that lies within, knowing in what we have believed. And if we have the faith, we will know that in which we have believed is able to keep us against any circumstance that may arise in our whole experience. Conditions may arise to make us lose confidence in individuals, but it doesn't necessarily follow that we lose faith in the *ability* of the individual. Losing confidence in an individual does not always make us love the individual any the less, if we are able to have faith in the *abilities* of the individual. Confidence partakes of a different phase of life entirely.

"By faith Enoch was translated that he would not see death; and was not found, because God had translated him; for before his translation he had this testimony, that he pleased God." *(Heb. 11:5)* From whom did he obtain this testimony? From whom may we obtain testimony as to whether we please God or not? It has been given, "The Spirit itself beareth witness with our spirit, that we are the children of God," *(Rom. 8:16)* and "God is Spirit and seeks such to worship him." *(see John 4:24)*

This individual, seventh son from Adam, was able to know within himself that he pleased God—pleased him so well that he was able to even forego the pangs of death itself. If that was done once, it may be done again. If the way is shown, we may do the same ourselves. And here the way is shown—that by faith we may be able to know what God would have us do, irrespective of the world or what those outside may say. If we are on the Lord's side, who can be against us?

"But without faith it is impossible to please him; for he that cometh to God must believe that He is, and that He is a rewarder of them that diligently seek Him." *(Heb. 11:6)*

Then the eleventh chapter of Hebrews goes on to reiterate all the various individuals throughout all the ages who, in some particular way or manner, have manifested their faith by their works or, in other words, they *believed*, they *had faith*, and they *acted* just as if they believed it! Even though many of them were persecuted, many of them were sown asunder, and many of them lived in caves even as the beasts of the field, yet they were not satisfied to keep other than that faith they had professed. How many of us live according to that which we profess to believe?

How many of us ever undertake to prove God to ourselves? How many of us have ever had an actual experience of *knowing* that we had a direct answer to that asked in prayer? How many of us have ever had the experience of knowing that we had to choose either this way or the other, and in prayer have had God Himself tell us the current path? I dare to say that many of us are afraid to make such a test. It has been said that, "It is a fearful thing to fall into the hands of the living God." *(Heb. 10:31)* I believe it is, unless we know from within that we are pleasing God.

Have we ever tried to serve God through being the answer to someone's prayers? Have we ever made a test that was the answer to someone's *faith* in God Himself? We cannot do anything *for God*, as He has no need of our weak abilities. We have need of His strength, but in ministering to the children of men, God has chosen us to be *His* ministers. He has chosen us to carry out their prayers, their supplications. And if we lose faith in our fellow man, it is more often because we have lost confidence in ourselves.

But let's not lose faith in God because an individual fails to do his duty as we have seen it! Possibly it is our failure to accomplish that which God has asked of us, as we can too often only see our own point of view—that in which we have already believed. If we use that *in faith*, then we are given more and more. His promise has been, "Ye are not tempted beyond that which ye are able to bear." *(see 1 Cor. 10:13)* If we put our whole faith in individuals and their personalities, we may be very sure it will not last. If we put our faith where it belongs, we will be as the elders who were able to obtain a good report—and we will know whether we are doing right.

Faith, you know, is very much like an old country man put it: "If God commands me to jump through the wall, it's my job to do the jumping and God's job to put me through the wall." We say that's blind faith. It is *not* blind faith—not if we are able to obtain a good report, as the elders did. "For they that say such things declare plainly that they seek a country. And truly, if they had been mindful of that country from whence they came out, they might have had opportunity to have returned. But now they desire a better country, that is, a heavenly: wherefore God is not ashamed to be called their God: for he hath prepared for them a city." *(Heb. 11:14-16)* They seek a city without foundations, whose builder and maker is God. *(see Heb. 11:10)*

If our faith is the working kind, if we know that our faith is properly placed, we will seek to obtain a report on our faith—not from our wife, brother, or neighbor, but from God Himself! For He is faithful to perform all the promises given, and He will certainly give us knowledge pertaining to our faith—no matter in which direction it may be placed!

"Wherefore seeing we also are compassed about with so great a cloud of witnesses, let us lay aside every weight, and the sin which doth so easily beset us, and let us run with patience the race that is set before us. Looking unto Jesus the author and finisher of our faith . . . " *(Heb. 12:1-2)*

During the Four Weeks Before the Lecture on "Numerology" (Apr. 12, 1931) . . .

In Virginia Beach: Of most significance for the Cayce work this month is the "gathering" held at Cayce's home on March 28, as advised in the work reading before the preceding lecture. This "pre-organization" meeting and a second gathering that follows on May 9 mark a turning point in the organization and outreach of the Cayce work.

A work reading (254-55) one week before the March 28 meeting recommends that the new organization be called the "Association *of* Research and Enlightenment." (When the application for an organizational charter is prepared in June, young friend and future author Tom Sugrue will suggest modifying the name slightly to the "Association *for* Research and Enlightenment.")

Of the eighty or so invited from all over the country, about thirty-five attend the meeting, and many others have written letters expressing their feelings about experiences with the work. In this collection of lectures representing Cayce's beliefs, it is appropriate to include excerpts of comments made at this critical meeting by both Edgar Cayce and his son Hugh Lynn, who will eventually take over the leadership of the work. (Minutes of the meeting are preserved as reports associated with the March 23 work reading, 254-55.) Edgar Cayce opens the meeting with this "charge" to those present:

Friends, I hardly know how to express myself at seeing each one of you here this afternoon. While we come together for a very definite purpose, I believe you will say when you have left the meeting that it was an unusual meeting. It is not that we may know how *to carry on the work . . . that I have been doing and you have been interested in, but as to whether we* shall *carry on the work. Each one of you has signified by your coming here that it will be carried on, that it must be carried on. I believe that you will agree with me that if this be God's work, the way will be shown us . . . There has been, or was, an organization [A.N.I.] which was proposed to carry on the research work, that has been ordered disbanded. I was the individual around whom most of that was built. Now, as to whether that is to be carried on and as to what purposes and what aims shall be set are the questions before you.*

Each person present is then asked by David Kahn, who is chairing the meeting, to "tell us if it means enough from past experiences to go on with the work."

After thirty-three others have spoken, the twenty-four-year-old Hugh Lynn Cayce, says:

You all must know, each and every one of you, what an occasion this is in the lives of those who . . . have contacted this work closely. Now, I want you to forget for a moment that I am the son of Edgar Cayce. I am just a soul hunting for something, going somewhere—most of us don't know where—looking, searching, for something. By the very presence of each of you here, by the words that you have spoken, you have manifested an interest in something that will make others' lives more worthwhile. Each of us as we have contacted this man, just a man—a highly developed man it is true, but just a man—are here . . . to promote and carry out the information, to give to the world the information that comes through this man. If to me, to you, it is worth while, as each of us gets a glimpse of the life, of the understanding we are to carry on to the others, then each of us is going to get what we are looking for. Our lives are going to represent the ideals and purposes that we believe in. We are the representation to the world of this work. Now, let us all get together. Let us think together. Let us be of one mind. Let us try to give to the world a little of life, of understanding, of truth. Let us try to help each individual that we contact to realize the Spirit of the Creator that is within each and every one of us. This man's work is but to emphasize, to bring out, in each individual, that understanding, that knowledge of the Divine which is within. Now, all of these things that are spoken of we must include—for we get exactly what we ask for in these readings—the physical, the spiritual, the mental . . . Let us give to every man what that man is seeking. Let us be able to approach the laborer in the street and give him what he needs to realize his connection with his God. Let us be able to approach the college professor and give to that man or that woman that which he or she needs to know and understand a little more of his connection with his God. Light—we have each just a little bit. Let us pass on the results of the work . . . the truths that we gain through this man.

I am just as I have been for thousands and thousands of years: ready, willing, to do my part, whatever it may be.

In his closing comments, Edgar Cayce emphasizes his view of how readings may be requested. Then he responds sensitively to his son's comments:

. . . We know, as has been given, when God spoke to Moses or through Moses when he was deserting or leaving his people, don't think that you are going somewhere else to find God. You have to seek for yourself. If this work, this phenomena, which manifests through me, is of God, the individual has to seek. Now, if we are going to put it on the basis where anyone can come along and ask that somebody will ask someone else to ask, personality will enter into it. God is not an institution. He is not a personality. We are manifestations of Him, and if we minister, we are ministers for God. You can't do much for anyone else unless they seek. You can always be willing, and your very smile, your very expression, gives the person the opportunity to ask for aid and help. Did you ever see anybody who had a frown on that you were willing to go up and speak to? One of the things I think of about the chiropractors is that their motto is "Keep Smiling." You know, when we look for light, we have to turn our face toward the sunlight. Don't turn your back on it. And it is the same way with people who are sick.

I want to be free, of course. Not free that I may enjoy anything for myself—I don't mean that. I want to be free that I may be the better channel for the manifestation of the way in which I have heard it expressed.

You don't know, you can't possibly know, what this meeting has meant to me. To hear so many people express themselves about the work being something glorious! And there is one more thing: There are few men who live to be a hero to their own children. To see the love that has been expressed by that boy this evening, to know what the work has meant in his life, has made my life more worth while. I often remember, as many of you have often heard before, what Sam Jones said. He was a very, very wonderful man—a very droll man in many ways. He often expressed it in this manner: "If you want to know whether a man has any religion or not, or if there is any stability in him, or what he professes, ask his cook, or ask his boy, and you will find out." I feel very much the same way.

Following that part of the meeting, Cayce gives work reading 254–56 for this purpose:

> . . . You will tell us what is the proper and correct manner in which to proceed under the existing circumstances and conditions. The purposes, ideals, as have been selected by this group, the name which has been chosen, and the three names suggested for manager. You will advise us who would be the best fitted person for general manager, considering all conditions in each individual, and answer the questions.   254-56

The Source reiterates the importance of purposes and ideals of the individuals of those planning the new organization. The specific abilities and motivations of several individuals are reviewed as candidates for management responsibilities.

During this four–week period, Cayce gives forty–seven readings, several of which (in addition to those noted above) provide information and guidance about the present and future of the work, focusing on several potential money–making efforts:

Another work reading continues to emphasize how individuals must approach the work and commit to it for the long run. Gray Salter asks about the supervision of activities relating to the expanded manufacture and distribution of mechanical appliances, batteries, and medicines, so that the operation may be self–supporting. Hugh Lynn Cayce asks about a department of research and distribution of data from the readings that might also become self–supporting, although the Source expresses many cautions about how such information would be expressed with proper qualifying conditions. Tom Sugrue also asks about his own competence to "undertake the labor of studying, editing, and compiling, the data other than medical, connected with the work." (254-55) The Source suggests steps for his own development as he undertakes such study.

Two readings raise the possibility of "more than a million" in treasure buried in White Horse Hill in Virginia Beach. (3812-6, -7) (These are the only two readings on file relating to this exploration, which did not result in recovery of any treasure.)

A reading on Atlantic University was requested by its president, Dr. William Moseley Brown. Apparently, the existing Board of Trustees is holding tight to its control of the foundering school, and Dr. Brown is trying to find ways to keep the school operating in spite of them. Finally he asks: "Can a settlement be effected with the present board of trustees?" and the Source replies pessimistically with: "By either conforming to their wishes or by making definite demands and going about to *act* in that way and manner!" (2087-7) This will not be resolved any time soon.

About the lecture on "Numerology": Late in March, Cayce requests a reading on numerology in preparation for this lecture. (5751-1) The interpretation of numbers 1 through 12, for example, comes directly from that reading, which calls the form of numerology "Talismanic" and indicates it is based on the Talmud. The details of interpretation may be different from other forms with which the reader is familiar.

This lecture is given in the "living room" (according to Gladys Davis's notes) at the Newcastle Hotel in Virginia Beach, a hotel originally built in 1926. (A modern ten-story Newcastle is still in operation at the same location—12th Street and Atlantic Avenue.)

Numerology

Sunday, April 12, 1931
Newcastle Hotel, Virginia Beach

There is so much being said about *numerology* just at this time—especially through some of the broadcasting stations—that it is possibly worth our while to consider it and see from this consideration whether there is anything practical about it, or if there is anything we may gain from a knowledge of numerology that will mean anything to us in our everyday life.

Various people have arrived at their conclusions regarding numerology from many different angles. Most conclusions as to the effect of numbers on our lives have come from the ritualistic orders of the ages. As there was the faith or confidence in that order from which they derived this numerological conclusion, to that extent did they give credence to the manner in which numbers were supposed to affect the lives of individuals.

Is there a source of information regarding numerology that may be relied upon? First, let's get this truth: The effect of numbers on our life is present, whether we think so or not. What we think doesn't alter the circumstances. As to how we use, abuse, or apply what we think, that's an entirely different thing. Just as it is in astrological influences. They exist, whether we feel that they do or not. The moon affects the tide, whether we say it does or not. There are other changes that will enter into even that experience, as we see verified before us twice every twenty-four hours, and they are the astrological influences.

Just so with numbers. What offsets that influence in man's experience—whether it be astrological, numerological, or what not? Man's application of what? That given him which makes him different from the rest of the world—his *will*, his *soul*! If he is forewarned, if he has a knowledge concerning the effect of the various things that exist in the world, then he can be forearmed against that effect, or work in cooperation with it for his own best development. A man who has no knowl-

edge of how the tide comes and goes may put himself in a very uncom-
fortable position if he goes to a place where the tide rises very high and
takes no thought of what will happen if he remains in that place until
the water comes in. He can't make the tide go back. Such things are
governed by immutable laws. So is the science of numbers.

Possibly the most popular method of arriving at our numbers is the
Talismanic, or that taken from the Talmud itself—which is a combination of the ancient Persian or Chaldean, Egyptian, Indian, Indo-China,
and such. Some systems of numerology use the numbers from one to
nine. In the Talismanic, they run from one to twelve. Why? There were
twelve tribes of Israel, twelve stones were placed in the midst of Jordan,
there were twelve fountains in Helim, and twelve Apostles of Christ
were set over the twelve tribes; and twelve thousand people were set
apart and chosen.

Thus, people felt that on certain days, certain periods, certain times,
certain things affected them more than they did at other periods. There
was not a complete number until they had reached twelve. Why? They
had been called in a certain direction. They were to be complete in a
certain number or certain group. That is the record as we have it.

Then, what efficacy did they give to numbers? How did they judge
them? The following is the Talismanic method of reasoning:

One—there is nothing before One, there is nothing after One. One is
the beginning of all things. One God, One Son, One Spirit. One, then, is
the beginning of everything for every individual. As they come to a
consciousness, it is a first, or a beginning, or a oneness that each individual must reach to come to an understanding of all the rest. All pro-
ceeds from One. All comes from One source. Then, if you are a One, you
are a producer, a creator—not a good judge, perhaps not a good lawyer,
possibly a fairly good businessman. You are a home man—you build a
house, and all those things that go to make up a oneness.

Two is the first division, and is the first weakness that may be seen in
numbers and the greatest strength that may be seen in numbers. Or, to
make a comparison, we may say an individual whose number is Two is
capable of as great or greater heights than a One individual, but he is
also capable of the meanest, smallest, lowest things imaginable. If the
strength that he may obtain from One is from the *One* source (which

means God Himself), then the strength is magnified. Also in the division, it may make for the greatest weakness, for he turns himself away from the light itself and becomes that which is weakness within itself.

We also find that we can reason scientifically with numbers. Do you know that two people can't make much more noise than one? It takes three to make more noise than one. Then it takes five to make more noise than three. It takes nine to make more noise than five. You who are interested in feeding people know that it will cost you about as much to feed five people as it will to feed nine. Now such conditions exist! After you have reached the point of nine, then it will require thirteen to make much difference. In color combinations, if you attempt to cover one color with another, it requires more than one to cover one color. Why? It's just the ratio of numbers. It's just numerology in action.

Now, I understand that if we believe in such things, we become what we call superstitious. Well, that's what superstition is! People thinking of all these things irrespective of what produces them. What produces them? One Source. Those things applied *with* God's force mean something! Without Him they mean nothing.

We are only able to visualize so many colors. There are colors above and below, but they are not perceptible to our senses. They run in tones. In music there are half beats and half tones, and they require all of these to make a full whole tone. The same thing in chemistry, the same in metals—a combination of the various ones makes all the changes. There is required at least three metals to change its potential effect. There is required five combinations to change its whole makeup. If it's made of twelve in combination, it makes an entirely whole change. If that be true (and it is! seek it out for yourself), then there is some value in numbers.

How far may we apply it? You will find that certain numbers have an attraction for you, and certain numbers seem to follow you wherever you go. What produces that? Because there is an attraction that actually exists, as it does in metals, in color, in music, and in nature itself. If you want to change the whole trend of your life, change one letter in your name—just one letter—and it will change your whole life. You may think that's foolish. Just try it! That's the only way you can find out. You may say that just thinking about a change could bring it about. That's true, but what difference does it make—just so the change comes? That which we hold before us will either carry us down or carry us up and onward. If we experience a thing, it gradually becomes a part of us.

Three is of the Godhead. *Four* is one of the weak numbers, as it doubles the Two, which is a combination of strength and weakness. *Five* makes a change. It changes the whole effect. *Six* becomes a quieting number for every individual—it's double strength of the Three. It is also that just below *Seven*, with its spiritual influence in individual lives. *Eight* shows a combination of strength and weakness, as it doubles the Four. *Nine* makes a complete cycle. *Ten* is a return to the oneness of things. *Eleven* is both strength and weakness and usually means a traitor. Beware of the time when your number comes to Eleven, and remember that all of these numbers come to you at one time or another. Eleven makes the traitor to whatever influences you have been attempting to govern your life by. *Twelve* makes the full completeness.

Now, how do we compute our numbers? Different ways. The Talismanic idea gives that you have a material number and a spiritual number. The *material number* is obtained by adding the letters of your name. The *spiritual number* is obtained by the addition of the birth month, day, and year. Whatever your number may be, your individual activity is influenced by that association. If you are living in a house where the number of the house does not cooperate with your own number, they are bound to be conflicting.

You can apply numbers on the other fellow better than you can apply them on yourself. If his number is Five, he is changeable—you can't always depend on him. If his number is Eight, he is conservative—very good businessman and you can usually rely upon him in business matters.

This doesn't mean that you should allow numbers to rule you. Not at all. It is just that, having a knowledge of numbers—and knowing that such influences do exist—you can use them for your own good. What was the first commandment of God? Subdue the earth and all that is therein. That means that we should have a knowledge of these things.

We know they exist because we see them in nature. Do you know how you can tell the flowers and vines that are poisonous from the ones that are not? By the number of points on the leaves. Numerology runs through the whole nature scheme of the universe. Why does it? We don't know, but it simply exists! How was the greatest heart stimulant that man knows today first discovered? Somebody in studying numerology found that a flower growing in the backyard had so many points. She knew that this number of points added to a different number of points in another certain flower would produce a strength—a oneness. She experimented—she used it. It worked! Very few physicians in this country today would attempt to practice without the use of digitalis, one of the greatest heart stimulants.

We could continue to say "Why, why, why?" but where does it get us? We simply know such things exist! We could continue to ask, as the child does, "Who made God?" We can only say God is. The very fact that we can't answer that question proves that God is! He has made this whole universe and set in motion all these various things in our lives.

Possibly your experience as a Two would be different from another's experience as a Two. Why? The very number itself indicates a weakness in one, or a strength in another, or a weakness or strength in either individual. If your number is Nine, you have completed a building up and are ready to alter your whole influence in life. You may know that such an influence exists. As to how much it is going to affect you depends upon the application of your own self to these conditions in your life. What is to be the criterion? God's forces made manifest within your own life! With His will and your will made One, the strength is always present—whether your number would be a Four, Two, Twelve, or what not. The influences, then, would be that you had to overcome these conditions. If your number is Two or Four or Eight or Eleven, you know there are certain things for you to watch in your own self—certain weaknesses that exist. What? They have been builded throughout the eons of time, and they are present. Watch your step!

If you place yourself in the hands of the One that is ruling all force, "If God be with you, who can be against you?" There is no place in God's word where He ever tells us to divide or subtract—it's always *add*, and you add to this, knowledge—and to knowledge, add patience—and to patience, add temperance, and so on, until you reach that same oneness.

During the Week Before the Lecture on "Vibration" (Apr. 19, 1931)...

In Virginia Beach: During this week, Cayce gave seven readings, including two more in the "buried treasure" series for the Kelly's Ford site in Culpepper County, Virginia. From the second of these readings requested by Hugh Lynn, this intriguing story emerges:

Question: Please describe the burying of the treasure at the time it was buried.

Answer: As we find, this the indications: These the conditions as surrounded when L.N. George, the paymaster here, received the money in gold and in silver. There was more than a washing tub full, and the preparations were to pay off, and they were in the tent—or the keeper here on the side of the hill, that came from the bridge that used to cross over same—when they were attacked in the early morning—the fires were all burning for the preparations for the meals—they were attacked from the south by the Confederate forces, and this was hurriedly dug by the side of those rocks in which the camp fires, or the foods were being prepared for that particular portion of the tent, see? of the camp—paymaster's—when it was hurriedly dumped in. Afterwards George and those associated with him—one was first taken prisoner, others were killed as they fled northward and toward the east—see? Whole washing tub full. Others, you see, were scattered in other places—these were of much smaller denominations.   3812-9

About the lecture on "Vibration": Cayce would have appreciated the slang expressions about vibrations—for example, someone or something giving off "good vibes." This expression came into usage in 1967, according to the Merriam–Webster Dictionary.

Like the preceding lecture, this one took place at the Newcastle Hotel in Virginia Beach.

Vibration

Sunday, April 19, 1931
Newcastle Hotel, Virginia Beach

Sometimes we confuse *vibrations* with *emanations*. They mean entirely different things. Both have to do and deal with the *psychic* influence in our lives. Often the question is asked: What is meant by psychic influence, or what is the psychic apparatus within the human body? Vibration is something in motion. It doesn't matter whether it has a definite, decided motion—moving in a certain direction continually—or whether it moves only partially in this, that, or the other direction. It is motion or something in motion.

We usually illustrate *vibration* with such as a violin string, or something set in motion for a definite purpose. When we consider it from the scientific standpoint, the same thing happens with numbers. The difference between a flower and a piece of cloth is that rate of vibration at which its elements, its atoms, its forces broken up are vibrating. That's how things are created. *Emanation*, as we know, means thrown out, or pushed out, or emanating from, moving out of, or moving into a certain direction. This movement of emanation as it comes from something is at the vibration (or the motion it takes or produces is the vibration) with which that object associates itself.

The scientific terms as to the rate of vibration are existent. Those who have made a study of such rates know that each element has its radiation. The thing we can use best as an illustration is radium itself, because of its emanations and its high vibratory rate. It has certain emanations which may be effective to certain things as it contacts those. We know there are elements that have an attraction one for another. Because of their rate of vibration, they have this attraction. Life itself begins from one element, one unit, one direction of vibration. And as it increases, it divides itself, and by dividing itself, it creates a greater vibration.

In the same way, the body itself is built up of atomic forces. All the atoms have their own rates of vibration. If we can determine from the vibration within our system just what has been disturbed, we may be able to add that rate to our body that will either break down or build up another portion to break down the vibration that has been created by an element entering into the body.

Why does life ever become humdrum to us? Because we do the same things over and over, and we find that our idea—or our ideal of it— makes us incapable of really living. Can you change your vibrations? Can you change your number? Can you change your outlook on life? You can! It's possible! How? By understanding that such things exist. If we can know what it is that affects us, and how it affects different portions of our system—physically, mentally, spiritually—we can go about to change those effects.

I knew a lady once who had gotten tired of living—nothing seemed worthwhile. She began to understand something about the psychic forces that may manifest through individuals. She had an experience herself. Later she said to me, "I just wonder what I used to do with my life before I found out there was something real." The real things in life are the things you can't put your finger on, that you can't see, that you can't get hold of with your hands.

When a person's body is built up, we find that individual's vibration at a certain given rate. Just as you pour water into a funnel, the water will always move in the same circle in a given funnel. Individuals always will vibrate to the same rate, unless there is some alteration in the individuality. Then the response to a given condition or circumstance will mean a different thing. How? By the environment, by the various conditions that affect an individual. The various conditions under which the body thinks, moves, reasons, and works—and very often the very things the body eats—may change the vibratory rate. You who live a great deal on meats vibrate at a different, lower rate than those who eat other things. Now when the body is building, all the organs vibrate at their own particular rates of vibration. The lobes of the liver, the brain itself, the heart, the digestive system, each gland of the system—each vibrates at its own peculiar rate of vibration.

When illness occurs or a portion of the system is attacked by something outside—a cold, congestion, fever, whatever it may be—it is centered about those portions of the body that are affected by this changed vibration. Consequently, throughout the years, various forms of applications have been made for the human body. They are not all wrong, they are not all right. The trouble is in giving or finding what is wrong in the vibration of that special condition in the system, whether cancer, arthritis, neuritis, or any other ailment.

It has been found that certain vibrations from outside will respond to certain vibrations inside. That's how medicines are built up. That's why the taking of drugs to prevent certain conditions gradually tears down a portion of the system. They are changing the vibration from its normal activity to an abnormal activity. If you move an individual out of his ordinary mode of life, he is stumped—he doesn't know what to do with the forces around him.

The physical organism is the same way. Each atom, each corpuscle within the physical organism, is a whole universe in itself. It has its own peculiar little cells from which there is a certain vibration emanating. Each one works in unison with the other. When the body is in perfect accord, when a body is perfectly well, each atom, each vibration of each portion of the system is working in unison. When various forms of applications were developed, it was found that the releasing of pressures in portions of the system, and also various mechanical treatments, have their value for the human body. That's because they are responding to something within the human makeup, something that has gotten out of tune, something that has gotten so that the vibrations do not accord one with another. A violin may be out of tune by one string being too slack or too tight. The same may take place in the body. Each individual, on account of its vibration, is emanating that which is known as the *aura*. Life itself is an emanation from Life as a whole—God—call it whatever you choose.

There are physicians who diagnose their cases by vibration. A certain medicine is held before a light, and it throws off a certain vibration. They keep on experimenting until they find a medicine that responds to the vibration thrown off from the individual.

If you are standing in a dark room and cannot see, you can tell by the vibrations whether one, two, or three people are approaching. You can tell by the emanations that are thrown off from the individual. If

your vibrations are in attune with another's vibrations, you immediately feel drawn to that person. Then you should be very sure that
vibration, or that emanation, is coming from the same source from
which you yourself have your life. It comes back to whether you are
attuned with God's laws—God's forces that may be manifest in nature—
or whether you are out of attune. It doesn't matter whether you believe
it or not—it just *exists*! It just *is*, as the universe and all the forces in the
universe just *exist*. They simply *are*!

Moses asked, "Who shall I say that God is?" *I AM THAT I AM!* (*see Exod.
3:13-14*) That means us, too. We are either in accord with those vibrations that come from the source of life itself, or we are out of tune. Is it
any wonder, if we go to the basis of it, that an individual is able to help
himself physically? Now, by taking thought, the Master said, we can
neither turn one hair white or black, but by putting some force into
activity, we are able to visualize through that psychic force within us
(which is innate within each and every individual). That's why we go
into the silence, or go into periods of concentration, or even why we
pray. Prayer itself is nothing else but the attuning of all forces to the
God force within us. The nearer we are capable of changing the carnal
mind—the mental mind, that takes in everything else outside—then the
psychic force, the God force, or the subconscious force is able to act
from within. And we may be very sure that our own spirit (which is the
source of all our emanations or vibrations) will tell us whether we are
in attune with that God force or not.

"My Spirit beareth witness with thy Spirit, whether ye be the sons of
God or not." (*see Rom. 8:16*) If we close out this physical consciousness to
the extent that we can turn within, we may know very well whether we
are vibrating with that emanation, that force in God or not. If it is within
that source—which is life and light itself—why can't we help our physical body? Why can't we create within our own individual self? We very
certainly can, for that is life itself! How may we do that? It's the same as
of old: "Put away all the cares of this life, wash yourselves with clean
water, and consecrate yourselves this day, for I, Jehovah—I, God—*I THAT
I AM*—would speak with you."

If God is the same yesterday, today, and forever, He will speak with
us—and we will know whether we are in attune with those forces that

give life itself, or whether we are out of attune. It will help our physical bodies, it will help our mental bodies, it will make our emanations—our vibrations that go out, as seen of men—an entirely different thing, if we often commune with that within so that we make our whole physical being vibrate to that one emanation, that one Source from which life itself in every form comes.

During the Nine Days Before the Lecture on "Psychic Phenomena" (Apr. 28, 1931) . . .

In Virginia Beach: During these nine days, Edgar Cayce gave sixteen readings, most of them physical readings. Eight of these were given on the same day, including physical readings for Cayce's father, L.B. Cayce, and for his son, Hugh Lynn.

About the lecture on "Psychic Phenomena": This lecture is not one of the Sunday afternoon lectures, but is one of Cayce's only other public lectures on record in 1931, so is included in this series. It took place on a Tuesday evening at the Monticello Hotel in Norfolk, Virginia. At the end of another "buried treasure" reading, the following exchange took place:

> Question: Please suggest the general line of approach to the subject of "Psychic Phenomena" which should be made by Edgar Cayce in his talk before the Norfolk meeting tonight.
> Answer: That should be made as the spirit or the form gives itself expression in the actual activity of the hour, for if the individual has so lived, so conducted self in the way, the promise remains "In the selfsame hour will it be given thee what shall be said."
> 3812-10

Early in the lecture, Cayce refers to three cases of apparent psychic phenomena known at the time: Madame Paledena, Mrs. Piper, and the "case of Marjorie." Madame "Paledena" is Eusapia Paladino, an Italian medium who had been under observation for many years. Mrs. Leonora Symonds Piper was a Spiritualist medium who was born in 1859 and died in 1950. Renowned psychologist William James said of Mrs. Piper: "To upset the conclusion that all crows are black, there is no need to seek demonstration that no crows are black; it is sufficient to produce one white crow; a single one is sufficient." She became to him the "one white crow"—the one honest Spiritualist medium whose existence proved that not all Spiritualist mediums were dishonest. (For more information, see James's "On Mediumship" and other articles on the Web at: www.survivalafterdeath.org/articles/James/)

Appended to this lecture is a question and Cayce's answer about psychic phenomena from an earlier lecture.

Psychic Phenomena
Tuesday, April 28, 1931
Monticello Hotel, Norfolk, Virginia

This subject is so large that I'm sure no one expects me to cover the whole ground in this short talk. There have been many volumes written on the subject. The phase of psychic phenomena that I hope to present to you is that phase that has involved me. You all recognize the fact that very few individuals through whom psychic phenomena are demonstrated ever attempt to address groups regarding their work, or regarding that phase of psychic phenomena that manifest through them.

Psychic phenomena have been taboo for such a long while that, when we even speak of them, people immediately think of ghosts, weird happenings, spiritual seances, and things of that nature. I have no comment regarding such phenomena. It has been my privilege to meet individuals who have made a study of psychic phenomena, who have written volumes concerning them, but there are few who attempt to tell what their personal experiences have been with psychic phenomena.

When we go to define the word itself, we find that the dictionary says psychic force deals with the mental, the spiritual, and the soul forces of individuals. Now, when we think of it in the terms as usually studied—by such groups as the American and British Psychic Research Societies—the phase they have studied has been principally such cases as Madame Paledena, Mrs. Piper, the case of Marjorie, and such phenomena.

To many, there is another phase entirely to psychic phenomena—one which is worthy of study. When we go back into history (which to me is sacred history), do you know where the first lines are drawn as to what are psychic phenomena? Where does there come a division as to what is real and what is not?

When Moses was sent down into Egypt to deliver the chosen people, he was told to take the rod he had in his hand, and with his companion, or with Aaron his brother, he was to go before Pharoah, and God

through him would show mighty wonders among the people. As he
went before Pharoah, he cast his rod down and it turned to a serpent.
The magicians cast their rods down and they also turned to serpents,
but Aaron's rod and serpent ate up all the rest of them! Then there
began what is called the plagues in Egypt—all the water was turned into
blood. Aaron stretched out his rod over the waters, and they turned to
blood. The magicians stretched out their rods, and the water turned to
blood for them. They brought the plague of frogs. Then followed the
first instance where blood is drawn from the body. The magicians attempted to do the same thing. Nothing happened. They turned to
Pharoah and said, "The finger of God is in this thing!" (see Exod. 7:9-8:19)
That's the division I want to draw. When we know, when we are convinced, when we see by the results that the finger of God is indeed in
what is taking place, then we know whether the phenomenon we are
seeing and experiencing is of divine origin or otherwise!

We say all force, all power, comes from one Source. With that I agree.
But when there is the misapplication, life itself—or phenomenon itself—
does not fail to act, whether directed properly or misdirected. Just as we
see people born among us who are mentally deficient or physically
disabled—and apparently such afflictions have nothing whatsoever to
do with themselves (I say apparently)—yet the phenomenon of life itself
moves on just the same. At some point, some condition in the phenomenon has been misdirected, or guided away from the purposes of the
all-powerful, but moves on just exactly the same. Then we know there
is the correct way, the correct understanding, of phenomena, and there
is a misunderstanding, a misconception of what is proper and what is
improper.

Now as to how we shall judge, there is no better way than the Master
himself gave, "As ye sow, so shall ye reap!" (see Gal. 6:7) "By their fruits ye
shall know them!" (see Matt. 7:20) There possibly wasn't a greater parable
than the one He gave, "The wheat and the tares are growing up together. Don't root up the tares now, else the wheat will be destroyed
also, but the time is coming when the wheat will be gathered and put in
the granary and the tares will be gathered and be burned." (see Matt.
13:24-30) Now, who is to be the judge as to what is the proper way and
manner of conducting research into the mysteries of life, or the myster-

ies of nature as we see them? Only by their fruits are we able to judge them. Only by the results individuals obtain who delve into the phenomena of life!

Continually I am asked by people who have just come to know me, "Are you a spiritualist?" "How did you ever become interested in psychic phenomena?" "Are you a medium?" "Are you this, that, or the other?" It has always been my desire to be able to answer for the faith that lies within, and it seems to me that if one cannot answer for the faith that lies within—or that one professes to live by—then such a one is not at his best. For we live by faith, day by day. If we don't know why, how, or what we believe, or why we believe it, we are indeed getting far afield from what the source of life would have us be.

What is life itself? What is the phenomenon of life? Where and how do the various phenomena manifest themselves? To my mind, through my experience, this condition exists: We have a physical body, we have a mental body, we have a spiritual body—a soul. Now, each of these has its own attributes. Just as the physical body has its divisions that are all dependent one upon the other—some more dependent than the rest— so does the mind have its source of activity. So does it have its various sources that manifest themselves in various ways through this individual body. So does the soul have its attributes and its various ways of gaining, maintaining, or manifesting itself among men. The psychic force is a manifestation of the soul mind. Many of you already know my views as to the subconscious mind.

Now as these various phenomena may appear, it doesn't necessarily mean that they appear from what may be termed the disincarnate personalities. If the soul is in the proper accord with the source of life, may not the phenomena be what directed *Aaron* in his activity, rather than what directed the *magicians* as they presented their activity? For if such phenomena come from other than the One Divine Source, it must reach the point where it must fail. The Master was in accord with the One Source of all good, and I think so were many of the others who at various times presented their bodies as a living sacrifice "holy and acceptable unto Him." (*see Rom. 12:1*)

So, it must be possible for any of us to be in accord with the One Divine Source of all information, if we will but pay the price. Often I have fallen far short in presenting myself as a living sacrifice for the manifestation of whatever source might manifest through me. On such occasions, I may be called a *medium*. I hope that I may be rather a *channel* through which blessings may come to many, rather than a *medium* through which any force may manifest other than God Himself. For if it is of God, it must be good. Or, if it is good, it must come from the All Good, which to me is God. This, I trust, is the type of psychic phenomenon that manifests itself through me. Only through the soul are we able to gain access to the throne of God.

Where have we been told that the kingdom of heaven exists? The Master gave it over and over again, and compared it to almost every condition we can imagine. "The kingdom of heaven is within you." *(see Luke 17:21)* That is the source from which all types of information may come. Then unless we have our own personal experience, it cannot mean a great deal to us. It may be interesting—it may even be worthwhile—but until God is our God, until whatever source we have chosen as our ideal source of information is ours, it cannot mean all it should mean. Then, what we each should do is have our *own* experience.

Have you ever asked anyone why he or she belongs to a certain church? Why is it that so few seem to really know, or to give a satisfactory answer to that question? Most people would say, "Oh, my father belonged to that church" or "My mother belonged to that church" or "I felt I ought to join some church, so I just joined that one." Is that a good answer? Is that a good answer to *ourselves*? It *isn't* if we have gotten to where we can think! We reach the place where such an answer doesn't satisfy. We have to come to know the Source of that in which we have believed—that in which we do believe—the Source from which emanates what we hope to build our souls upon. Our souls are what we have to present to our Maker. Our experiences through this life, the phenomena that we pass through here, have much to do with the type, class, or kind of bodies—soul bodies—we will be able to present to that Maker. Are we very sure that we know what we have believed in, and why we act in the way we do toward what we profess to believe? Many of us profess this, that, or the other. How many of us act in a manner in keeping with what we profess to believe?

When we are little children, do we seek for sources of information from some outside source first? If parents are living right with their children, do they allow them to go to other sources first for the foundation on which they build? Are they just as sure of the source from which they are receiving information? If they are in touch, in close association with the Source of All Good, do they want someone else to pass out that key to the source of life to those dependent upon them? No! There are few children who do not first seek their information from their father or mother. Just so it should be with us. When we are seeking to know the phenomenon of life that manifests to us through our soul forces, or through that which we term psychic sources, from what source do we want to receive it? God has seen fit to endow individuals with some peculiar phase of life that is yet scarcely understood, to give us an inkling and an understanding of what the source and the forces in life may mean. But the real source must come to us as our experience, not as someone else's experience!

I think that we have often misconstrued the meaning of the Master's words, "I am in the Father and ye in Me." *(see John 14:20)* Only as we are in the Father and He in us are we able to be of assistance to each other. We can awaken that desire, for the soul seeks its source of supply—as well as its companion, which is not of this earth. It is a companion with the physical being. Through psychic forces, we see various manifestations in life, but let's be very sure that the source is of that emanation—that vibration, that light and color and understanding—which comes from the Source of All Good—which is God!

[The following question and answer occurred at the end of the earlier lecture "What Is the Soul?":]

Question from audience: What is the explanation of "the phenomena"?
Answer by Mr. Cayce: There have been so many explanations given by others, very seldom have I attempted to give my own explanation of *my* interpretation of the phenomena. Possibly none of my associates would agree exactly with me. I have said from the beginning, the phenomenon that has manifested through me is possible in every individual that I have ever contacted. It is possible within each and every one of you. It *manifests* daily. Not in the same degree perhaps. Possibly it's ca-

pable of manifesting in many of you in a much higher degree than it has ever been manifested in or through me.

There has been the promise of old, "If ye forsake not my ways, I will ever abide with you." *(see John 14:16-17)* You can draw your own conclusions from this. Understand that I'm not claiming to be any very good man. For remember this: The man that is more often spoken of as being a man after God's own heart–if you judged him according to *your* idea of morals–he was the most immoral man spoken of in the Book–David. There is nothing in the whole category of sins that we say has to do with morals in human life that is not laid against that man. Yet over and over again, the text is made to say, "I will do this for my servant David's sake, even unto the third and fourth generation." *(e.g., see 2 Kings 19:34)* Why? The *man* David lived as he saw within his own self, doing what was necessary to meet the needs to keep before him–and those he was associated with–his concept of *his* God.

How many of you live that way every day? That *everything* you do is of such a nature that no one meeting you does not know that you are living your concept of your God? Whether you think so or not, that's what you *are* doing. If individuals are willing to lay aside enough of their own personality and individuality to give the Holy Scripture the opportunity to speak through them, it will come in some form or manner.

What is my explanation of the phenomenon? It is the speaking of the spirit through me, whether you want to call it the spirit of John Smith, Will Jones, or who! It's the speaking of the spirit through me. All spirit is of God. Where will it carry your soul? Where does it speak from? It's where it has been carried by the life lived by that individual.

During the Twelve Days Before the Lecture on "The Aura" (May 10, 1931) . . .

In the U.S.: A government report estimates the current per capita wealth at $2,977 per person, while the U.S. Treasury predicts a billion dollar deficit for the year.

On May 1, the Empire State Building opens in New York, becoming the world's tallest building.

In Virginia Beach: Cayce gives twelve readings during this period, including another reading on the "buried treasure" in Culpepper County, Virginia. Remember that Hugh Lynn and the others see this as a potential source of much-needed income for the A.R.E. The searchers seem a little frustrated, and the response appears somewhat impatient:

> Question: How thick is this rock?
> Answer: No matter how thick, if it's to be searched through—then seek!
> Question: Is the depth down to the rock struck in the bottom of the excavation the correct depth?
> Answer: If it was, the treasure would have been uncovered if it was wholly so—would it not? Let's understand that forces in nature, forces in man, forces in the soul of man, sources as are in the realm of man's undertakings, are being used. Use each in their respective sphere. We are through.   3812-11

About the lecture on "The Aura": Most Cayce readings referring to auras are yet to be given, so the sources of Cayce's aura information for this lecture are not known. He mentions, however, experiments he himself participated in under a "student of psychic phenomena" who talked with him about auras. Cayce will later prepare a complete pamphlet on "auras"—one of the few complete booklets he will ever write.

Cayce refers to "hearing Sam Jones once talk" about a man who "got religion." In the Sam Jones Tabernacle in Cayce's hometown of Hopkinsville, Kentucky, Cayce heard not only Sam P. Jones himself, evangelist and builder of the barn–like hall, but also other itinerant evangelists like Dwight Moody, who privately encouraged him to fol-low his inner guidance about serving God.

This lecture was apparently repeated at the Ragged Robin in Norfolk on October 12, 1932.

The Aura

The *aura* is the result of a condition that exists with the *entity*. The term *entity* does not mean just the physical being, but the mental and spiritual being as well. The activities of the physical being, we know, are controlled a great deal by the mental being. The mental being is that which builds up or retards our spiritual being—our soul being. Consequently, the aura is a result—not a cause—of a condition within the individual self.

Before trying to define the aura, we would have to show from what premise we are reasoning, or what we have assumed to exist without question. All force is a manifestation of some form of life. The four elements—earth, air, water, fire—are made up of various forms of life, and we depend upon them for our physical existence. We are assuming, then, that these elements are an expression of Creation. For it is from them that life as we come to know it in this plane is made up. Then as these elements are a form or a portion of Creation, we as human beings—or as finite minds—react to these various forms that go to make up Creation, creating that within ourselves which emanates from us.

We call light a form of fire. No one knows what electricity is. We know some of the things it will do. We know various forms of electricity. We know that it takes on various forms according to the number of units that make up a form visible to us. But there are many forms of electricity *in*visible to us that we depend upon every day for our very existence. This, then, is just one of the creative elements. We come into existence in the earth as a portion of those elements making up the whole human being.

As we react upon those elements, there is the variation according to our reaction. The triune exists throughout creation, changed or altered by its reaction in that state or form that it finds itself, going to make up that basic force of the other element necessary to bring it to an experience, a manifestation, or a form of existence to the human being. So, as we react to these things, we take on certain elements that vibrate or emanate from us. In the throwing off of energy, the wave lengths are active upon these things about that element. Now, as we have builded within ourselves, and as radiation and reaction form into color, we also throw off energy.

The aura is that which we as individuals radiate or throw off. What produces it? Our reaction to all forces in nature that go to make up what is creative within us. As the creative portion reacts, then we are able to see that reflection or activity the creation itself is having upon the individual, or the reflection of the creation, or the Creator Himself. In other words, our own individual reaction to creation makes within our mental being—and reflects through our physical representation in the earth—the spiritual element that is creation! It is the reflection of what we are! Or, what we are speaks so loud one cannot hear what we say. That's another way of saying, "Thoughts are deeds and may become crimes or miracles." (see 136-54, 240-2, 257-71, 505-4, et al) We become that which we constantly hold before us, and that to us is Truth. Truth grows. Our perception grows. Our vision, or visibility grows. By that I mean the soul. "Man looketh on the outward appearance, God looketh on the heart." (see1 Sam. 16:7; also 262-69, -86, -91) That spiritual self within that allows us to vision what is reflected in the individual life is what is termed in the spiritual sense the *aura* of an individual.

We carry our aura around with us every day, and whosoever is able may read it. The aura determines the characterization of the individual. It becomes so clear that, as the Book says, "He who runs may read," provided he is already in attune himself. For he would have to be in accord and have to know what he is looking for. In another place, the Book says, "You are to be as wise as serpents and as harmless as doves." (see Matt. 10:16) An individual mind is only able to catch or grasp a thing by comparing it with something else in nature. It is like an old minister who said, when speaking of how Adam named all the animals, "When Adam looked at the sheep, he looked so sheepish that he just called him a sheep; when Adam looked at the fox, he looked so foxy that he just called him a fox." We have given names to various things we see manifested in nature. Sometimes we see in an individual a manifestation we are unable to describe, other than to say, "He has a wonderful personality." What has made it? What makes a beautiful individual?

I remember hearing Sam Jones once talk about a very ugly man who "got religion" so strong that it shone on his face, and he became one with a beautiful countenance. The spirituality, whether we have it or not, is expressed in our faces. It is stamped there because what we think, what we constantly think within, gradually takes shape, and it shines as a halo about the individual. Such a halo exists about each and every individual. The psychic force within an individual is the relation of the mental being to the soul being.

A few years ago, I went through a series of experiments under a student of psychic phenomena. He told me that he knew from his experiments that there was such a thing as an aura. It was his theory that, as the blood courses through the veins, it runs in the form of a figure eight through the whole body, and sends out to all the outer portions of the body that constant vibration which we call the pulsation. But it sends it out through the circulation between what carries the blood flow to the heart and what carries it from the heart—the capillary circulation. As it goes in and out, it is very much like the heat waves, or the pressure on the barometer, or the ocean tide as it goes up and down by the motion of attraction pulling to and fro. As that goes on in the system, it throws out from the body that which we really are.

What we have thought and what we are building within our bodies is a result (not a cause) of our manner of living! As this is thrown off, as the power or force is in motion, it gives off that which to our senses becomes color. It begins from the lowest color (as in the spectrum), from that leaden or gray, or a misty foam. Then it turns into that orange or dull red. Then it forms into that which becomes as a glow, as we reach to the higher. If you follow these same things in the form of electro-therapeutics, the low form of electrical forces are those which are incapable of being felt, but are very much like that form in lead, or that which comes from the low, baser metals. As we come to the red, we come to that which is the more penetrating. As it gets higher and higher, it turns into another color of orange, then gradually into blue, into purple, into red, and then into white. Those are the colors you may expect to see about individuals—those shades or tones as of the spectrum itself. Of course, there are those shades of green, also.

The doctor who experimented with me found that he could actually measure and weigh the aura. Well, what good is that? Just this: What do we want to carry around with us as our ideal or idea of the Creator, or of creation? If we are *carnal-minded*, we may stay in the red a long, long time. (Many who have the bookkeeping idea know what that means! It is on the wrong side of the book!) Many who are *spiritual-minded* will reflect that which is of the spiritual forces, that continuity of life itself. Our ability to carry on not only in this life, but also in the life to come depends upon that which we have builded—not that we build so as to have a beautiful aura, but that we may have a beautiful life! The aura is the *result* that happens as we go along in life. As we alter or change our life, as we think differently, as we are carried further towards the mark of the higher calling as is set in Him, we carry with us that attunement which others may see. We reflect constantly what we are *doing* with the creative force that belongs to us, which is a gift from the Creator Himself!

Do we know anything that is any more free than the air we breathe? As we respond to creative forces, we gradually reflect that which becomes our aura. What good is it? What may we learn from it? How may we apply it in our own lives? Act in such a way to the other fellow that we constantly give him the impression that we are spiritual-minded. Just as we react, just as we act toward the other fellow, just as we give out—or as I heard a man describe the other day, the fellow who doesn't give will never be able to receive. A closed fist never gives or receives, but the open hand, while giving, receives, and that is a very good illustration of this. We live that which draws us closer to creation itself. We create within our own beings not only health, not only life, not only a beautiful aura, but that which gives out to others, makes life more worthwhile, more worth living for them as well as for ourselves.

During the Two Weeks Before the Lecture on "Relativity of Force" (May 24, 1931)...

In the U.S.: Many Americans, no longer able to pay the rent or the mortgage, move with their families to makeshift settlements of tents, packing crates, and other modes of creative construction. These "Hoovervilles" lie at the outskirts of many cities and even in some city parks, once they attain a foothold. For food, many of these same Americans rely on the bread lines and soup kitchens set up by charitable organizations. The renowned gangster Al Capone is among the first to establish a soup kitchen in Chicago and to tell merchants to give clothes and food to the needy at his expense.

In Virginia Beach: During these two weeks, Cayce gave twenty-seven readings. During a new "buried treasure" reading, the Source acknowledges the searchers' disappointment and urges them on with the information that "the cache is almost wholly intact." (3812-12)

Exploring additional ways of bringing in new income, as well as for making the information and remedies available to more people, has become an important goal for many of those close to Cayce. A reading for businessman David Kahn includes some qualifications about the preparation *atomodine* (subsequently spelled *atomidine*):

> In relation to Atomodine . . . while in a condition or position for distribution, in a manner—is not a *perfected* article as to its greater worth; yet this may be distributed as an *individual* article of value or may be combined with others in the distribution of same . . . In those necessary changes, as we would find to make it more a valuable article, would be in some of the preparations or compounds as they are put together. Were those properties of the iodine in its original state shot through with so many volts of electric current, then its combination and its usefulness as a non-poisonous article in the combination would be made.

This has been outlined before, yet not understood. Necessary that some laboratory tests be made as to just the quantity, or just the quality, of the product before its combination in the boiling together.

Readings later this year will address this product again, moving toward its eventual distribution, as well as its application in many future readings.

About the lecture on "Relativity of Force": Before addressing one of his more difficult topics, Cayce is at his most humble, prefacing his lecture:

Many times in a tobacco field, I have seen a little worm making a tiny hole in a leaf. From his viewpoint, he was doing the very best he could, but he was making an awful mess of the tobacco. I remind myself very much of that worm when I tackle a subject like this.

Relativity of Force
Sunday, May 24, 1931
Newcastle Hotel, Virginia Beach

"Relativity of force" is the relationship of one thing to another. I do not intend to explain any of the theories of eminent scientists through the ages, but simply my concept of it. Necessarily, we must touch upon things that have to do with scientific problems, such as whether man evolved from the monkey or whether he has had *spiritual* evolution.

As the earth came into being, man must have (in some form or other) inhabited it many eons before animals even could have lived on the earth. I don't say he existed as a physical human being, but the *soul*—the concept—must have been in some form that was equal to the conditions that surrounded all forces as they operated in nature. As they began to develop, man gradually took on form. He became a living soul, occupying a position *relative* to that he had occupied, to what he *is* to occupy, to what he *will* occupy!

As man developed, and as he became a *thinking* human being, he began to get farther and farther away from causation. To every cause, there must be an effect. Man comes to that point of reasoning, and if he holds to that, he gets farther and farther away from God! Why? Because he is setting up his own *self*, his own *ideas* (I didn't say ideals) in contrast to what *really* exists!

We say there is no time and no space. Man lives by those very things. If we were able to view this earth and man in the earth from the position that the sun occupies, as the earth turns about it, what time would it be? Three o'clock, noonday, or when? When would the time change? It wouldn't! It wouldn't change so far as the vision of that physical mind, as related to the earth, is concerned. The position or the relative forces would change, but the time would not change. It would always be *one*. It *is* always one, relatively speaking.

As man reasons, he is conscious through the five senses. He is not able to get hold of a thing ordinarily unless such happens. He is not able to grasp an idea unless he can see it, feel it, hear it—unless it comes through his senses. Senses, then, are material—they are confined to those things that pertain to man and that which is about him. Man has never found *what* is the causation of *any* force manifested outside of himself or within himself! Such a thing is not capable of being known with the senses. Yet we all say we live, we exist, we can see objects and know they are there. How do we know they aren't something else than what we think they are?

That's where we come to those things presented to us by our response from within ourselves to those things our senses have conceived as being existent—just as we say it is morning and evening and it is the first day, and it is morning and evening and it is the second day, etc. Then we say, in seven days the Lord created the heavens and the earth, and all that in them are. *Relatively*, yes! Relatively! Whether that means as *we* see it with these senses *now* or not, we do not know! We *cannot* know.

There is nothing we can learn from any philosophy—any schism or ism—that isn't in the Bible. Relatively speaking, we get away from it because we do not apply *spiritual* things to *spiritual* aspects of our life; but we attempt to make for the *physical* conditions about us *spiritual* truths that will govern them. It doesn't work! Why? When we say, "If the God I serve or the God I worship isn't something I can see in my *everyday* experience—if He cannot come down so I can understand Him— then I want none of Him!" And we create in our own minds, then, a God who has eyes because He sees. He must have ears because He hears our prayers. He must have hands so that we may be "in the shadow," as it were, of His hands.

We create what our own minds can grasp in terms of what we know, and we forget what is back of all these things. We have lost the *relative position*! When we stop to think that there are very few of the stars as small as the earth, and that there are many out there that we can't see, how do we know they are bigger? As we read the Bible, it says the moon and the stars were put in place for man's use, and they become the signs, the seasons, and years, and they are all subject then to *man*, and they are for *his* use, according to all these things.

Well, you say, what's the difference? We have created for our mind that we are so all-important that God made all of these things just for us! If we were viewing the earth from the position of the sun, or from the position of any of the farther stars, how large would it be? In comparison, it would hardly be a pencil point on an area of half a mile, yet we want to say how all these things are set and that they are for *our* own convenience! Why do we want to say that?

Relatively, it's true—*if* we have grown big enough within our inner self, within this soul that must have lived eons of time before even the earth came into existence, if we are capable of opening that soul sufficiently to be all-inclusive of all the things of which our body is composed. Our body contains forces that are equal to all that exists in the whole universe, even though we are so tiny, so small—a living body, though, not a dead one! (Many of us are dead and don't know it!) But if we are living, if we are thinking, if we are doing and being, our physical body contains those same elements that go to make up all the universe—*all* the universe and something even more! That spark, that soul, that we are continuing (when we live carnal-minded) to clamp down and down, so that it becomes hard to ever realize from the acts of the individual that he even *has* a soul, or ever expects it to live on. But the only thing that is big enough, or that can grow up big enough to encompass, to understand all this that exists *is* the soul—*if* we have enough faith, even as much as a grain of mustard seed!

Faith comes of what? Can faith come of anything that is material? No! It comes of something that's bigger than all of that. If you have faith even as a grain of mustard seed, you can say to this mountain, "Be removed!"—and it would be removed! Do we grasp, then, how big the soul is, that God would have us be one with him! It is a portion of us— it is that which keeps the body together, yet it is big enough to encompass all of this space about us, and it is also capable of being crowded down even to where one *portion* of the soul, the faithful portion, may not be even as big as a mustard seed! That isn't the way we ordinarily think of the relationships of individuals.

How would we apply these things? How would we set out towards these things? How would we think towards these things? As we begin to grasp some of the mysteries, some of the understandings may come of why there is not *always* the same effect from a cause. There is cause, and its reaction is an effect. That is of a material force. That is the way man judges conditions. We combine certain elements—they will always produce the same thing.

There was a little tree in the back yard. It was beautiful when it was all in blossom, and then as the blossoms fell, the fruit began to appear. It was filled, yet numbers of them fell, and the rest grew to full fruit. Why? What caused it? What were the different elements? Scientists would say, well, something that happened at this point, or some element was lacking at that point, and it would go so far and no farther.

A block of wood cut from a tree in the forest may make a beautiful doorstep in front of our home. To the household, there is something sacred about the gathering about the front steps. It can't be described, but nothing else can take its place. From that same tree, there may be made a communion table for a church. Those who have gathered about a communion table know that it carries with it something sacred such that nothing else just fills its place. It has reached not a family, but a community. That's *relative* position. Is that created in the mind of the individual, is it a harkening back to that something within that may be all-encompassing for the whole universe? Or which may be so tiny, so small, that even one portion of that soul—the faith portion—will not fill a mustard seed? Or so big that it may be all-inclusive, encompassing, that it may gather about it as a line that may be set up for a whole nation, as the totem pole set up for a whole group of people. Look at the flagpole, carrying an emblem which stands for something to a whole nation. The *spirit*, the *life*—that companionship of the soul that is within *every living atom* that exists in the universe—is of *one* Source: The spirit is of God! If we know that *companion* of the soul, then we know what we are going to do with it. That's the whole question.

How do scientists explain why cause and effect do not always follow just in the one straight line? They cannot. Why? Because the world and all that is in it has been *appointed* of God, and He has said, "If ye would obtain mercy from Him, show mercy unto the man next to you." *(see James 2:13; Luke 6:31)* In doing the things He has given us to do, we are awakened within, and we come to a knowledge and an understanding of His ways that to the ordinary man are past finding out. The way has not been closed to any. We may not be able to explain why we believe in Him, but our own acts day by day will show to others *how* we believe in Him. For as we act day by day, we show to the man next to us our conception of our God. And if our God is a material being with all the attributes we create for Him within our own selves and our own activities, that's all He can ever amount to. If it isn't that which knows the *spirit* of things, and that which can awaken the spirit that is within each individual, it can't grow sufficient to encompass the whole earth.

During the Two Weeks Before the Lecture on
"Personality and Individuality" (June 7, 1931) . . .

In the U.S.: President Hoover asks the country to remain "steadfast" during this "Valley Forge" of depression. He feels that for the government to provide "charity" to even the most severely affected Americans would rob them of their motivation to care for themselves: "The way to the nation's greatness is the path of self-reliance."

The deficit forces the U.S. Treasury to sell $800 million in government bonds to maintain operation.

In Virginia Beach: Eighteen readings were given during these two weeks, including one more in the "buried treasure" series, answering additional questions about the search location.

The most significant event of this period is the meeting on June 6 to organize formally the Association for Research and Enlightenment. A work reading on June 1 provides recommendations about the form of the organization, its governance by a board of trustees representing various regions of the country (e.g., Western, Eastern, Southern, Central) with a smaller executive board, classes of membership, etc. The Source comments on the qualifications and potential roles of specific individuals. (254-57)

The meeting on June 6th takes place at Cayce's home with "sixty or more present," according to a Cayce letter reporting the meeting. During the discussion, Cayce sees a figure in white clothing and a turban— apparently Persian—sitting on the stairs and nodding agreeably about the suggestions and decisions being made. This same figure had appeared to Cayce years before warning him about his early associates in Hopkinsville. Within a few days, a charter is approved and the Association for Research and Enlightenment is incorporated in Virginia Beach.

At about this same time, Morton Blumenthal sends a sheriff to the Cayce home with an eviction notice, informing the family that they must move out of their home by July 1. Until now, Cayce was under the impression that Morton had given him the house, but he does not put up any resistance. In his memoirs, Cayce says, "It was perfectly all right, if he just hadn't plain lied about it—that I just dislike in anyone." (from *Edgar Cayce—My Life As a Seer: The Lost Memoirs*, p. 235)

About the lecture on "Personality and Individuality": This lecture returns the series to the Presbyterian Church in Virginia Beach.

Cayce refers briefly to Charles Lindbergh as a "great man" or at least a "noted" man at the time. (He completed his famous solo trans–Atlantic flight four years earlier.) From a view about ten years in the future, his life will represent an interesting example for the point Cayce is making: "It isn't the fame that lives on. Fame is only for the moment. That which really lives on is the individuality of the individual, or their abilities to meet any and every condition that will enable the lives of those who follow in the same path." Consider how Lindbergh meets the tragedy of the kidnapping of his son in less than a year (March 1932). Further consider how Lindbergh later (1936–38) openly supports the ideas of Adolf Hitler and the Nazis in Germany (including the sterilization of "defective" individuals). In fact, for his efforts on their behalf, he is awarded the Service Cross of the German Eagle in 1938 by Hermann Goering, Hitler's second–in command. Might such experiences have an impact on his individuality?

Personality and Individuality

Sunday, June 7, 1931
First Presbyterian Church, Virginia Beach

So many books have been written on *personality*—how to acquire it, the key to personality, what is personality, the psychology of personality, and such things—that it seems unreasonable for an individual like myself to attempt to say anything else about it, or to attempt to explain the difference between *personality* and *individuality*. However, most of you know that I tackle big jobs.

Some years ago, I met an East Indian under very unusual circumstances, it seemed to me. That evening we were at dinner together. This was the subject of his lecture. Perhaps some of you have heard of him, as he is a very noted lecturer. During the discussion that evening, he asked me what I thought was the difference between *personality* and *individuality*. I answered him in this way: "Personality is what you want the other fellow to *think* you are, and individuality is what you *really* are!" That's it!

Since then, we have had a great many instances in our information where it has touched on how one may acquire personality. That's a different tale. There must be an *individuality* before one can acquire a *personality*. There must be! Your individuality is *what you are*—the sum total of all your experiences throughout the earth's plane, no matter whether you have lived once or a thousand times upon the earth! It is the sum total of *all* your experiences upon the earth and what you have done with them, what you have done about them, or how you have reacted towards them.

Now that is *spirituality* also. Your individuality is motivated by your spirituality, for, unless it is alive, there is no spirit in it. If you haven't any spirituality within your whole makeup, you may read and study all the books in the world on the subject, but you'll never have a personality that will influence anyone for good.

If you would gain personality—that something for which individuals are sought, that manner or way of putting a thing over—first start to acquire spirituality, or individuality. If personality alone has gone to seed, a man may have a wonderful personality for the moment, but it will not last very long. It will soon pass out of the picture, and he becomes just a shell or—as the Master expressed it—he becomes a whited sepulcher, full of dead men's bones. (*see Matt. 23:27*)

Let's go back just a moment. Perhaps you will disagree with me on this. Man's advent into the world was possibly millions of years ago, when he came as a voice upon the waters, or as the wind over the waters. That was his soul—or man as his soul—when he first became individual and separated from God, the Creative Force Himself. As the earth became a place upon which man might take form, and evolution as we know it began to go on through the earth, man became more and more personal—more a *personality*—and he got farther and farther from his *individuality*, or his soul—that which is life itself. He will continue to get farther and farther away unless he, by his association with the Spirit from within, harks back to that Source from which he emanated.

Some of you have studied along such lines and know what I have reference to—how the physical evolution may have gone on in the earth—which has nothing in the world to do with man's ever having been a monkey. For man has been a voice and, if he has any of God in him today, he is still a voice. For that which goes out is that individuality shining through the personality of the individual, or what the individual has done with his environs and his circumstance, as to whether he has kept them in line with that from which he came and to which he is returning. For man's experience in the earth's plane is to determine as to whether he is a fit associate for God or not! That's true, isn't it? He has been given the privilege to come into the earth and to manifest in these ways, through the dual conditions that exist—through personality and individuality. If he makes the one with God, he is a source, or whatever we may call it. If he has so shelled himself about [enclosed himself in a shell] that it is this *I*, this *Me*, instead of the great *I AM*, then he has allowed his personality to overshadow him, as to separate himself entirely from his ability to become one with the source of all creation.

Now, that is my interpretation of my feelings in the matter. As said of Moses when he came down from the mount, his face shone, his personality shone so—because he had been so close to God—it was necessary for him to put a veil over his face, even that the children of Israel might look upon him. (see Exod. 34:35) To all of us, that which attracts to us an individual is their personality. That thrown out from them, that they would have us feel that they are—we are attracted by that. If the basis of that *personality* is not founded in their *individuality*—what they really are, their spiritual selves—it soon becomes shallow and means very little, and the individual soon loses all the attraction he may have had—unless we are like-minded. For all blackbirds flock together—they don't try to associate with jays or crows.

It's the same with us. If we are like-minded, we will naturally come together. If we are shallow and it's only a front we are putting up, if it's only that personality that we want to shine and there's nothing of the reality back of it, naturally we will drift along together, but we will fall out—and we do fall out sooner or later. If it is the continuity of life, we will really gather more and more and more. For the thought, the will, the direction of whatever power we may see is constantly directed in that one purpose that finds an answer in every individual we may contact.

So if we are the sort that the better people know us, the better they like us, we may be very sure that our individuality shines out through our personality. If we are of the sort that are glorious to meet for a few minutes, but not the sort to do this, that, or the other with, then we are hollow, we have become as sounding brass, or as a tinkling cymbal. (see I Cor. 13:1) Then it's time for us to stop and take account of ourselves to see if we have a *personality*, to see if we have that faculty spoken of as *individuality*, and awaken within ourselves—our inner selves—the spirituality or individuality (for they mean one and the same thing). The farther man has gotten away from the subconscious, or the soul consciousness, the more his personality has shone out. But as to whether the personality was the lasting kind or simply just a reflected light that lasted for only a little while depends on the individuality back of it.

The man who has individuality, his whole experience lives on and on in the minds and the hearts of the people whom he serves; for "the greatest among you is the servant of all," (see Mark 10:44). And it isn't *personality* that's the servant of anyone, unless it is backed up first by real *individuality*, real spirituality within the individual. God makes us our individualities—we make our personalities. If we are using the wrong kind of material to build a thing, we may be very sure it will be a poor structure. The same with the personality. It will be a very poor front we are able to put up before those we contact from day to day, unless it is builded with the right sort of material.

There is so much said about people growing farther and farther from God, and so much said about people growing closer and closer to God. It depends entirely upon how the individual is making use of every force within his own experience. We often read how we may contact certain influences by creating that "bold front." I disagree with all such. If we want to be able to make a bold front, let's have something behind it so that, when the light is thrown out, others may see there is something real! We can put up a bold front, but unless there is some spirituality behind it—some individuality behind it—the bold front won't do us any good. That which we cultivate grows. If we are cultivating personality and haven't cultivated the real thing, it makes the personality go to seed very soon. If we cultivate our relationship to God, the personality will shine out in such a way that it is worthwhile for others to contact us. Our personality lives on in the earth—it doesn't live afterward. We give it up. We leave it here. It's the personality we know of individuals who have lived in the earth's plane and have made, we would say, names for themselves.

There were wonderful individuals, wonderful examples, but rather did they become examples from their spirituality possessed and made use of, rather than just personality that shone out before me. As we come to know individuals, even those who have passed—those who have made history—it isn't those little things that shone out at the time, but the whole individuality back of them.

There was a discussion between two men—men very able in their fields—as to the personality of Abraham Lincoln. One said his personality as known of men was very little—he loved to tell dirty stories, he wanted to tell those things that would attract for the moment. The other said it was his individuality—his ability to meet any circumstance whenever it arose in his life—that made him a great man. The personality cannot enable one to meet hardships, for when it strikes obstacles, it soon fades away. Individuality, or spirituality, enables us to meet any condition that may arise in our lives—and smile about it all the while. We say Lindbergh is a great man at the present time. Rather is he *noted* at the present time—that's all we can say of any individual. They usually become great, or greater, after they have passed into the Beyond. We do not know what one is going to make out of his life—what it will mean to the world is yet to be seen. He is simply noted for the time being. He is a famous aviator, sure, but being famous doesn't mean a very great deal. Now, if that lives on and he is not forgotten four years after he dies, why it would be a different thing! It isn't the fame that lives on. Fame is only for the moment. That which really lives on is the individuality of the individual, or their abilities to meet any and every condition that will enable the lives of those who follow in the same path.

If we understand that God would have us reflect Himself in our lives, in our personalities, then we know the difference between individuality and personality. We all come from the One Source. Our beings are the gift of the Father, and as we do with that gift as He would have us do, the individuality and personality are the natural result.

During the Two Weeks Before the Lecture on "Hypnotism" (June 21, 1931) . . .

Around the world: On June 17 in China, British troops arrest a Vietnamese nationalist leader who later adopts the name Ho Chi Minh. [In 1942, Ho will be arrested again in China, by Generalissimo Chiang Kai-Shek, only to be released to the U.S. Office of Strategic Services (OSS)—predecessor of the CIA. Ho will return to Indochina and, working with the OSS, help rescue Allied pilots shot down over Indochina. Ho Chi Minh will support the U.S. effort during World War II and is perceived as a friend of the only nation he sees capable of aiding in his country's independence from France. The future U.S. involvement in Vietnam will be yet another story.]

In Virginia Beach: During these two weeks, Cayce gives twenty-three readings. These include two more readings for the team trying to locate the buried money near Kelly's Ford in Culpepper County, Virginia. In their continuing frustration, the team asks "Are there any Forces trying to prevent recovery of this treasure? If so, why?" and "Are there any influences in the community that would prevent these recovering the treasure?" The Source suggests there may be others with interest in the treasure, but this group should persist in its search, reassured that "it is here!" Unfortunately, nothing is ever recovered from this site. "Buried treasure" does not seem to be an answer to A.R.E. finances.

About the lecture on "Hypnotism": As Cayce points out, a forerunner of hypnotism was practiced in the 1700s by a German physician, Franz Anton Mesmer, using magnets to assist in physical healing. He called it "animal magnetism" and published a report on his findings in 1779. This later became known as "mesmerism."

The term "hypnotism"—reflecting the Greek word *hypnos*, meaning sleep—was created in 1842 by Dr. James Braid, an English surgeon (not by a French doctor, as Cayce suggests). Braid concluded it was not the magnets that induced hypnosis, but something within the patient. He attempted to standardize induction techniques.

In 1922, Emil Coué published a book on *Self-Mastery*, in which he promoted self-hypnosis and proposed the popular self–help phrase referred to in the lecture: *Every day, in every way, I get better and better.*

Cayce refers to the then–declining interest in hypnotism as a form of stage entertainment, which has effectively disappeared since Cayce's time. On the other hand, what was still deemed questionable about hypnosis during his lifetime has been replaced by widespread acceptance and application of hypnosis in the healing process, including for the change of habits such as smoking and overeating.

Hypnotism

Sunday, June 21, 1931
First Presbyterian Church, Virginia Beach

H ypnotic influence is recognized by the medical profession as dif-
ferentiated from narcotic influences, though the activity of certain
drugs is very similar to conditions produced by hypnotic influence.
Both may produce in the brain cells a condition causing an inability of
certain parts of the body to perform their normal functioning, whether
produced by suggestion or any of the many phases of such influence.

The first individual to give the name *hypnotism* to such influence was
a doctor in France in 1800. As a young man, he began the practice of
what is now known as hypnotism. Since then, the greater amount of
study and the only great schools of hypnotism are in France. No doubt
you know the history of Mesmer and *Mesmerism*. Now, Mesmer called it
a different condition entirely, yet in all general ways the subject passes
through the same experiences in hypnotic influence as in mesmeric
influence. Also Mesmer proclaimed that there was an invisible fluid
that passes from the operator to the subject, which later scientists have
described as *ectoplasm*. Whether it's the same thing or not, we might
have more of that in *spiritualism*.

My first experience with hypnotic influence was forty years ago. The
first time I ever saw anyone hypnotized was by a professor or doctor
who called himself Hart, the Laugh King. I have seen him hypnotize at
least two hundred people in an audience of five hundred. The suscepti-
bility of persons to hypnotic influence, I believe, is about 95 percent.

As to the condition that takes place, there are possibly four distinct
stages. Of course, many of the students of hypnotism—or many of those
who use it as a profession—tell you there's seven, eight, ten, or twelve
stages. Possibly so, but you have to draw a very fine line for those differences. There isn't very much difference between the first stage of
hypnotism and taking a good hot bath. The same condition exists in the
body. When you take a good hot bath and feel sleepy, it is produced by

161

the drawing away of the blood from the brain or the active forces of the brain.

Many very fine men have studied the various forms or conditions that might be produced by hypnotism, and the benefits that might be derived from it. There is a great school of hypnotism in Nancy, France. Many of you have heard of the man who originated the saying, "Every day in every way I am growing better and better." He was one of the students of that school. There is also a hospital in Paris where most of the operations are performed under hypnotic influence, rather than anesthesia.

In my own experience, when I was operated on for appendicitis, the physician in charge had me put myself to sleep. Then he gave me the anesthetic, for he was afraid I might awake during the operation. Possibly the influence under which I place myself is very much akin to hypnotic influence. Whether it is the same thing or not, I do not know. Many of the men who have made a study of the phenomena manifested through me have termed it *self-hypnotism*.

In the first stages of hypnotism, the ordinary nerve forces refuse to function. This is called the power of suggestion, or control of one mind over another. As to whether that is the condition or not, I am not prepared to say, because I do not know whether it may be done entirely by suggestion or not. It is certainly true that, if a subject has been hypnotized very often by the same operator, just by looking at the person he will be able to make that individual lose consciousness. Not only will he lapse into the first stage, but into the second—that in which the sympathetic nerve system refuses to function or to coordinate with the rest of the body. Or he will reach a little lower stage in the same operation, which is called the *somnambulistic*—the stage in which you lose not only consciousness, but something that has the power of knowing what goes on *during* that period or *before* that period; and yet the next time you are put into that state you will remember everything that transpired during the time you were in the hypnotic state.

The first stage is what we ordinarily see in performances on the stage, where they make monkeys of everybody—just to entertain people. Such things do happen and can happen. What activity takes place is still a moot question with many people. Whether it is something that happens between individuals or whether one has the greater power over the other or not, I do not know, but it does happen, and people know that it happens. What it is has not been decided by the scientists, or those people who even practice it. Apparently, it is one of those phenomena that comes and goes in prominence.

A few years ago we used to see many hypnotists performing on the stage. Gradually that seemed to go out of fashion. Now, there are many who actually use it in their practice. It has not yet been determined as to how great an influence may be had upon the life of another by continually putting them under hypnotic influence. Whether it is possible for one to force another to commit a crime while under the hypnotic influence, I doubt very much. I believe the best minds will say the same thing. However, I believe it is possible for one to continually use an individual and gradually build into their minds that which they desire them to do and possibly force them to do things, or train their subconscious mind to the point where things they had once considered against their morals will agree with the operator's ideas. For you *can* fool your subconscious mind!

You will notice from the first symptoms of hypnotism that it operates upon the voluntary muscular forces, or voluntary action of the nervous system. In the deeper stages of hypnotism, we reach the moral and mental fiber of individuals. After all, there is nothing outside of the universe—outside of the human being in the universe—which is not contained within a normal physical living body, even to God Himself. Then the activity of one portion of a normal mind, acting upon the forces within another individual, may overbalance on one portion. By what? That which controls all of the physical organism, which is *suggestion*, carried by the mental being, the physical being, or even the soul being itself. Then it may partake of all those influences. As to what good can be done with it, that is another question entirely.

Like many of the things that can be made very valuable to the human family, hypnotism is also a very dangerous thing—just as I said about being able to be a mind reader, or telepathist, or influence other peoples' lives. It is a wonderful thing to possess that ability within self to influence another individual, but it is a detrimental thing if you misapply it or misuse it! Just so with the ability of individuals to hypnotize, to gain control over the voluntary forces, so one cannot voluntarily do anything of himself. That's the first influence over a hypnotized person. He cannot of himself do anything except what he is told to do. Then, to be hypnotized is to turn the faculties of your personality over to another person, and for *that* person's personality to control *your* personality. Hypnotic influence, or hypnotism then, is merely one of the phases of human experience through which one may be operated upon. Anyone may develop so as to be able to hypnotize another. Anyone can keep from being hypnotized. I believe that hypnotism, properly used, can be made one of the greatest boons to suffering humanity. If used improperly, it can be a curse.

During the Two Weeks Before the Lecture on "Psychoanalysis" (July 5, 1931) . . .

In Virginia Beach: In response to Morton Blumenthal's demand that the Cayces vacate their house, they move from the 35th Street house to a small house on the oceanfront, Wright's Cottage—ironically, right across the street from the former hospital. They will be able to watch as it is converted first into the Cape Henry Hotel. Within a year, Edwin and Morton Blumenthal will turn it into the Princess Pat Hotel. Another irony: Their loss of their much-beloved home and its garden echoes what many across America are experiencing in the wake of the stock market crash. Without consulting Edgar, Gladys begins to contact members and prospective donors to seek funds for purchasing a home for the Cayces.

Since the closing of the hospital, Cayce's health and demeanor have been deteriorating. He experiences neuritis and a recurring loss of his voice. Partly because of the move and partly because of his ill health, he gives only six readings during these two weeks, four of them on June 29.

About the lecture on "Psychoanalysis": In the early moments of this lecture, Cayce refers to three *divisions* of psychotherapy, one of which is *psychoanalysis*. The other two are *autosuggestion* (related to the preceding lecture on hypnosis) and *"new education"* or *"new thought."* The term "New Thought" is usually associated with the spiritual philosophies of Charles and Mildred Fillmore (founders of the Unity movement) and of Ernest Holmes (founder of Religious Science and *Science of Mind*). If that is what Cayce is referring to here, it is interesting to see these spiritual philosophies—which emphasize, for example, "change your thinking, change your life"—included as one of Cayce's "divisions" of psychotherapy.

It is also interesting to consider where the practice of psychoanalysis was in 1931 and where it is in today's world. Freud's *The Interpretation of Dreams* was published in 1900, and in 1909 he gave his first lectures in the U.S., which became the basis of a book published in 1916. In 1931, psychoanalysis was still not widely accepted, as Cayce points out. Actually psychoanalysis as a significant mental health "treatment" hit its greatest popularity in mid-twentieth century. Today psychoanalysis—a very long process, as Cayce points out—is but one healing approach among an arsenal of mental health treatment modalities, including some that seem to be effective in relatively short periods of time, such as pharmaceutical products.

Psychoanalysis

Sunday, July 5, 1931
First Presbyterian Church, Virginia Beach

The subject of *psychoanalysis* is really a subtopic of *psychotherapy*. At least it is so considered by those who accept any phase of the phenomena at all, and it fits in very well with the subject we last discussed—*hypnotism*. The three divisions given by those who have found psychotherapy worth studying are autosuggestion, new education or "new thought," and psychoanalysis.

Psychotherapy itself means the study of the mind and its activity in general, so if I divide it up—talking first about one phase and then about another—it is only to become more specific and avoid confusion. I will try to stick close to psychoanalysis as a phase of psychotherapy.

Psychoanalysis, new thought, and autosuggestion are just other names for "new education" or "higher education"—though not that higher education that deals with the development of man's mental phases. Psychotherapy has been rejected by medical men for a number of years. Recently some of the leading men of the profession, such as Dr. Mayo and others who are considered authorities, have accepted certain phases of it. They accept, however, more of the autosuggestion than of the psychoanalysis. This latter is almost a personal product of Dr. Freud.

I have had, in my limited experience, several contacts with individuals and physicians who have used, in one way or another, the various phases of psychotherapy. Psychoanalysis as taught by Dr. Freud deals with the suppression of suggestions that have been given to the mind of a person during his formative stages, usually during the developing years of childhood. Dr. Freud has carried his theory to sex as a basic cause of most nervous diseases. Certain people even go so far as to say that the majority of nervous troubles which manifest in a neurotic or neurasthenic condition arise from suppression of the mind during its developing stages of childhood. When we come to that phase of it, we find that most of those people who treat such conditions psychoanalytically require from one to two years' study of a case before they complete a diagnosis. The suggestions are taken from the dreams of the patient during this period of investigation, and all dreams are interpreted according to the Freudian system of dream symbols, or a system similar to it. Under such circumstances, a psychoanalyst can only treat about six patients a year, and it follows that it requires a lot of money to be psychoanalyzed.

As to the difference between psychoanalysis and the phenomena manifested through me, I can explain that in a few words. Often there are conditions in people's lives that are the result of former experiences. The information as it comes through me takes the whole life as one, whether the individual has lived seven times in this world or seven hundred. At any one time, the individual is a sum total of what he has builded for himself throughout his experiences in the earth's plane. Naturally, this leads us into reincarnation.

Psychoanalysis only takes in the one life, the one advent into the world of experience. According to the psychoanalyst, those things, those ideas that have been impressed upon the body during that formative stage of the mind's development are what affect it both physically and mentally. And if one becomes overbalanced, there are certain nervous disorders coming about from it.

A psychoanalyst whom I knew had been treating a patient for three years. She obtained a reading for him through these channels. Her history of the case agreed with the reading in some respects. She claimed that the condition arose from an experience when the young man was a child. His nurse took him to a park, and a conversation between herself and a policeman made such an impression on the child that it produced the nervous condition that grew worse as he grew older. She had discovered this from the dreams he had had during the three years she treated him. The reading, in slight contrast to this, had a great deal to say about the boy's former appearances, and how he had acted in relation to other individuals in a former appearance. It pointed out that he merited this condition, and stated that, in order to overcome it, the help of a stronger personality and will was necessary.

Now, although I do not know the outcome of this case, it seems to me that, despite the conflict as to the cause of the boy's condition, the strong mind and dominating personality of the psychoanalyst—put forth in a sympathetic effort to help the boy— would produce the conditions necessary for cure.

In the field of psychoanalysis, I think we all ought to have something we can use ourselves each and every day. I do not believe in people living in the past to such an extent that they dwell on it, becoming melancholy and morose. That is usually a sign of old age, when life is almost over. Yet, I do believe in individuals stopping occasionally to take account of themselves, analyzing their own activities, pondering why they like this, dislike that, why they are affected by certain associations, and what brought these conditions about. Then they should have something to compare these with. To do that, they must have an *ideal*.

Each and every individual must have an ideal. Just as in the psychoanalysis of an individual it is necessary to set a certain standard by which every portion of the individual's mind and physical condition is gauged, so in the analyzing of self there must be a standard to go by. We must have a standard—an ideal—and we must analyze ourselves and measure the result by that ideal. As to what the ideal should be, that is a personal matter. If an individual determines that what he wants in the world is fame and fortune, or an easy life, or just to "get by," if he has that for an ideal—a life of no hardships with nothing to overcome and the world owing him a living that he's going to get—then he will be a hanger-on and gradually go down to the level of his ideal—or rather the level to which such an ideal must eventually bring all who cherish it. An individual's life and environment in this plane is the sum total of all his experiences and his reactions to them, whether considered as one individual life or as all the experiences he may have had on the earth's plane.

My idea is that psychoanalysis should be used to measure ourselves to a standard. This may sound like uniting Christian Science with Psychoanalysis. They are as far apart as east and west—at least they are considered so—but I think that all the force, all the power that may come from an ideal is of one source. It is up to the individual as to what he does with that force or that power that is able to manifest through him.

There is latent within each and every individual that ability to analyze self and surroundings. And if each does that, there will be little time for analyzing other people. I would suggest that each individual analyze himself, questioning why he reacts against or toward certain circumstances, conditions, individuals, etc., and then measure those things by a standard or an ideal. In so doing, he will find that New Thought, Autosuggestion, New Education, Psychoanalysis, Christian Science, and any other of the sects or isms have their inception from one Source, and individuals have merely separated them into divisions and given them names to suit their own convenience. Such divisions or schisms or isms tell you that you have to go to the other fellow when, in reality, all the help that anyone can possibly get must come from the divine forces latent within them.

During the Two Weeks Before the Lecture on "Reincarnation" (July 19, 1931)...

In the U.S.: An epidemic of polio in the summer of 1931—over 30,000 cases—results in more than 4,000 deaths, in spite of some advances in research on the disease.

The University of Chicago Press publishes the first edition of the "American Translation" of the Bible, with J.M. Powis Smith and Edgar J. Goodspeed as editors and two of the translators. John 1:1 is translated as "In the beginning the Word existed. The Word was with God, and the Word was divine." An earlier version appeared in 1923. A 1939 edition will come to be called "the Goodspeed Bible."

In Virginia Beach: The charter for the "Association for Research and Enlightenment" is granted on July 7.

During these two weeks, Cayce gives seventeen readings. Of these, a work reading (254-58) reviews the proposed by-laws for the new organization (A.R.E.) and discusses several questions about membership and leadership. The source says that, once the by-laws are set, they are to be kept "inviolate." "Once turned in an unmindful direction, brings discord."

About the lecture on "Reincarnation": Not surprisingly, Cayce first addresses reincarnation from the "evidence" presented in the Bible. He then refers to an early "horoscope reading" and subsequent readings which mention "former appearances." He cites a specific example from a life reading in which the woman was able to verify a past existence in a most unusual way.

This is one of the first lectures in which several audience questions were recorded. They are included at the end of the lecture.

Gladys's notes suggest this or a similar lecture may have been given two years earlier, but that cannot be confirmed.

Reincarnation

Reincarnation is a question that is occupying the minds of people today, possibly more than at any time. It has long been considered a part of Eastern religions, so that we have cause to consider it foreign to Christianity. For many years I was taught that and believed it and taught it myself. However, I doubt if anyone who has really studied the Bible or the Scriptures could say that it was not contained in that Book.

Throughout the ages, the question has been asked, "If a man die, will he live again?" (see Job 14:14) One of the poets gave, "Dust thou art, to dust returneth"—this was not spoken of the soul. Consequently, it has been generally considered that if a man live again, it is his soul that lives. Then, to the Christian way of thinking, a man only has one life. As a man dies, so is he departed, or as the tree falls, so will it lie. (see Eccl. 11:3)

There are many instances when the Master said "Ye must be born again." (John 3:7; see also 1 Peter 1:23) And He said that we must be born of the water and of the blood. When questioned regarding these things, he did not clarify them—He knew that we did not understand. He said to Nicodemus, "Art thou a master of Israel, and knowest not these things? The wind bloweth where it listeth, and thou hearest the sound thereof, but canst not tell whence it cometh, and whither it goeth. So is every-one that is born of the spirit." (see John 3:1-10)

The disciples asked the Master, "Who did sin, this man or his parents, that he was born blind?" Jesus answered, "Neither hath this man sinned, nor his parents; but that the works of God should be made manifest in him." (John 9:2-3) Now, it wouldn't have been possible for the man to have sinned in this world (as we know the world) into which he was born blind. They must have believed that the man lived before, or else they wouldn't have asked such a question.

Again, the Master said to His disciples that some of them would not taste death until they had seen the Son of Man come in His glory. After

six days, He took with him Peter, James, and John, and went up to the
Mount of Transfiguration, and there they saw Moses and Elias. The disciples, or at least Peter, recognized them, and wanted to make it a per-
manent thing—wanted them to remain with them forever, which wasn't
to be at that particular time. But as they came down from the Mount,
Peter and John asked the Master, "Why, then, say the scribes that Elias
must come first? And Jesus answered and said unto them, Elias is come
already, and they knew him not, but have done unto him whatsoever
they listed. Likewise shall also the Son of Man suffer of them. Then the
disciples understood that He spake unto them of John the Baptist." (see
Matt. 16:28; Matt. 17:1-13)

In another place, He said, "Verily I say unto you, among them that
are born of women there hath not risen a greater than John the Baptist;
notwithstanding he that is least in the kingdom of heaven is greater
than he. And from the days of John the Baptist until now the kingdom
of heaven suffereth violence, and the violent take it by force. For all the
prophets and the law prophesied until John. And if ye will receive it,
this is Elias, which was for to come." (Matt. 11:11-14) Later Paul said, "The
first Adam brought sin into the world, but the last Adam brought life."
(see 1 Cor. 15:45) Whether that's figuratively speaking or not is for us to
determine within our own experience.

Always there was within me a feeling that did not find answer in
what was ordinarily given as the answer for such feelings. How is it that
some people we meet we immediately feel as if we had known them all
our lives, and others we have known for years in this life and still do
not feel close to them or understand them? I don't believe anyone can
answer that unless there is more than just this life. I'm sure none of us
feels within ourselves that this span of life is all there is to life, for we
remember that many writers in the Book give, "You do not live again
unless you die." (see Job 14:14) Nothing lives again unless it dies. Even the
grain of wheat, if it dies, it lives again. But it doesn't live again unless it
dies, bringing forth that which will propagate its own self.

That in itself seems to be an answer, or a reason for believing that
each individual will have that opportunity to choose to come into the
earth's plane, even as the Son of Man chose to become our Savior. He
chose that. It wasn't forced upon Him. It isn't forced upon the indi-

vidual to enter the earth plane again. The individual may use the opportunity to manifest through the earth's plane—that he may make manifest God's love—because we are each a portion of Him, and it isn't a forced issue with me. We may work out our own salvation through whatever sphere we may find ourselves. We have an opportunity to come into the earth to make manifest what we may have gained through whatever experience we may have passed. God gives us that opportunity. It is our job to do the working out. He is willing to aid us in doing the job right, but it's our job—and we have to do it! Too often we want to do the work *our* way and take the credit to ourselves.

The first information we had about reincarnation in the readings came through what was called then the horoscope reading. It gave more about the planetary influences upon the individual, the personality, and what could be made out of this life. Then it told about why such a personality or individuality existed. For we know that the *individuality* is what the individual really is, that which has been builded within the individual, so that the shining out through this we call flesh makes the *personality* of the individual. The personality, then, is a reflection of the person's individuality and what we are today. Our personalities that are seen before me reflect all that we have builded within our own selves, whether it has been done through one life or a thousand lives.

Then the information in the readings spoke of former appearances in the earth plane. As I saw more and more of such information, I came to think—as a certain lady expressed herself to me one day—"I have often wondered what's the snake in the woodpile. Now I know—it's reincarnation."

There are two groups of individuals who do not accept anything that pertains to reincarnation: These who are very orthodox in what they call Christianity and those who are of the spiritualistic faith. According to their own teachings or their own beliefs, they cannot accept it.

Now reincarnation means that the individual, the entity, lives again. At first it was hard for me to separate that idea from transmigration, but now I realize that they are entirely different.

A reading told a certain lady that she had lived about ten thousand years ago in what is now New Mexico, and that she had made certain marks, certain hieroglyphics, which were still to be found in that location. Later she wrote me that she had gone there with a group of friends and had found the marks just as indicated. Now, I had never been to New Mexico and neither had she—in this life. When she saw those indications, something answered within her so that she knew she had lived there and had made those marks.

That's the same way with us. If the information tells us that we were associated with certain individuals during certain periods in the earth's plane, and we see in the present an exact replica of the description of former associations—and the reactions that would naturally come from such associations—we are bound to see the consistency of it.

At the present time, I am very much interested in seeing two people meet whom I know from the information in the readings were sisters in a former incarnation. I think I know exactly how they will react to each other when they do meet. Such experiences might not be proof to some people, but I can only give instances that have been brought to my attention, and let others decide for themselves. We either have to accept all of it or reject all of it. Of course, that is the way we should be with our religion, but most of us take one little portion and run away with it, and reject all the rest.

[Mr. Cayce responded to questions from the audience.]

Question from audience: Do you think that when a soul enters the earth plane, it knows what sort of environment it is coming into and the conditions it will have to face?

Mr. Cayce's answer: Yes, I think it must know that it is entering the environment which is necessary for its own development, and it must know the whole outline of the life and the purpose of it. It knows this is its opportunity to pass through that experience necessary for its development. Just as when God made Saul king, He must have known what was going to happen—and it hurt Him to know that Saul was going to prove so faithless, yet he was given the opportunity to become the greatest king the world had ever had. Then God raised another man who was given an opportunity to show the world what could be done by ruling over such a people. Just the same with a soul, and I do not believe that a soul enters until the breath of life is drawn. The soul doesn't enter at conception.

Question: Is the soul sent here, or does it come of its own desires?
Cayce: Comes of its own desires, for desire remains throughout all development of man, or of the soul, whether we speak of material, mental, or the soul portion. Desire goes right through, and is possibly the motivative force behind the soul. For without a desire to do a thing, we can't get very far. We don't begin to build until the desire is created, and the course the desire takes depends upon whether it has its inception in Truth or Untruth.

Question: If the soul knows so much, why does it have to do all these things over again?
Cayce: It's very much like we have in school, I think. We have to go over and over a lesson, for it is not to be merely rote. In other words, as a man's religion should be–not just because it is the thing to do, but because it is the reality. We go over and over a lesson in mathematics until we know not only that it is rote, but that we can get an answer by doing that. We have to know the principle of the thing, or the basis of it. Man goes over and over his lessons, and necessarily under much different environment that it builds that which is lacking–or he has the opportunity to build that which has been lacking in the soul development, that has kept it from understanding its relationship to its Maker.

Question: Are we not reaping what we have sown in the past, and is not the earth today reaping some terrible tares it has sown?
Cayce: The earth changes continually because it is for man's indwelling. As the earth changes, man has to conform to those changes, which have been necessary for his own upbuilding.

Question: Do you believe that every human being has soul?
Cayce: I believe that every human being has a soul–that which makes it akin to the Creator, that which is given an individual that it may become a companion to the Creator. As we see in the forces all about us, Nature herself desires companionship. So does God! He gives us the opportunity to be His companions by giving us a soul–which we may

make a companion with Him, but we have to do the making. He is willing to aid us and will assist us if we will allow it to be, but we have also been given a will, which we may take from or add to.

[Audience questions relating to reincarnation from an earlier lecture:]

Question: Why do so many of us in our previous entities appear in Egypt? *Cayce:* I haven't studied this phase as much as some of them. According to the numbers so far whom we have had information about, there are comparatively few from Egypt, if you take it from the total numbers on whom we have had life readings.

Let me tell you another question that someone asked me the other day on this same thing. "I like this idea of reincarnation if it didn't appear that all of us were princes and princesses at some time." All of us were some great individuals at some time. We are all *gods*, every one of us—and have been and *will be*, if we will only live like that and not live like devils! Because an individual may have been a servant doesn't necessarily mean he hasn't been a prince.

It is much like the story I heard told from the pulpit some time ago: A lady who was very wealthy had died. She went to heaven and met Peter at the gate. As she went through, she wanted to know where her home was. He told her: "Go right down that street and after a while you will find the place you are to live." As she went down the street, she noticed a beautiful mansion, and she said I know this must be my home. "No, this is for the little boy that lived next door." Well, then, surely it is this one over here. "No, that's for your cook, for the life she lived." Well, you certainly don't mean that this little mean hovel over here on the corner is for me? "Yes, that's just what you lived—that's your size now."

Now, the position that we occupy in this experience is that we have earned in the life we have gone through. Whether that be riches, position, power, abilities in one direction or another. As we apply ourselves, that is what we build in our lives. According to the information we have had respecting former lives, there were possibly in the beginning five places in which man's appearance in the earth came. Now you will say, do you find that in the Bible? I do. You say, well, how do you get away from the story of the Garden of Eden? I don't get away from it. That's only just one experience of one of the men, or one experience of the nations or of the whole peoples there at that time. As people have lived from these various experiences through the earth's plane, they are called into being according to that which they in their position find would be necessary for their development. Do you understand that?

If, in the minds of two people who have come together with an intent and purpose in their heart and being, they bring into being that vehicle through which–if you had the opportunity to develop under *that* environment–it would bring you the desire of your soul, and then you enter. Now, that's it! That's the whole thing. Will carries on just the same, all the way through.

God is ever the Creator of that through which the individual may enter and may develop. He is ever giving you the opportunity, even as when man had so far gone astray as to be directly disobedient, He immediately began to prepare the way that man may come to that lost estate. That He may be able to bring that individual portion of Himself, that makes man so entirely different of all creation, He begins to prepare that–even as when He sent His Son into the world that He, in man's estate, lives as man, so that man passes through just the same trials in all things tempted, even as you and I. Yet there could be nothing spoken against Him, except he was very radical in his views.

Now, that's what you say of me. I have had people say to me this, over and over again, "The phenomenon I see manifested here–done through the things you say–is wonderful, but you tack on something that is too radical for me."

Now, I *think* I speak only as the Spirit gives utterance of my understanding. I don't want any of you to have *my* views–you *couldn't* have my views–you want to have your *own* views–they are *yours*. It is *your* God that you want to go to, not mine. Now, if they be the same God, we will find it all in one, for all of us live and move and have our being in the same God. How individual is it? So individual that His spirit is ever with each and every one of us, and it is our individual souls that have to answer to Him for the deeds done in our bodies–not in someone else's body–and it doesn't matter how many bodies we may have.

Remember: One of the great teachers in Israel came to the Master by night and said to Him, "I perceive thou art a great teacher. Won't you tell me something about this?" And He said, "Ye must all be born again." The great teacher said "How is it possible? Can a man when he is old enter again and be born of woman?" And the Master said, "Nicodemus, have you been a student so long and yet haven't learned this?" Of what did He speak? (see John 3:1-10)

Let's hear any of you declare unto me the meaning of the most beautiful chapter–or a portion of the most beautiful chapter–in all of the whole Bible, unless it refers to that when it says, "The meek shall inherit the earth." (Matt. 5:5) Tell me that literally, and tell me that any meek man will ever inherit anything here! In other words, it says this: Who is going to be the man that has the power of wealth in the earth? He that is meek and humble before Me. There are your men in positions of place and power, and there is the man spoken of through these very things: "He that is pure in heart shall see God." (Matt. 5:8) Tell me what it means if it doesn't refer to another experience other than that in which one little cycle of life passes?

Question: What do you do with heredity with reference to reincarnation?
Cayce: That's where your heredity and environment bespeak the truth, rather than untruth, of reincarnation. The psychologist gets up to this point and says there's something in the child's life that made the man what he is. Well, what made it in the child's life? The hereditary condition is just that very thing that I answered you a moment ago as to how an individual came into being under circumstances when two persons with an ideal–it may be only an idea–came together for a purpose–that those individuals bring into being a condition, an environment, an hereditary condition, that through all the stages that a soul has developed or retarded such that the individual may, through that particular hereditary, environmental earthly, have that place which will develop it! That individual! Is that plain enough? Isn't it?

By the way, let's don't say transmigration. Do you know the difference between transmigration and reincarnation? I knew a man who had a second wife. He also had an old white mule that he took very good care of, because he said his first wife's soul had gone into that mule. She must have been mighty hard-headed! That's when people believe in transmigration.

There is a definite understanding given in the Bible concerning that. There was a certain rich man, and he fared sumptuously every day. And there was a poor beggar who lay at his gates who begged that the crumbs from the table might be given him to eat. In time, the rich man died and also did the beggar. In hell, the rich man lifted up his eyes and saw this beggar in Abraham's bosom, and he prayed that this beggar might come and cool his brow and quench his thirst, even with a drop of water. He was told, "There is a fixed gulf, impassable. The position you occupy is one you have builded yourself, even as that that the beggar occupies," and he said then, "Well, if he can't come to me, let him go back to earth and warn my brothers that they don't come to this place of torment," and the answer was, "If your brothers won't hear what they have in their *own* hands today, even if one rose from the dead, they wouldn't need any more." *(see Luke 16:19-26)*

Just the same as it is if your soul has ever been one that is capable of being in companionship with God, it still has it and isn't one of the common herd of which man was made control over. Then, the only thing that will prevent you from ever being developed to that position is your own self–for it is God's will. God has prepared a way that you may be one with Him through the ways that He has given you, that His Son has shown, and they are only this: "Thou shalt have no other god before me, and thou shalt love thy neighbor as thyself." *(see Luke 10:27)*

Anyone that *does* those–not merely says "I believe that"–but goes out and lives it day by day in their actions, in their walks in and out before Him, are indeed children of God. And as He has said, "Don't be fretful about what may come in this place, that, or the other. Ye will *not* be tempted beyond that which you are able to bear." *(see I Cor. 10:13)* It is your will as to whether ye yield or not. It isn't *His* desire, but for your own development many things come about.

Now Christ suffered, and in suffering–though He were the Son–yet learned He obedience by the things which He suffered Himself–for you, for me, for the world. There is no such thing as development except under adversity. Most of that we create ourselves–first in our own imagination, and the Mind is ever the Builder.

Let us hope that the mind in you will build *your* soul body in such a way that when the Spirit returns to the Creator, it may carry you with it!

During the Four Weeks Before the Lecture on "Evolution" (Aug. 16, 1931) . . .

In Virginia Beach: During these four weeks, Cayce gives fifty-two readings, several of them relating to the business and activities of the new A.R.E. For example, in Virginia Beach, Cayce gives a reading for A. C. Preston as the new business manager with guidance about several current A.R.E. business decisions. (Two and three days later in New York City, Cayce gives physical readings for Preston, who has become seriously ill.)

A reading for Tom Sugrue addresses his writing abilities and some manuscript plans, both for A.R.E. and for himself. Sugrue asks: "Who can best collaborate with Edgar Cayce on the complete story of his life and work, and what literary form should it take—autobiography or biography?" (849-9) It will be eleven years before Sugrue publishes the milestone Cayce biography *There Is a River*.

Another interesting reading is given for the musician, Vincent Lopez, who asks several pointed questions about Cayce's problems at this time. Most of the answer is given by the Archangel Michael, "Lord of the Way," who first spoke through Cayce in July 1928. When Lopez asks what role he can play to help Cayce at this crucial time, Michael directs him to first make himself right with God. (Michael will speak up in several readings in the coming weeks.)

In August, a local member, Florence Edmonds, asks Cayce if he would give a series of readings to a group of local members interested in studying the information in his readings. Her sister Edith even provides him with a list of questions for the readings. The first of perhaps his most significant series of readings—the 262 series of "Study Group" readings—will be given in September.

About the lecture on "Evolution": This brief lecture begins with another Cayce disclaimer about his ability to contribute anything to the understanding of this topic. Of particular interest are his responses to several questions from the audience.

Cayce reveals something of his attitudes about Darwinian theory when he says, " . . . not that we were ever monkeys or crawled up out of the sea." His own beliefs about the stages of human evolution may seem to some people even more far-fetched than did Darwin's theory of evolution at the time it was published.

Evolution

Sunday, August 16, 1931
(Location Not Recorded)

Evolution is a subject that has interested the greatest minds of the world. I do not say that I have had any special revelation, and it may seem very daring on my part to attempt an explanation or interpretation of evolution. It is my own, for you to accept or reject as you think best.

If you have considered the various subjects we have discussed since I began these talks, you will readily see that the natural outcome would be for us to discuss evolution. I believe in physical evolution, but I would like to define what I mean by physical evolution. If we have entered into the world more than once, let's hope that we have been on the ladder going upward. Not that we were ever monkeys, or that we ever crawled up out of the sea. As we consider the first six chapters of Genesis, let us understand that possibly a few lines oftentimes includes many millions of years instead of days. I don't mean to change the text, but to compare all that is said, instead of taking one part and attempting to make that mean the whole thing! There are included in a verse or chapter many eons of time. But, I would like to present a more comprehensive phase of evolution.

When the earth became a fit place for man's indwelling, man appeared in the earth—not made of any one thing that was already created, but of all things that were already created. For if man was given the authority—by the Authority—to subdue the earth, man must have been composed of some of everything that was in the earth. If an individual is given the injunction or the law that he is to subdue a thing, then he must be made up of that thing. Else he cannot subdue it.

Then man is the only thing made that may live with God. The common theory of evolution holds that evolution stopped when it came to Adam and Eve. That's where the evolution of man *began*. That we are composed of some of everything that is in the earth does not mean that we are the whole thing, any more than it does that, because we are gods in the making, we are gods. We are in the evolution of that stage where, applying the will—that gift to us by the Creator, by God—we may build to be that. Just as He showed us in the creation of the earth, first the heavens and the earth appeared in them. Not of that already made, but that made by Him, His Mind!

Mind, then, is that which evolves, that which builds. For with the conceiving of Life, it came into existence, as it may come into existence for us, if we know how to apply the law pertaining to Creative Energy itself. Being, then, the offspring of God, we are gods in evolution. The evolution may be down even below the monkey, or it may be up to the Godhead itself. For there is nothing that can prevent an individual (who has received the approval of God) from becoming one with Him, yet not the Whole, but with the consciousness of being able to be one with that Whole and able to preserve or maintain the *individuality* all the way through—not the *personality*, for that must merge into God-likeness.

The process of bringing personality and individuality into oneness with Him is evolution, as I understand it, as I have gathered it, as I read it, and as I see it in nature about us today. We know, we recognize the fact, that those things we see in the earth are a portion of us, but that which will enable us to control those things is not of that same creation. For God breathed into man that which might be a companion with Him, that which nothing else had.

Yes, they all have souls—as animals, as the blade of grass, as anything that lives—but it is, through common God-consciousness in life itself, without the ability to do other than fulfill that purpose for which it was created, which is to show man his way to God! Everything that has been created, of which man is made, is evolving, is developing, so that it may point the way for man to approach the Creator and become one with that Creator.

[Mr. Cayce responded to questions from the audience.]

Question from audience: Does not the blade of grass have a spirit consciousness, which is in man the soul consciousness?
Answer by Mr. Cayce: We see Life in a blade of grass. The Spirit of God is

within it. That's Life. God is Life. The blade of grass has a God-consciousness—that is, a universal soul-consciousness. It is by that that man's spirit becomes a portion of God, through dwelling upon it. For what we eat we will surely become, whether meat, fish, or flowers—but some flowers are poison ivy, just as others are beautiful.

Do you see what I mean by a universal soul-consciousness? It has not reached the power to use an individual mental consciousness. Mind builds! The mind of God brought the earth into being. I believe that the mind of man may attain to that position where it, too, may create worlds and rule over them. No wonder there are new stars being found continually!

Question: Do you mean the individual split souls may attain to that position, or when those two souls meet that make the one soul?
Mr. Cayce: That brings up another phase entirely. We would have to say where they split first. I mean that we, as individuals, may be given—or will be given—the opportunity to manifest that portion of God which is within us, so as to become rulers of universes.

Question: Suppose we don't desire to become rulers of universes?
Mr. Cayce: Then we wouldn't be individuals, could never have been. For we would be satisfied with a universal consciousness and have no desire to go farther, just as with an individual who has builded a concept of heaven paved with gold, or just a harp by the river of life. Would any other heaven ever satisfy that individual? I myself cannot conceive of any individual, any offspring of God, not desiring to manifest upon that it may rule over. Can you?

Question: My idea of ruling would be to help those who have not found the way.
Mr. Cayce: That's ruling. That's ruling as God rules us. Here is the whole thing before us: Life has developed before us—it is developing before us now. What are we going to do with it? If we use it to become one with Him, it is being used in the same manner that brought it into being—and we become one with the Creator, yet are sufficiently individual to know that we are not the "whole cheese." My idea would be, then, here's

a universe in your name—what are you going to do with it?

That was given to the Son of Man. That was given to many of the leaders. So it must go throughout the whole universe.

Question: Regarding the blade of grass, do you think it has the opportunity to develop, or does it stay at one stage?
Mr. Cayce: The greatest development anything in the world can have is to fulfill its mission, that for which it was created. "Consider the lilies how they grow; they toil not, they spin not; and yet I say unto you that Solomon in all his glory was not arrayed like one of these." *(see Matt. 6:28-29)* The blade of grass remains in its own consciousness. It is its own universal consciousness and fulfills the purpose for which it was created. We should be able to continually take lessons from Nature herself. So few of us find the purpose for which we were created, much less carry it out.

Question: Does not the grass fulfill its purpose much more quickly?
Mr. Cayce: Today it is, tomorrow it is in the oven—but it has fulfilled and sustained its portion. More often it may enter in through its same consciousness, for unless the grain of wheat dies it cannot bring forth.

Question: Wouldn't the blade of grass be more beautiful if cultivated?
Mr. Cayce: So would our lives and souls be more beautiful if cultivated in the light of God's love.

Question: Then we all need help.
Mr. Cayce: We all certainly need help. That's why the Son of Man came into the earth, and why He descended into hell, and why we pray for those that have passed over.

Question: If a person ruled materially in another life and lost, would he bring into this life a fear of power and rule?
Mr. Cayce: That's answering what different phases of an individual's development might be. We all have to pass through those experiences necessary for us to understand the Whole. If a fear is brought over, then it is necessary to pass though an experience to overcome that fear.

I believe, though, in forgiveness of sin, and that we should forgive even as we expect Him to forgive. As we forgive, it will be forgiven us. "If ye will be my people, I will be your God." *(see 2 Cor. 6:16; also Jeremiah 7:23; Ezekiel 11:20)*

He has made us free-willed. The evolution, the development, is going on. Are we going up the ladder, or are we going down? Are we satisfied to become just the universal consciousness, or do we want to be individual and at the same time one with Him? He made us as individuals. We want to go back to Him as individuals.

During the Two Weeks Before the Lecture on "The First Ten Minutes After Death" (Aug. 30, 1931)...

In the U.S.: In their efforts to help employees lessen the continuing impact of the Depression, on August 23 the Ford Motor Company implements a new policy requiring its employees to grow their own vegetables—or to give up their jobs.

In Virginia Beach: During these two weeks, Cayce gives only ten readings—seven of them on one day. From August 20 through August 29, he gives no readings.

Cayce occasionally finds time for his favorite hobby, fishing—not always without unfortunate consequences. In late July, he wrote to a friend: "For the last week I have been crippled—did a very foolish thing—went fishing in my bare feet and the sun blistered them, or scalded them, or burned them—so I've been worse than someone with gout. Just beginning to be able to get about again." (From background for 294-126)

About the lecture on "The First Ten Minutes After Death": This is the second or third Sunday lecture presented in the Cayce home, Wright's Cottage, just across the street from the former Cayce Hospital. Remember they have just moved to this cottage in early July. Living right at the beach makes the story in the following lecture all the more real and poignant.

The First Ten Minutes After Death
Sunday, August 30, 1931
Cayce Home, 67th Street, Virginia Beach

A s to the first ten minutes in eternity—or the first ten minutes after death (for I think we are now living in eternity)—this naturally has to be very speculative—unless we accept experiences of individuals who have in some manner known transition. And, "If they hear not Moses and the prophets, neither will they be persuaded, though one rose from the dead." (*Luke 16:31*)

My approach to this subject is rather unusual. I must tell you an experience I had recently while on the train going to Kentucky. It was the first time I sat down to meditate on this subject. A young man came in the smoking room and said to me, "Well, I have just come to. I was drowned day before yesterday at Virginia Beach. My brother was not revived and is being taken home in his coffin on this same train." If it is possible, I want to convey to you his experience, as he told it to me, just how he felt when he sank into the waters out here in the Atlantic Ocean.

He knew he was going. He felt himself give out of strength. As he sank into the waters, he realized that it was the bluest water he had ever seen—everything was very, very blue. Yet he was happy in the consciousness that he was with his mother, though he knew she wasn't in the water, as she had been buried back in Kentucky. Yet he was very conscious of her presence, and she urged him to make at least one more effort. He did not know that he ever made an effort, yet now he was physically alive, but not conscious of anything that had passed since he left Virginia Beach, or since he had been taken from the water. He was not conscious, he said then—that he had even been put on the train to go home with his father and brother who had helped to save him.

He answered my question without my even asking. As he expressed it, there is no difference in the living physical experience and the unseen experience, except as to the knowledge that the world unseen to us is not populated with the *seen* world. Do we get just what that means?

When death comes to an individual, he knows that he has passed from what we call *life* into what we call *death*. There's no fear in death if there is no fear in life.

As to the other side, I feel that the following was a real experience and is as near an illustration of what happens at death as it would be possible to put into words. On going into the unconscious state to obtain information for an individual, I recognized that I was leaving my body. Immediately you ask, "With what did you recognize that fact?" We are made up of a dual personality. There is one portion which holds very close to the earth no matter how much spirituality we may have. For we remember, "My God, my God, why hast thou forsaken me?" (Mark 15:34) If the Master cried that, what must it be to us mortals who hold so strongly to anything pertaining to heart when we come to the passing from one condition or phase of life to another? Life, of course, in its *essence* is a continuity—it is a oneness, and it's just the change that takes place.

I passed into this state with the consciousness that I was to seek information for this individual. As I left the body, I was only conscious of that portion of the body—or that something—that was seeking. There was just a direct, straight, and narrow line in front of me. On either side was fog and smoke, and many shadowy figures who seemed to be crying for me, or begging me to come aside to their state, or to that state they occupied. As I followed along, the way began to clear. The figures on either side grew more distinct. They took more form, but there was a continual beckoning back, or the attempt to sidetrack me or bring me aside from the purpose. Yet with the narrow way in front of me, I kept going.

After a bit, I passed to where the figures were merely shadows attempting to assist, and they urged me on rather than attempting to stop me. Then they took on more form, and they seemed to be occupied with their own activities. When they paid any attention to me at all, it was rather to urge me on.

I came to a hill where there was a mount and a temple. I entered this temple. There was a very large room—very much as in a library—and the books of each individual's life were very large. For each individual's activities were a matter of actual record, as it appeared, and I merely had to pull down the record of the individual for whom I was seeking information. I have to say, as Paul, "Whether I was in the spirit or out of the spirit, I cannot tell," (*see 2 Cor. 12:2*). But that was an actual experience.

When the Master spoke to Jairus's daughter, what was her state of being? We remember He did not allow the whole crowd, not even all of His disciples, to listen at what He said when He entered this chamber. But as He took her by the hand and called to her, she came back. (*see Mark 5:35-42*) From where? Where was that being? The physical body was there. We know there must be a separation of life and the physical body, but *where* was that individual soul, the soul that lives on? Where *was* it? Had it left the body, or was it just dormant?

When speaking of Lazarus, He said, "He is sleeping," and His disciples said to Him, "If he sleeps, he does well," and then He told them plainly that he was dead. (*see John 11:14*) So the soul must have passed. We know there is builded that in the life of Lazarus which we may use as an illustration or a lesson as to how our lives may be builded, as to how we are called, and as to how the soul *continues* for the time being about the earth's plane.

We have had information that "This body, or this entity, has not yet realized it has passed from the earth, or has not realized it is dead." Again, "This individual has just realized it has passed from the earth plane." That is, it has just become wholly conscious of the "inter-between" or the borderland. Borderland means one thing, and the inter-between, or shadowland, means another. When a soul, then, passes from the physical body—provided it has builded that which allows it to be present with creation and Creative Forces—then it continues to build. As said by the Apostle, "To be absent from the body, to *me*" (and so it should be with each of us) "is to be present with the Lord." (*see 2 Cor. 5:8*)

If we are present with the Lord, we may be very sure as to what our experience is. I have seen a few people—some very near and dear to me—pass into the borderland, or pass from life to what we call death. I have heard them give expression to what they saw and heard. Stephen, when he was stoned, said, "Behold, I see the heavens opened, and the Son of Man standing on the right hand of God." (*Acts 7:56*) How these words must have stuck with Paul throughout his labors in the earth!

Our experiences, we may be very sure, will *not* be the same. To say

what the experience of an individual might be in the first ten minutes
after death would be the same as trying to tell a bride how she will feel
the first ten minutes after marriage. No two would feel exactly the same.
We all know this, however, as we live day by day, as we apply the abilities and talents we have been given: When we pass over, our experience
will not be very much different from passing from one room to another,
for "In my Father's house are many mansions, and He has prepared a
place, that where I am ye may be also." (see John 14:2-3) It is up to us how
we furnish our room in that mansion. If we furnish it with beauty, then
we know just what our first experience will be on awakening in the
shadowland. It will be just what we have put there! If it has been a life
of hate or of selfish desire—then those things must be met in exactly the
form we have builded them, either in this life or the next. If it has been
a life of love, a life of self-sacrifice for another, then those things most
nearly representing that will be those encountered as we pass from one
experience to another.

[Mr. Cayce then responded to questions from the audience:]

Question from audience: How would you name the various places?
Answer by Mr. Cayce: That is just a matter of your own language, trying to
put into words that which would represent the individual's idea.
Whether we say purgatory, hell, or what not, it is merely an expression
of that passing, or transition. The Book expresses it, or as given in the
Apostles' Creed, "He died, descended into hell," and he passed through
that experience. Or, as He said Himself, as Jonah was in the belly of the
whale, so must the Son of Man—or the body of the Son of Man—be in
the tomb so many days. (see Matt. 12:40)
    As to the transition to the inter-between, borderland, or the like, it
means the different developments of the soul through the experience
from one sphere to another. It would be just as passing through its
various spheres of consciousness as a child. When the breath of life
enters into the body and it becomes a living soul, it must be very close
to that source from which it emanated, and it has a physical body now
to gradually get into motion. The child is trained away from its experiences. When we are born *out* of the physical body, we must pass through

the same stages of development.

Why was it that, when Lazarus was raised by the Master from the dead, he didn't always remain alive? Would we not reason from the physical–human viewpoint that if he could have remained alive throughout the ages, many more would now be converted to Christianity? Why couldn't he remain alive? He was given life by the Son of Man, or by God Himself through the man Jesus. Why couldn't he have remained alive, as a living example throughout all the ages? Because, by doing so, he would have lacked the development in earth's plane, and because "There will not be a sign given unto you, until ye have made yourselves right!" He would have remained a sign for each generation. The individual must seek that which will develop itself in its own plane. So Lazarus was called back for only the moment.

Question: Mr. Cayce, when that boy was drowned, why was he able to come back and his brother not?
Cayce: There was a stronger urge from the other side for him to come back. He had something yet to accomplish on this plane.

Question: Does this inter–between or borderland have a location in the universe?
Cayce: If we make it a location, yes–otherwise, it is a state of consciousness, or state of *being.*

Question: Some claim that the astral plane is two hundred miles from the earth. Is that true?
Cayce: I do not know. I only know that I passed through somewhere and I got to a place. Where that place is, whether it's just over the other side, I don't know. I saw myself leave the body. Then I didn't see the body, but I was following that line to obtain the information.

Question: Don't you think that, while contacting lower entities, you were just passing through those planes or states of consciousness?
Cayce: States of consciousness, which–to my mind, as I think of it–were very close to the earth. Whether we say that's up or down, whether it's a million miles or what not, doesn't matter. For we pass beyond time

and space, but there must be a place, we say, for it is hard for us to get any conception of an idea in the material plane without being able to put our fingers on it. We can only have our own personal experiences, and I believe each one is a lesson to us. But we can't ask others to believe them. We can only use them as steppingstones to that consciousness of the home in which we would like to live. Think of what our homes would be, builded with many of the thoughts or furnished with many of the thoughts we have about people from day to day. Wouldn't we hate to live in such a house? Well, it is up to us as to whether we have to do it or not. God has prepared a way, that we may know just where we are going, and He is willing to help us. But He can't change our course! We are the only ones that can!

During the Month Before the Lecture on
"What Is Spirituality?" (Sept. 29, 1931)...

Around the world: Underscoring the continuing worldwide economic catastrophe during this period, the financial crisis in Great Britain results in collapse of the Labour Party government, followed by austerity measures that provoke riots in London, Liverpool, and Glasgow. The government devalues the pound sterling and prohibits converting currency into gold. The eminent Danatbank of Germany has already gone bankrupt.

In Virginia Beach: At this critical time, the Cayce work experiences a remarkable shift, represented by several of the fifty-two readings during this month:

Remember the request by the Edmonds sisters prior to the lecture on "Evolution"? A local group is looking for guidance from Cayce to study his work and become more spiritually attuned. That group includes Miss Esther Wynne, a high school teacher. On September 1, Miss Wynne asks in a reading about her future: "When should she definitely connect herself with the work of the Association for Research and Enlightenment?" The response is: "As soon as the department of the study groups, or lessons, have been put on the basis where these may give that proper remuneration for the efforts of those that are to *conduct* such field of operation." *(307-3)* This anticipates the development of those lessons, which is about to begin. Miss Wynne will have a central role in that development, as well as in the eventual A.R.E. study group activities

On September 14, in the Barrett home in Norfolk, Cayce gives the first reading in response to the request "made by those present. These individuals came together for the purpose of forming a group to study the information received through the psychic forces of Edgar Cayce." *(262-1)* This first meeting of the "Norfolk Study Group #1" includes twelve local members (including Esther Wynne) as well as Gladys and Mildred Davis and Edgar, Gertrude, and Hugh Lynn Cayce. Others will join the group as it continues to meet, get readings, and work on the lesson materials. This "262 series" of readings that begins tonight continues for almost eleven years, providing the material for twenty-eight lessons eventually published as *A Search for God*. (The second 262 reading is given to the newly formed study group on September 20.)

The morning after the first study group reading (September 15), Cayce has a dream about that first meeting and its reading. In the dream, Mildred Davis (Gladys's cousin) tells the group they will have a special "healing circle" consisting of six of the group members. Such a healing group does begin to meet and will have its own series of readings (the "281 series") beginning in October. That group becomes the prayer healing group known as the Glad Helpers, which still meets every Wednesday morning at the A.R.E. in Virginia Beach.

About the lecture on "What Is Spirituality?" The location of this brief lecture on a Tuesday is unknown. Like the preceding one, it may have been at the Cayce home. The lecture itself is very brief with several questions at the end. It may have been stimulated by confusion Cayce has heard expressed between "spirituality" and "Spiritualism." In addition to the popular writings of Madame Blavatsky, Spiritualism has drawn new interest to itself through the work and writings of renowned individuals such as Sir Arthur Conan Doyle and Sir Oliver Lodge, a British scientist and ardent believer in survival after death.

What Is Spirituality?
Tuesday, September 29, 1931
(Location Not Recorded)

I wonder if we make the proper differentiation between *Spiritualism, Spiritualistic Influence*, and *Spirituality*! No doubt we all in a vague way have an idea of what *Spirituality* is. But do we know how to apply it in our everyday lives so that it becomes a living, vital thing—rather than something applied to people we more often think of as being moralists or sober, long-faced individuals without the proper conception of the pleasure that comes with true physical living?

Spiritualism may be at times applied to Spirituality in action. Again we often think of Spiritualism as applying to those conditions wherein man at times delves into communicating with departed personalities. For example, Saul was fearful of the outcome of affairs in his life when he sought out the Witch of Endor and asked that she bring up from the dead the spirit of Samuel—he who had anointed him King and who had counseled him during the earlier part of his reign over Israel—seeking from him reassurance, believing (as he must have) that life in its continuity of existence might bring him aid. *(see 1 Sam. 28:5-15)* Just so, we at times may seek from our loved ones or our acquaintances or even individuals in various positions in the affairs of the earth who, having passed into the beyond, are still interested in earthly conditions and who are willing and anxious to aid others in carrying out their ideas. Hence, we seek for information from such sources.

This we term *Spiritualism*, or adhering to that which may be given from unseen sources or the spirit realm. This is questioned by many. Many have no patience with such communication—neither as to those sources nor with individuals who indulge in such. There are few, I really believe, who would absolutely deny and be able to prove that such a realm and such communication does *not* exist and that it is *not* at some time or another the experience of a great many individuals.

Before turning to Spirituality, let us consider one other term often confused with Spirituality. What do we mean by *Spiritualistic Influence?* That influence which comes from unseen sources, but conscious to an individual by comparison in the material plane, such as the "Spirit of '76," or the "Spirit of India," and from such influence one often feels that it is of untold value in their experience. Possibly it is true—possibly it is not true in every case. Much might be said on this particular phase of human experience, but as I have already said, Spirituality is our subject.

Then what is *Spirituality?* It is the quality of being *spiritual* as opposed to *material.* God is Spirit and seeks such to worship Him. *(see John 4:24)* Then, Spirituality and its activity in the hearts and souls of mankind cannot be reached by any philosophical reasoning, hence cannot be questioned, as would Spiritualism and its directing influence, or Spiritualistic activity and its directing influence. For to reach conclusions from our experiences in Spiritualism or Spiritualistic Influence, we must go through some form or another—some routine or rote—to induce some power in an unseen realm to manifest itself that we may become cognizant of the forces upon which we become dependent. *Spirituality* is the directing of our actions through the Spirit of God Himself. It is that as was promised to us, "If I go away, the Comforter will come" *(see John 16:7)* (or the Holy Spirit will come), and, "He will abide with you always." *(see John 14:16)* "Take no thought of what ye shall say, for in the self-same hour will it be given you what ye shall say or what ye shall do." *(see Luke 12:11-12)* Do you see the direction, or is it too indefinite?

Let's put it another way. "This is He that came by water and by blood—Jesus, the Christ." Not by water only, but by water *and* blood. And "It is the Spirit that beareth witness, because the Spirit is Truth." *(see 1 John 5:6)* Now, if we are guided by the Spirit (the Holy Spirit), we may be sure that it is Truth.

As we have learned from some of the other discussions, such as "What is Truth?" what would be truth to one might not be truth to another. Hence if we reason from the philosophical standpoint, it becomes rote or ritualistic, but if we reason by the directing of the Holy Spirit, it is Truth. If we have gone through certain forms to prepare our imagination, or if we have come to rely upon some consciousness that is awakened by going through some formula, are we sure that it isn't an influence outside ourselves that is not of Truth?

Spirituality, then, is applying day by day, in every way, those lessons as were given by the Christ in the earth. For He comes as a promise, having fulfilled the law, became the law, subject to all of those influences as we are today, subject even unto death. But He overcame death even as He overcame all of the ritual that pertains to law. For He fulfilled the law, and now sitteth at the right hand of God to make intercession for us. And having promised us the gift of the Holy Spirit that would guide us day by day, if we are guided by this—not for self-aggrandizement—but that His will may be done in earth even as it is in heaven, in so doing, we enable those we contact to see in our activities the knowledge that we have been with the Christ and the Truth! *That is Spirituality!*

[Mr. Cayce then responded to questions from the audience.]

Question from audience: What is true physical living?
Answer by Mr. Cayce: Letting that mind be in you which was in Jesus Christ, who thought it not robbery to make Himself equal with God, but made Himself of no estate that He might, through His association with men, make a way for man to know God the better. *(see Phil. 2:5-8)* Then, living in Him is true physical living, for He wept with those who wept and rejoiced with those who did rejoice, and really lived James' definition of true religion: "True and undefiled religion is visiting the widow and orphans in their affliction and keeping one's self unspotted from the world." *(see James 1:27)* That is true physical living.

Question: Was *Saul* wrong in endeavoring to obtain counsel from Samuel through the Witch of Endor?
Cayce: There had been a command given to Moses that those that had familiar spirits or who were witches were to be banished from the congregation of Israel. And, as the text is given concerning Samuel, Saul had put out those who had familiar spirits, or who were wizards. But in his extremity, he had asked that such a one be sought. When he appears before the Witch of Endor and she asked who he would talk with, he told her "Samuel." Saul recognized that he had sinned, and he must have hoped that Samuel would make intercession for him, but God

alone is able to forgive sin. Then, it must have been wrong for Saul to
have endeavored to obtain counsel, for Samuel's first reply, "Why
troublest thou me," saying in so many words, "You have already by your
own actions lost the privilege of having God speak to you through
dream or through Urim," for through dream or through Urim or through
a prophet was the way God spoke to His people at that time. *(see 1 Sam.
28:6)* So he had not the right to call on Samuel.

Question: Is it not better to seek to be guided by the Holy Spirit rather
than by departed spirits?
Cayce: To be sure.

Question: How can we best attune ourselves to be conscious of the Holy
Spirit's guidance?
Cayce By doing day by day that that we know to be His will–by making
our wills one with His, or, not as "I will," but as "May Thy will be done in
earth as it is in Heaven," *(see Matt. 6:10)* and we become, then, spiritually
conscious that He is directing and guiding our way.

Question: How may we manifest our better selves?
Cayce: In Him is the individual's best self, as the seeking for understanding is that that makes the way open for Him to set in, by the individual's
efforts. The desire in self–mentally, spiritually, physically–opens the way
that He may manifest through the activities of self! Hence, "*His* will–not
my will but thine, O God, be done in me, through me!" *(see Luke 22:42)*
    This does not hinder nor prevent the use of the pleasures in physical
living, but it does forego the abusing of the privileges in Him. For we
being free in Him, the law becomes of no effect in Him. But would we
defy the law, we become subject to the law, and the law of love is made
of no effect in us. So, in the manifesting of the better self, law becomes
of no effect and love becomes active in our own selves.

During the Two Weeks Before the Lecture on "Where Is Heaven?" (Oct. 11, 1931)...

In Virginia Beach: The eighteen readings during this period include the third reading in the "262 study group series" and the first in the "281 healing group series." In that first healing group reading, those present are reassured that "Each as are gathered here are fitted in their own particular way for a portion of that work designated by the group as the healing group." This is immediately followed by this caution: "Hence, when once chosen, and the face set in that direction, that as the warning, as the threat." One does not undertake this work lightly or without commitment. Their overall purpose and ideal will be to "lose self in love and service to others." (281-1)

The study group reading is especially noteworthy because it gives them—and us—the first of the powerful affirmations in *A Search for God*—the affirmation for Cooperation:

> Not my will but Thine, O Lord, be done in and through me. Let me ever be a channel of blessings, today, now, to those that I contact, in every way. Let my going in, mine coming out be in accord with that Thou would have me do, and as the call comes, "Here am I, send me, use me!" 262-3

About the lecture on "Where Is Heaven?": The records indicate that this may have been given on October 12 instead of the 11th. Like the preceding lecture, this lecture is brief, unidentified as to location, and followed by several questions. Its ideas help to round out the basic topics Cayce has addressed since he began the lectures two years earlier under much different circumstances and expectations.

Where Is Heaven?

Sunday, October 11, 1931
(Location Not Recorded)

From our teachings and—more often, I would say—from a longing within our own beings, most of us think of heaven as a place of rest, where all tears and sorrows are wiped away, a place beside the river of life, or the river of life flows through its grounds. There is no night there, no need for the sun.

How oft have we heard, "In my Father's house are many mansions; if it *were* not *so*, I would have told you. I go to prepare a place for you. And if I go and prepare a place for you, I will come again, and receive you unto myself; that where I am, *there* ye may be also. And whither I go ye know, and the way ye know. Thomas saith unto him, Lord, we know not whither thou goest; and how can we know the way? Jesus saith unto him, I am the way, the truth, and the life; no man cometh unto the Father, but by me." *(John 14:2-6)* Also, "And it came to pass, while he blessed them, he was parted from them, and carried up into heaven." *(Luke 24:51)* If His disciples, who had been with him, didn't know where He was going, how may *we* know where heaven is?

We are so prone to jump at conclusions or to draw comparisons without considering just how we may know something of the subject. So, in drawing a comparison here—if we know something of the inhabitants of the place, something of the dwelling place of the Father (for He said He went *to* the Father)— then heaven must be God's home. And truly the heritage of every man and woman—for we *being* God's children and brothers of the Christ—are heirs to that throne, that home, wherever it may be.

But how much do we know of God the Father? How well are we acquainted with His home? Would we recognize it if we suddenly found ourselves therein? Are we not very much as the three blind men who went to see the elephant? One stumbled against the side and said it was very much like a wall. One stumbled against the leg and said it was very much like a tree. One found its tail and said that surely an elephant was very much like a rope.

The Master, we remember, drew such comparisons of heaven as likened unto the grain of mustard seed, the ten virgins—five foolish and five wise—Lazarus and the rich man, and so forth. In each of these parables, we find that, in the preparation for entrance into the kingdom, it was necessary that a change be made, or that a definite stand be taken by the individual seeking. Very much as if we would start out for any city—there may be many roads leading there, many byways, but there is *one* direct way we may take.

As to locating heaven, we know that the Father and the Son are there. Then it must be very much like love—for God is love, and the Son manifested love. Then again it is very peaceful there, for as He said, "Peace be unto you—My peace I give unto you." *(see John 14:27)* It is also very much like hope, very much like mercy. For if we would have mercy shown us, we must be merciful to others. But telling what we may expect to find there is not telling *where* it is.

Is heaven, then, a place? May there be metes and bounds put about it? May we draw a line over it? Or is it only an imaginary line we may draw, as we speak of the equator about the earth?

We see our loved ones born into this world, and as we look into their faces and eyes, we see, as it were, the blue of heaven, the smile of an angel. Are they, then, gifts from heaven? Are they but strangers in this mundane sphere who have been at home in heaven? Did they come from the Father, Him in whom we live and move and have our being? He the author of life and we merely His children? This, to me, seems almost to answer itself, for we *must* believe the Son came from the heaven of heavens that through Him we might have access to the Father. It is true, then, that He *is* the way if He came down from heaven and ascended back to heaven. Then heaven must be *up*. Not in the sense that we think of over and above something else, but in that sense that we are beneath that to which we have direct access by the activities of our own being. Then where is heaven? Where is God? In Him we live and move and have our being. Then *in* us, *about* us, *over* us, *under* us—all about us—is heaven.

What makes the change as to the place we dwell? The very activities of the inhabitants of a place make the greatest change as to whether it be lovely or otherwise, as to whether it lifts up or degrades, as to whether it brings hope or despair. Then we all may find the way, for the way has been prepared for all. "Whosoever will, let him come—for the bride and the spirit saith 'Come.'" (*see Rev. 22:17*) That which would prevent our knowing where heaven is, is in ourselves only.

Heaven may be within you, for "The kingdom is within you." (*see Luke 17:21*) Heaven may be in the love light in someone's eyes. Heaven may be in the song that awakens within you the relationship you bear to that King of Kings, that Lord of Lords. You may or may not be a long way from home. Heaven *is* the heritage and home for all who will let "*His* will be done" in them.

If we have created within our own minds a heaven that is builded with the cares of this world, or deceitfulness, or riches, or if we have by comparison set metes and bounds about the heaven we long for, will we not occupy just such a heaven? How long will it take us to get out of this? Will we be satisfied always with being in the shadow? Will we be satisfied always with being just in *hearing* of—not knowing altogether—the source? The Master said of John the Baptist, "There is none born of women greater than John the Baptist, yet the least in the kingdom of heaven is greater than he." (*see Matt. 11:11; Luke 7:28*) Why such a statement? What prompted it?

People thereabouts were drawing comparisons concerning the life of John, who had the rights to be a high priest, yet would have none of that. Rather he chose to be the voice in the wilderness: "Make your paths straight, for the kingdom of heaven is at hand." (*see Matt. 3:3; Mark 1:3; Luke 3:4*) How was it said of him that the least in the kingdom of heaven was greater than he? For like so many, poor John—under persecution, under tribulation—doubted, and he sent to ask, "Art thou the Christ, or shall we look for another?" (*see Luke 7:20*) What was the Master's answer? His answer may give us an inkling as to what heaven may be: "Go and tell John the things ye have seen—the blind see, the deaf hear, the lame walk, and the poor have the gospel preached unto them." (*see Luke 7:22*) Or that love that makes us think first of the other fellow, rather than ourselves, *gives* us a glimpse of heaven, and we—God's agents, God's children—may, through our activities here now, make for others that experience of glimpsing something of the glories of heaven. We know that now we see through a glass darkly, but *then* we shall know as *we* are known. *(see 1 Cor. 13:12)*

Where is heaven? "To be absent from the body is to be present with the Lord" *(see 2 Cor. 5:8)*—provided, to be sure, that our lives, our acts, our thoughts are such that they build in the hearts and souls of men that which is in keeping with that kingdom. For we are heirs of a kingdom, and just as it is necessary for an heir to conform to those rules for one in such a position, so may we—if we have not lost that birthright—be heirs of that kingdom.

Then where is heaven? Where God is!

[Mr. Cayce then responded to questions from the audience.]

Question from audience: What is the meaning of "Seek ye first the kingdom of heaven and all these things shall be added unto you?"
Answer by Mr. Cayce: If we have the knowledge of God's laws, and God has made heaven and earth–and all that in them are–then, *knowing* that law prepares us for the receiving of that portion of the earth's blessings for our own use, to the developing of such necessary to be developed within us. This, to be sure, applies to the necessities of life, and even the luxuries, but being content–not satisfied–with the lot He has seen fit to place us in. For it may be the position necessary for us to catch that necessary glimpse of heaven, or it may be the door to the entrance into the kingdom for us.

Question: Are there not many who attain the necessities and luxuries of life without first seeking the kingdom?
Cayce: No. *Someone* has first sought the kingdom, for not only the iniquities but the blessings are visited unto the third and fourth generation. This same question was asked poor old Job by his comforters, and he answered it.

Question: Who is the judge as to whether we are worthy to enter the kingdom of heaven?
Cayce: "Judge not, that ye be not judged." *(Matt. 7:1)* Just as our being able

to see and know heaven by the deeds we do in the present, just so is the judgment passed, *not* by someone else, but by the acts of our own selves. No one can separate us from the Father save ourselves, for we are free-willed. The Book says we all shall stand before the judge in the last day, *(see Rom. 14:10)* and the sheep shall be separated from the goats, *(see Matt. 25:32)* and he will say, "Depart from me, I never knew you." *(see Matt. 7:23)* But does it say He will do the judging, or that any individual will do the judging? Doesn't it rather imply, or say, that standing in that presence will make us know within ourselves where we belong?

Question: To one who abides in the kingdom of heaven, are not all things perfect?
Cayce: Spiritually speaking, yes. Perfection, in its real sense, may not be reached in earth–only comparatively so, or relatively so.

Question: How may we obtain heavenly bliss while still on earth?
Answer: "As ye would that men should do to you, do ye even so to them." *(see Luke 6:31)* Or possibly better, as He said, this is the whole law: "Love the Lord thy God with all thine body, mind, and soul, and thy neighbor as thyself, for this is the law and the prophets." *(see Matt. 22:37-40)* In doing this, we may obtain heavenly bliss here on earth. While we may not be understood by men, we will have that bliss that comes from being and keeping in His presence.

Question: What caused man to leave the heavenly state?
Cayce: God created man that He might have companionship, but He gave man free will, that he might become One with Him–which can *only* be with or through will–"*Thy* will, not mine be done." *(see Matt. 26:42)*
   Man, as man, may only inhabit that portion of the universe which he has builded through his own activities. All of heaven and earth is made up of and from one Force or Source. Man, then, left heaven or is in heaven according to what he does *with* that Force, making for himself a heaven or a hell, or an earth, or some other place of experience.

Part Three

Other Public Lectures

1933-1935

INTRODUCTION TO THE OTHER PUBLIC LECTURES

The Cayce lectures in the first two series—most of them presented on Sunday afternoons in Virginia Beach—were introduced by brief notes on what was going on in the world, in the United States, and in Virginia Beach, especially in the life of Edgar Cayce. The lectures that follow in this section are presented without national or international context or introductions to individual lectures. The comments below highlight both the near-fatal crises yet to occur, as well as the shift in the direction of the work.

As pointed out earlier, Edgar Cayce's Sunday lectures consist of his clearest "waking state" presentations of his own beliefs about key spiritual and metaphysical topics. A review of the topics covered by these Sunday lectures suggests that most of the significant topics were addressed during this period. They become, in effect, his first step in approaching the public with this information—his first step of advocacy.

The six lectures that follow are given over a two-year period from 1933 to 1935 after sixteen months without any lectures recorded. This hiatus may be partly the consequence of critical events that remind Cayce to take nothing for granted: Cayce loses his credit for groceries and the utilities are turned off, forcing him to collect debris on the beach to burn in the cottage's fireplace for heat. Then when money becomes available to travel to New York to give readings, that visit culminates in a further disaster: On November 7, Edgar, Gertrude, and Gladys are arrested in New York City for fortune telling. The court rules as follows:

"After seeing the People's witnesses and the three defendants and their witness, on the stand, and observing their manner of testifying, and after reading the exhibits in the case, I find as a fact that Mr. Cayce and his co-defendants were not pretending to tell fortunes and that to hold these defendants guilty of violation of Sec.

899 of the [New York] Code of Criminal Procedure, Subdivision 3, would be an interference with the belief, practices or usages of an incorporated ecclesiastical governing body, or the duly licensed teachers thereof, and they are discharged." (*The transcript of the hearing is appended to work reading 254-59.*)

Although the charges are dismissed, this event—coupled with all the other personal crises of 1931—takes its physical toll on the man. At the end of November, he is severely depressed and has ominous dreams. In December, a reading interpreting his dreams (294-128) warns that he might be drawn back into the spirit world unless he is held here by his friends. The local members, including the Glad Helpers, rally in support and undertake special prayer efforts. Gladys reports positive change within days. Gladys intensifies her efforts to find member support for buying the Cayces a home.

The Cayces later view this organized "rescue" effort by friends and members in many locations as a reinforcement for the need to reach out with the spiritual ideas and lessons through such efforts as the preparation of *A Search for God*. That shift in emphasis probably contributed to the near-abandonment of the formal Cayce lecture as a significant outreach effort. They had served a purpose all their own—providing a record of Edgar Cayce's own personal spiritual philosophy. His first "audience" has always been *individuals* ("First to the individuals . . .) and small *groups* of friends and associates (" . . . then to groups . . . "). His lectures seemed to move him toward the larger audiences (" . . . then to the classes and the masses.") He will now return to his emphasis on reaching out to smaller groups—this time, groups specifically gathered for the purpose of developing personal spirituality through *A Search for God*.

The six lectures after 1931—between February 1933 and February 1935—take some of the Cayce information to wider audiences not only locally, but in Washington and New York. They are the last of the recorded Cayce lectures, except for presentations to local study groups and to annual A.R.E. Congresses.

What Is a Reading?

Monday, February 6, 1933
Norfolk Study Group #1 Open Meeting
Location Not Recorded

It is rather hard to describe something which has become so much a part of me—almost like trying to describe what my face looks like. I can show you, but I can't tell you. Some of my experiences and thoughts concerning the readings might be given. But as to what a reading is, I can only tell you what others have said and what has come to me as I have studied the effect created in the minds of those receiving readings.

First, I would say, then, a reading is the information that comes through me to the individual who seeks through this channel for information. That's almost like going around in a circle, but many who have seen readings being given know the process much better than I.

It would not be an exaggeration to say that I have been in the unconscious state (during which the readings are given) perhaps 2500 times in the last thirty-one years, yet I have never heard a single reading. How can I describe one to you?

Possibly those seeking an answer to that question—what is a reading, so that they are able to describe it to someone else—would get a better understanding by asking me questions.

Many who have never heard a reading have asked just how I ever knew I could give a reading. I never did know it—don't know it yet—except by taking another's word for it.

When I prepare myself for the unconscious state, I pray—and, as some have pointed out, I unconsciously have taken on many forms of the better adepts—that is, I press on the third eye (of which I was not conscious until someone pointed it out to me). On losing consciousness, the name of the individual is given to me, with the address at which that individual will be during the time of the reading. It is said that I repeat this very slowly, until the body is located. Then there begins a description of the condition that exists. On awaking, I feel as if I had slept a little bit too long, as we do sometimes when taking a nap in the daytime.

As to the validity of the information, that is always the question with every individual. I feel this depends upon how much faith or confidence the one seeking has in this source of information. Of course, I have ideas as to the source; but you can guess as well as I can. It would be merely a matter of conjecture, for even though I have been doing this work for thirty-one years, I know very little about it, very little. I can make no claims whatsoever. We all only learn by experience. We come to have faith by taking one step at a time. We don't all have the experience of getting religion all at once—like the man who got religion halfway between the bottom of the well and the top when he was blown out by an explosion of dynamite. But we all do have our own experiences and arrive at conclusions by weighing the evidence with a something that responds from within our inner selves.

There are many elements that go to make up the spiritual experience of an individual or entity—"entity" being the combined experience of an individual soul throughout its passage through time (what we call time)—through all the eons of time. The total makeup of the experience of that soul may be the source from which anyone may obtain information through any individual channel able to contact such.

To say that I am one of those who may lay aside their own personality sufficiently to allow their souls to pass into the universal source of knowledge to obtain information—that may be considering myself rather braggadociously.

Many might say they obtain the information through me from some departed individual or personality that would desire to communicate with them, or from some benevolent spirit or physician from the other side. This is possible, I am sure. If the one comes seeking that, then only that can be obtained. God in His goodness and love has made us so much a part of Him that He allows us to abuse the most glorious things that go to make up creation. Our will is the only thing that may save us or damn us—and it is up to ourselves which it shall be.

I believe this source does touch the universal. Not that I claim to possess anything any other individual doesn't possess. Really and truly, I do not believe there is a single individual who doesn't possess the same ability. I am sure many have a much greater ability than they are ever conscious of. Would you be willing, even once a year, to throw away—that is, pass entirely from—your own personality?

Many ask, how do you prevent undesirable influences entering into the work you do? To answer that would be to tell an experience as a child. When I was between eleven and twelve years of age, I had read the Bible through three times. I have now read it fifty-six times. No doubt many have read it more times than that, but I have tried to read it through once for each year of my life. But as a child I prayed that I might be able to do something for the other fellow, to aid others in understanding themselves, and especially to aid children in their ills. I believed that He would answer my prayers. I still believe it, and as I go into the unconscious condition, I do so with that faith, so that I believe that, if the source is not wavered by the desires of the individual, it will be from the universal.

If an individual's desire is so great to have communication from Grandpa, Uncle, or some great soul so that one directs the contact that way, then that must be the source. Do not understand that I am discounting those who seek such, for would God forbid any great soul to give that information? *What ye ask, ye shall receive* is a two-edged sword—it cuts both ways.

[Mr. Cayce responded to questions from the audience.]

Question from audience: What classes of people does the information mostly interest?
Answer from Mr. Cayce: In my opinion, the Jews. They have sought it more. I have asked many of them why, and more often they have answered that perhaps it is because they are a superstitious people. I do not believe superstition is the basis of their seeking, but that it is a real innate spirituality which makes the real seeker. And the more spirituality or faith an individual has, the more benefit I believe may be derived from such information.

Question: What has been the effect on the Jews in regard to your belief in Christ?
Answer: There is not a single instance, nor has there ever been, where a Jew has asked for information that it has in any way sidetracked the issue when it came to what is the saving grace in this world. That I think speaks for itself, rather than anything I might say about it.

The Visible and the Invisible
Sunday, February 26, 1933
Ragged Robin, Norfolk, Va.

A few weeks ago, I stood up to speak to a Sunday school class. Many more seats were vacant in front of us than were filled. Within myself I felt that I had something to say, and I wondered why so few were present. Then I saw an invisible audience—invisible to the rest present—fill practically every seat in front of me.

So we may rest assured there is the visible and the invisible. We have with us always an invisible audience to our acts—yea, to our every thought. If we could come to realize this more and more, we would know that His presence abides with us and that, if His presence abides not with us, it is our own fault, for we have blinded ourselves to those things which it is possible for us to make our very own.

We all recognize that we are passing through a period of stress, when we are all expecting something we know not what. Why don't we know what to expect? Why is it impossible for us to know what is going to happen? Isn't it because we have so blinded ourselves to the evidences about us?

We are told by many who have made a study of such things that we are passing through a certain position in the universe. As astrologers have said, we are reaching that place in space wherein the influences are beginning for the third cycle, or—as some others have said—that place where we may expect a new race, a new people, a new thought.

Admitting for the moment that this is true, are these influences bearing upon us because we are in such a position or are we in such a position because of what we have done? If we are in trouble, depressed, do not understand what is going to happen to us now, is it because of what we have done or what somebody else has done?

The same old question arises in our experiences day by day as is said was asked of God by the first man that brought death into the world, "Am I my brother's keeper?" (*Gen. 4:9*) We are still evading the question, blaming someone else for the position we occupy.

We are told that there are being reincarnated into the earth those individuals who occupy a position where they may wield a mighty influence, because of the position they once occupied in the thought of the world. And because of the astrological effect upon the earth's inhabitants, they are now coming into their own.

Be that as it may, do we all not occupy that same position now as to what we are going to do about it? It is because of what? There is a very good description reading something like this: We are all subject to the powers that be. There is no power that is not ordained of God. Then, is it because the Maker of the universe has brought us into this, that, or the other position, through the astrological influences, or because we as individuals have been and are being reincarnated in the earth's experience at this time? Is it not the plan of the Supreme Force or Power that we call God? It has all been laid out beforehand. Then, you say, "Well, you are a fatalist—what's going to happen is going to happen, and nothing can change it." No, that isn't answering the question "Am I my brother's keeper?" It is the same today as when that question was first asked.

We are studying along lines of thought pertaining to development of the inner man, the soul. We feel there is within us that something we term our soul—our entity, our being—which lives on and on.

We say this is a period of hard times, when we are all becoming afraid, wondering just what is coming to pass. It is a period when there are to be upheavals. How often have we been told about such things? How often have we thought on these things, as we have read about them or have experienced a vision of them from the unseen forces? We have all at some time or another been warned in visions, dreams, meditation, or prayer. What have we done to prepare ourselves for such happenings? "These things will come about," the Master said, "but the time isn't yet. There shall be wars and rumors of wars. There shall be earthquakes in divers places. There will be signs in heaven and brother shall rise against brother, nation against nation, but the time isn't yet." (see Mark 13:7-8)

All these things are coming about. Why? What was the warning beforehand? "If ye fall away, if ye go back and follow after those things pertaining to the desires of your own carnal influences, I will turn my face from you." *(see, e.g., Ezek. 18:21-24)* The invisible face, yes—that which we cannot see, that which we cannot feel with our five senses, but that which may be aroused within us that tells us whether we are following in the way He would have us go or not.

How do we know about those things? How do we find out? He has said, "And ye shall know the truth, and the truth shall make you free." *(John 8:32)* For, "My Spirit will bear witness with your spirit whether ye be the sons of God or not." *(see Rom 8:16)*

It doesn't matter how these warnings come to us now. We are in the condition—it is all about us—the changes are coming about. Yes, portions of the earth are going to be wiped away entirely in the next few years, I feel very sure of that. Immediately we want to know, "Will it happen where we are?" What difference does it make, if we are living right?

If we are overanxious about ourselves because we are living in the wrong place, we are like the people talking to the old lady who lived on the frontier. A man came by and said he was going to a new country. He wanted to make a place for his family of boys and girls coming on, but he certainly hated to leave all the friends he had at home. She told him, "Well, you'll find it just the same way out here. If you had friends at home, you'll have friends here." The next man who came said that he was glad to get away from the place he had lived so many years. The people there were all selfish and stingy, and he couldn't get along with them. She said, "Brother, you'll find it the same way out here. If you couldn't get along with the folks at home, you won't be able to get along with them out here. If you didn't have friends at home, you won't find them here."

It's the same way with us. If we are not ready, if we are not making our preparations, it will only be a matter of time before we must pay that penalty, if we don't happen to be among the first that may be taken away in a moment.

How do we know all these things are going to happen? We don't know, save by the signs that have been told us, that we are expecting, that we are experiencing. If we begin to fear, fear, fear, and believe—and believe and build it—what else could happen? "As a man thinketh in his heart, so is he." *(see Prov. 23:7)* As a man builds into his heart by his thinking (for mind is the builder), so is he.

Now, the outward appearances—the things visible about us—are mere shadows of the things that really exist and that are coming about. And when, as the Master said, we see these things coming about, we know it is because people have acted within themselves and towards their neighbor such as to bring them to pass.

Because God made Adam and put him in the Garden of Eden, did that make him sin? Or did he sin of himself? Because we are in the world, these conditions we have learned. The first command was, "Be fruitful, multiply, subdue the earth—gain the knowledge of all these things that are here." *(see Gen. 8:17)* There isn't a thing that isn't a manifestation of God. How do we treat it? Do we use it or abuse it? Do we give it its rightful place, do we show forth our appreciation for the things about us, or do we say, "Gimme, gimme, gimme," and try to draw it all into ourselves? Do we blame someone else for bringing about unfavorable conditions for us? "Am I my brother's keeper, or is my brother keeping me?"

Life isn't a bit different today from what it was a million years ago. Life is One—God is Life, whether in the oyster, in the tree, or in us. Life is God—it is a manifestation of Him. Man can make a beautiful tree, but he can't give it life. He can make a beautiful egg, but he can't give it that which will make it reproduce itself. What is that something that can reproduce life except Life itself, or God? The invisible that is within us, about us, and all around us—what are we going to do about it?

It doesn't matter how these things come about, yet it's wonderful to know—if we know what to do about it! Then if thoughts are deeds, our constructive and positive thinking will aid in building or establishing that which will bring peace, harmony, joy, love, the fruits of what? The Spirit! What is the Spirit! *It is that which we do not comprehend except by the application of it,* or as to what we do for the other fellow.

We had a very beautiful illustration of this same thought in our Sunday school lesson this morning. The Master had spent Himself in giving out to others—He had grown tired, weary. It was necessary that He rest physically, for He was then a man. Something had been taken out of Him to give constructive influence to that which had been destructive in the lives of those He had contacted. He was asleep on the sea. The boat began to fill, and the disciples became uneasy. They went and woke Him. "Carest thou not that we perish?" He rebuked the wind, and the sea became calm. (see Matt. 8:23-26) Did that power go out of Him or did it come into Him? It came into Him—the peace, the calm, because He was of the Creative Forces that would manifest. In the giving out, it came in. In our giving out to make this a better world for others to live in, the peace, the harmony, the understanding—fruits of the Spirit—come into us.

So, what are we going to do? Shall we go out and do wonderful things? Shall we stand on the corner and preach this, that, or the other? If we are called to do such, then we should do it. Or shall we speak the kind word to our next-door neighbor, to the child we meet in the street, to the lame dog we see, or to anything or anybody that is a manifestation of God?

It would be well if we could all get it into our minds and hearts that life itself is a manifestation of what we worship. What are we doing about it? Just being kind day by day, just speaking the kind word, just bringing hope to those that are losing hope, just bringing the cheery word to those that are discouraged. As we are able to do this, we give out what we have received. "Freely ye have received, freely give." (see Matt. 10:8) All are called, but not in the same way. Not all are called to be healers, not all preachers, but we each can do that our hands find to do, magnifying the spirit and the fruits of the Spirit—which are the unseen.

When doubts and fears arise as to whether we are going to be fed tomorrow or be able to pay the rent for the next six months, we can be sure that sin lieth at the door. That's what He has said from the beginning. We will not find it different, any more than the man who was looking for a new country and new friends. "As the tree falls, so shall it lie." (see Eccl. 11:3) What does that mean? The things we do today will make the manner of individual we will be tomorrow, or a million years from now. We don't die to be in eternity—we are already in it! It's just as important for us to understand from whence we came as it is to understand where we are going, because if we know from whence we came, we know what we are up against. We have to grasp the knowledge, and then use it for somebody else. If we use what abilities we have, then we will be given more tomorrow. We will be given the next step to take.

We don't have to be dishonest. Perhaps people dislike us more often because we are dishonest about our failures. If we have failed, let's acknowledge it—and not blame it on somebody else!

He has said, "If ye will come, I will lift you up—and will always be near unto you." That's what we have to do about it now. All the failures that are behind us, let's not allow them to bear us down. Let's use them as stepping-stones to better things. Know where we have failed, yes—but don't let our failures overcome us.

In Texas a few years ago, I found that the first question there is not "Who are you?" but "What are you doing about it?" The usual question where I come from is asked, "Who was your grandfather? and so forth," but not so in Texas. It is not *what* you have been, but what you *are* that counts. Not what you have done, but what *you are doing today!* Let's not talk about what we have done or what we are going to do, but what we are doing now!

Have we faced about toward God and said, "I am weak, I am unworthy, but I am willing to be shown"? And when we are shown, let's not blame it on somebody else, nor give the credit to ourselves. Because, as He said to the children of Israel as they went into the Promised Land, "Do not think because you are given the privilege of going into this Promised Land that it is because of your own righteousness, not a bit of it! It is nothing more than what should be the natural thing! It is unnatural for you to have wandered away."

The natural thing is to draw to that from which we have emanated. It is self-exaltation and selfishness that carries us away or brings doubt, fear, and all these qualities that bespeak of the visible things, or those making worry, hardship, and misunderstanding.

Whatever may be troubling us, let us take it to God, to Christ, and we will be shown the way.

[Mr. Cayce responded to questions from the audience.]

Question from the audience: Do you think it is a fact that present-day conditions, as we have them, are due to the fact that the unseen forces of evil are more active on earth today than they have been in the past?

Answer by Mr. Cayce: I do not doubt it, but I do believe that the cause of the unseen forces being more active is that those who profess to be Christians are too passive and not active enough!

You know, we have another illustration of that same thought in the Sunday school lesson for today. As the Master crossed the Sea of Galilee and came into the land of the Gadarenes, he met a man coming out of the tombs who, being possessed of the unclean spirit, was so strong that no man physically could bind him. We might say, that's our condition today—it can't be bound by chains or ropes. But the Master said, "Get out of him," and he got out. *(see Mark 5:1-8)* It is the same with us. We have been enjoying the fleshpots of Egypt through the last generation so much that we have forgotten God and wandered away. If the people who know will say, "Peace—be still" in His name, or in His name say, "Get out!" I verily believe the terrible condition of today will be just as the unclean spirit that said, "What have we to do with thee, thou Jesus of Nazareth?" *(see Mark 5:7)*

Question: How long do you expect this condition will prevail?
Answer: As long as we are doubting within ourselves. As soon as we become conscious that we can trust Him, it is over with us.

Continuity of Life

Thursday, December 14, 1933
Ragged Robin, Norfolk, Va.

First, let us understand what we mean by certain terms that we must use. Not being a scientist, I cannot speak in a scientific way and manner. I am not an educated man, so I cannot speak in the terms of a scholar. I can speak only from experience and observation, or from what I have read.

When we use the term "continuity of life," what do we mean by "life"? Do we mean that span from birth until death? Would it not be preferable to refer to life as the consciousness of existence?

With such a premise, I approach the question that has been sounded throughout the ages. It is one of the oldest questions man has considered: If a man die, shall he live again? What is death? What comes next? All of these sound the same note. We must each answer within our own self. But this is my belief:

I believe that when God breathed into man the breath of life, he became a *living soul*—an individual soul, if you please. The Spirit of God is life, whether in a blade of grass or in man. *The soul of man is individual and lives on.*

In the very first part of the Bible, we find it noted that man was forbidden to partake of certain fruit in the Garden. *(see Gen. 2:17)* In the partaking of that fruit, man became conscious of his being, and it was sin, for he was forbidden to do it. Then God reasoned with man that he must leave the Garden lest he partake of the tree of life and live forever. What did that mean? Just that? Or had Satan been correct when he said, "Ye shall not surely die if ye partake of this fruit!"? *(see Gen. 3:4)* What brought physical death to man? Error! The partaking of that which was forbidden. Did it bring death to the soul? No! It brought death to the physical body.

Now, to become conscious of our continued existence is to become righteous in ourselves. Then we may become conscious of our contin-

229

ued existence, whether in the physical realm, the spiritual realm, or whatever stage of development through which we may be passing from physical life unto spiritual life. As we pass through all the various stages, what are we attempting to gain? Righteousness within!

Jesus said that, if we had His consciousness within us, we should become conscious, or we should *know* what He has said to us from the beginning. What was the beginning with Christ? "In the beginning was the Word, and the Word was with God, and the Word was God." (John 1:1) So were our souls in the beginning. The Master said, "Ye say that ye have Abraham for your father. I say unto you that before Abraham was, I AM, and he rejoiced to see my day and he saw it and was glad." Then many of those to whom He spoke these words walked no longer with Him, but turned away. (see John 8:54-56) Why? He was answering that same question which had been bothering man from the beginning: "If a man die, will he live again?" He said to Nicodemus, "Know ye that a man must be born again?" When Nicodemus asked, "How can such things be?" He answered, "Are ye a teacher in Israel and knoweth not these things?" (see John 3:1-10)

What is it to know continuity of life? It is to be righteous within and to have the consciousness of the Christ within. For God is Life. Christ is Life and Light unto all that seek to know Him. Without Him, is there any other way? Not that He is the *only* way, but, "He that climbeth up some other way is a thief and a robber," to his own self! (see John 10:1) He *is* the Life. He came to represent that life, and the continuity of life is in the immortality of the soul.

Immortality of the soul is an *individual* thing. My soul is my own, with the ability to *know* itself to *be* itself, and yet *one with God*. (see 2030-1) That was the message Jesus gave to His disciples all the way through. "I of myself can do nothing." (see John 5:19) But the life that is within—and the gift of God working in you—will make you conscious of your relationship to your Maker. How do we become conscious of our relationship with God? By living the fruits of the Spirit! Spirit is the Life—and Light—that makes us conscious of immortality, which is the continuation of our oneness with God. If God *is* Life, we then must be His to enjoy the consciousness of being one with Him.

Continuity of life, then, is *being conscious of our oneness with God*, through the channel that has been set before us by the example that came into the world to show us the Way of Life.

The fact that consciousness exists after physical death is clearly pointed out to us in at least two ways that I would like to mention:

After Samuel passed on, Saul was still in trouble. He knew that Samuel had rebuked him for the manner of life he lived, yet he was in great distress and sought to know if Samuel would give him another blessing, although Samuel had passed from the physical plane of existence. So, Saul sought out a channel through which he might speak to Samuel—and spoke to him. We find that Samuel's consciousness had not changed one iota by having passed to the other side, for his first words to Saul were along the same lines that he used while still on earth, "Why troublest thou me? Dost thou not know God has rejected thee already?" (see 1 Sam. 28:15-20) Passing over did not automatically make Samuel know more than he knew when he was here—not one bit more—for the manner of existence he had lived in this plane had only developed him so far.

What did Christ say about this? "As the tree falls, so shall it lie!" (see Eccles. 11:3) When we pass into another plane, our development begins right there in that plane—just as our birth into the physical brings a gradual unfoldment and development in the physical.

Therefore, I believe it is a gradual growth throughout. What is Truth? Growth! What is Life? God! The knowledge of God, then, is the growth into Life—or the continuity of Life itself.

Another example of continuity is pointed out to us in the parable that Christ gave of the rich man and Lazarus. They had both passed into what we call the death state, yet both were conscious. (see Luke 16:20-26) Living, then, is being conscious of your experience—or conscious of where you are!

Dives, the rich man, lifted his eyes, for he was in torment. Why was he in torment? Where was torment? We want to have these questions answered in our own consciousness—in our own figure of speech—so that we can encompass what we are talking about. We want to give things metes and bounds. We want to tag them with names, and even so we may not recognize them the next time someone calls those names. We have gotten names for most everything, yet when we say a name, it even now means an entirely different thing to each one of us. It is our experience with what is named that makes the difference—it is our own development. The same thing may have varied meanings.

The place Dives occupied was his own building, his own development, and he was being tormented in a flame. Tormented in a flame of what? Fire? Well, he had the consciousness that it was fire, so it must have been something like it, for he wanted water to put it out!

It was a continued existence for that man, and he saw Lazarus in Abraham's bosom. He recognized Abraham, though he had never seen him. How? He recognized Lazarus, though possibly he had never paid any attention to him while on earth. How? You answer it. But he was *conscious* of the condition. He was conscious!

Most of us believe the Scripture—at least we believe that what is written there is for our knowledge and understanding. And if we *follow* that, we will come to a greater knowledge of Life—that is, of God. We will come to a greater concept of how great life *is*.

I would like to go into the subject of just what consciousness has to do with life and death, but that is reincarnation. Why are we not conscious of the continuity of life in the physical plane? Why do we not remember when we live again? We do not remember because we have not been righteous enough. Christ said that if we had His consciousness within us, He would bring to our remembrance all things from the very beginning! *(see John 14:26)*

As a child, it once bothered me a great deal that God spoke to the people in the Bible and did not speak to us. Now I believe that He does and will speak to us—if we will only listen. Often we allow the desires of our physical bodies to so outweigh our desires for spiritual knowledge that we build barriers between ourselves and God. We do it ourselves, for "He is the same yesterday, today, and forever," and He does not will that any should be lost. What prevents us from knowing more about Life or God? Ourselves! Nothing can separate us from the love of God but ourselves—nothing! It is *the will of man* that can make him conscious of the knowledge of God and of all Life. It is also *the will of man* that can separate him from his God, because he enjoys rather the pleasures of the flesh for a season. "I will satisfy the desires of my body now, rather than listen to the voice that may be raised within."

SEEKING INFORMATION ON

holistic health, spirituality, dreams, intuition or ancient civilizations?
Call 1-800-723-1112, visit our Web site, or mail in this postage-paid card for a FREE catalog of books and membership information.

PBIN

Name: _____

Address: _____

City: _____

State/Province: _____

Postal/Zip Code: _____ Country: _____

Association for Research and Enlightenment, Inc.
215 67th Street
Virginia Beach, VA 23451-2061

For faster service, call 1-800-723-1112.
www.edgarcayce.org

I choose to think that each one of us has an individual soul, that there is *One Spirit*—the Spirit of God—going through each and every one that makes each and every one of us akin. That makes all life and nature akin, for life in *every* form is dependent upon that force we call God. For as matter came into being, it was permeated with the Spirit of God that gives life, with its ability to carry itself on and make of itself that which has been determined by God that it should be. Man only, who was chosen to be one with God and a companion with Him from the beginning, chose rather to go his own way—as Adam. But He has prepared a way, through the Christ, who came into the world that we through Him might have life and have it more abundantly, that we might be more conscious of all periods of our development of the life of God that is within us. *(see John 10:10)* Christ Himself taught that we must test the spirits, and they that acknowledge Jesus the Christ has come in the flesh are born of God. The truth makes alive, and the life makes you free.

In closing I would like to give an experience which I have had at frequent intervals for many years, during the time when I am in the unconscious (so-called) or superconscious state. This experience has come eight or ten times while giving "life readings" for individuals. I remember nothing of the reading, but have a very vivid impression of the following. This may help you to understand your own experiences.

I know my spirit, mind, or soul was separated from my body and that it was seeking information for another. I passed into outer darkness—so dark that it actually hurt—yet there was a stream of light that I knew I must follow, and nothing on either side of the light must distract from my purpose to receive for that other what it was seeking in the way of aid for itself.

As I passed along the line of light, I became conscious of forms of movement toward the light. Coming to the next plane (if we choose to call it such), I realized that the forms of movement or figures were taking shape as humans, but rather the exaggeration of human desires. Passing a little farther, these forms were gradually lost. Still I had the consciousness that they were seeking the light—or more light. Finally, I passed through a place where individuals appeared much as they are today—men and woman—but satisfied with their position. The number of individuals in this state of satisfaction continued to grow, and then there were homes and cities where they were content to continue as they were.

Still following the light which grew stronger and stronger, I heard music in the beyond. Then there came a space where all was spring-time, all was in blossom, all was summer. Some were happy, some desired to remain, but many were pressing on and on to the place where there might be great understanding, more light, more to be gained. Then I reached a place where I was seeking the records of the lives of people that lived in the earth.

Don't ever think that your life isn't being written in the Book of Life. I found it! It is being written. *You* are the writer! As to how close it is going to be to your Savior and your God, you alone can answer. You alone. It is your soul development. It is up to us to answer. If we would reach that consciousness, if we would become aware of our relation-ship, we must live it here and *now*—and then the next step is given to us. That has been His promise, and His promises are sure.

[In 1936, Cayce reported the following incident:]

Some years ago I had a very warm personal friend who was an executive of the Western Union Telegraph Company in Chicago. We met quite often, and in our discussions of various subjects, the question frequently arose between us as to whether or not there was a survival of personality. It usually ended jokingly with one of us saying, "Well, whichever one goes first will communicate with the other."

During the last few years of my friend's life, we did not meet— but corresponded intermittently. Then I was notified of his death.

Several months afterwards I was sitting alone in my living room, listening to the radio. The program was Seth Parker's. Members of the group had decided they would sing songs which their loved ones had been fond of during their lifetime. One lady asked that they sing "Sweet Hour of Prayer." Another asked her *which one* of her husbands had liked that song. I remember that I was very much amused and leaned back in my chair smiling to myself.

Suddenly I felt as if there was a presence in the room. I was cold, and felt something uncanny or unusual taking place. The program was still on. When I looked toward the radio, I realized that my friend, several months deceased, was sitting in front of the radio as if listening to the program. He turned and smiled at me, saying, "There *is* the survival of the personality. *I know!* And a life of service and prayer is the only one to live."

I was shaking all over. He said nothing more and just seemed to disappear.

The program finished, and I turned off the radio. It still appeared as if the room was full of some presence. As I switched off the light and climbed the stairs, I could hear many voices coming from the darkened room. Jumping in bed and shivering from the cold, I aroused my wife. She asked me why I hadn't turned off the radio. I assured her that I had. She opened the door, and said, "I hear it— I hear voices." We both did.

What was it?

The Second Coming

Monday, May 7, 1934
Ragged Robin, Norfolk, Va.

This is a subject about which very little is known. Jesus Himself said that it was given only to the Father to know the time of His return. We have, however, two sources of information upon which we will draw for material which may be used in forming our ideas about this subject. We will turn to the Bible for part of our discussion and to information received psychically for a clarification of various passages and for further data. (Do not get the idea that "psychic information" means simply communication with "Uncle John" or "Aunt Sue," though it may mean that to some at this time. Rather, view it in a broader aspect as referring to the development and expression of soul faculties.)

First, what does the Master say about the Second Coming? How has anyone ever gotten the idea that there is to be a Second Coming? Let's look first at the New Testament book of John. Jesus said, "Let not your heart be troubled; ye believe in God, believe also in me. In my Father's house are many mansions; if it were not so, I would have told you. I go to prepare a place for you. And if I go and prepare a place for you, I will come again, and receive you unto myself; that where I am, there ye may be also." *(John 14:1-3)*

How often in the history of the world has a great religious teacher arisen? Plato sets the cycle at a thousand years. Judging from history, the period of time varies from six hundred to twelve hundred years among outstanding religious leaders. Do you ask, "Is that how often you say Christ has come?" No, I do not suggest that, but if we will consider for a few moments the following passages of Scripture, an interesting idea may be formulated: "In the beginning was the Word, and the Word was with God, and the Word was God. The same was in the beginning with God. All things were made by him; and without him was not anything made that was made." *(John 1:1-3)* "And the Word was made flesh, and dwelt among us . . . " *(John 1:14)* "He was in the world, and the world was made by him, and the world knew him not. He came unto his own, and his own received him not." (John 1:10-11)

In talking with the judges of Israel, the Master said, "I know that ye are Abraham's seed . . . If ye were Abraham's children, ye would do the works of Abraham . . . Ye are of your father the devil." (John 8:37, 39, 44) In the flesh, yes, they were the children of Abraham, but in spirit they were not. What did Abraham do? He was righteous—his deeds were counted to him for righteousness because of his faith in the One God. In the same chapter, we read, "Your father Abraham rejoiced to see my day; and he saw it, and was glad. Then said the Jews unto him, Thou art not yet fifty years old, and hast thou seen Abraham? Jesus said unto them, Verily, verily, I say unto you, before Abraham was, I am." (John 8:56-58) What do you think He meant?

If we turn to the fourteenth chapter of Genesis, we read where Abraham paid tribute to a certain individual, Melchizedek. No cause or reason is given, save the man came out in the place to bless him, a priest of the most high God, without beginning of days or end of life, a man not born normally, but a high priest of the living God. (see Gen. 14:17-20; see also Heb. 7:1-4) How does this fit with the above passage? Was this the Master, this Melchizedek?

Consider now the book of Joshua. Who directed Joshua when he became the leader of Israel? Who walked out to lead Joshua after he crossed the Jordan? The Bible says the Son of Man. The Son of Man came out to lead the armies of the Lord, and after Joshua's experience in meeting this man of God, all the children of Israel were afraid of him. (see Josh. 5:13-15)

From the above, let us draw a few conclusions and supplement them with psychic information. The Spirit of the Christ manifested in the earth many times before the coming of Jesus. At times, this was through one such as Melchizedek, and at other times as a spiritual influence by or through some teacher upholding the worship of the One God.

What has this to do with the Second Coming? First, there ceases to be a *Second* Coming in the light of the above. Further, by a consideration of the conditions that made possible His appearance at various times—or if you prefer, the one time as Jesus—we may be able to deduce certain facts about the return of the Master.

How did He ever come as Jesus of Nazareth? There had not been a revelation to man (of which we have any record) for over four hundred years. Did darkness and dissipation on the part of these people bring Christ into the world? If so, it is refuting the natural law "Like begets like." The laws of God are not refuted at any time. Never will we find them so. They are immutable, and they carry through any kingdom in this earth. And the things we see in this earth in the various kingdoms of their development are merely shadows of the celestial and terrestrial world. For we grow, as another of the writers has said, in grace and knowledge and in understanding. *(see 2 Peter 3:18)* By what? *Application in our lives.*

What brought about, then, the coming of Jesus? Was it not a sincere group of people seeking to make themselves channels through which this great thing could come to pass? That group was the Essenes, the most hated of all mentioned in profane history, and scarcely mentioned in the Bible. How many more times was Zacharias allowed to go up and offer sacrifice after he had been spoken to once within the temple? Never again. He had joined that hated group, making his son (who by lineal descent was a high priest) an outcast.

Did not Mary, the mother of the Man we worship as our Lord and Master, seek first her cousin, Elizabeth, the mother of the great Essene, John the Baptist, and announce to her the great tidings that the angel had made known to her? *(see Luke 1:39-40)* These people, then, *through consecrating and dedicating their lives,* their inner selves, made it possible for there to be *a meeting place of God with man* to such a degree that Jesus, the Christ, came into the world. If we will have a meeting place in our heart, in our home, in our group, in our church, we may have the Christ come. When we have prepared the place, He will come—and not before.

Is this sensible? Of course, it is if we believe the law that is set before us day after day: "Like begets like." What harvest may we expect from the seed we sow? How often the Master used that illustration in the parables! Those who purpose, desire, set, and live that which they desire to have in their lives—a knowledge of God—may obtain it. If we would seek God, we must first believe that *He is,* and that He is a rewarder of them who diligently seek Him. One doesn't go without the other.

When the way is made possible, He will come again. And He will come as He is. His Spirit is here always, for He said, "I will abide with you." *(see John 14:16)* Do we believe this? We say we believe He descended into hell and taught those who were there. We read it in the Bible, and we say that it is true. But we do not really believe it, else we would act like it. If we really believed it, we would never find fault with a soul in the world—never! If we believe He went into hell and taught the people there, the least we can do would be to refrain from condemning our neighbor because he does not believe or do exactly as we.

Jesus taught that our knowledge and understanding of God and our relationship to our fellow man come to us by the application of what He has given us through His own life. What is the whole gospel of Jesus? "Thou shalt love the Lord thy God with all thy soul, mind, and body, and thy neighbor as thyself." *(see Matt. 22:37-39)*

When is Christ coming again? When we prepare the way! A warning was given to a man of God that a certain country would be destroyed. But the man prayed and talked with God face to face, and God promised if there were fifty righteous men he would save it, and then—*finally*—if there were ten just men He would spare it. *(see Gen 18:24-32)* When there are possibly fifty—or a hundred, a thousand, a million, or perhaps the one hundred and forty-four thousand—the time may be here, the way may be prepared. When such individuals have united in their desires, in their supplications that the Christ physically may walk among men, then it will be possible for Him to come. He has said that whatever we ask in His name, *believing*, that will He give unto us. *(see Matt. 21:22; also John 14:13)* That is the promise He gave to us—the Man Jesus, the Christ, who was crucified. We look to Him. Why? Without Him, so far as this earth is concerned, there was nothing made that was made. It belongs to Him, the Creator and the Builder of this little world. He for our sakes became flesh. How many times? Answer for yourself. How soon will He come again? When we make it possible. It was made possible at least once.

It is our work to set the house in order, to prepare the path—by being kind and by holding no malice, hate, uppishness, snobbishness. When we live the life He has laid out for us, we will be making it possible for Him, the Lord and Master of this world, to come again. "I will not leave you comfortless, but I will come again, and receive you unto myself, that where I am there ye may be also." *(see John 14:3, 18)*

Practical Application of Psychical Information

Thursday, October 11, 1934
Hamilton Hotel, Washington, D.C.

Tuesday, November 20, 1934
McAlpin Hotel, New York City

Thursday, January 17, 1935
Ragged Robin, Norfolk, Va.

What is psychical information? It exists, call it what we will or may. We have a body, a mind, a soul. Whether we are aware of a soul or not, we have it just the same. It is that portion which lives on after the physical body has ceased to function properly. In our bodies we have a nervous system. That nervous system goes to every single portion of our bodies, and it is centralized in the brain. Consequently, many people have looked into the brain to see if they could find the soul there. They don't find it any more than they can find words there–even though the man with such a brain may have a wonderful vocabulary. But it is true that psychic information can be given out to others.

Then, we know–through the faculty of something we call *mind*–that something takes place. Does that something take place irrespective of the physical body? Can the mind function without the body? There isn't but one way to get an answer and that's psychically! Then we may know that we have psychic information, for we are acted upon by the things within us and from without.

Who was the first individual who ever had psychic information, according to our known records? I say Enoch. Although Eve was really the first to receive outside information, she got it from the Devil not from within herself. She did not receive it from anything that had a body, did she? It fooled her. She was mistaken, or was the serpent mistaken, or the evil force which tempted her? When she said, "We are forbidden to do this, for we shall surely die," the answer was, "Thou shalt not surely die,

241

for it is good to look upon." *(see Gen. 3:3-6)*

I don't think all psychic information is good to look upon. We have another illustration shown us very plainly. I have been told by some that I am a "spiritualist" and ashamed to acknowledge it. I'm not ashamed to acknowledge that I believe in spirit communication, but I am ashamed to acknowledge that I would listen at such communication before I would listen to God! And God has promised to meet us within. That's psychic information, isn't it?

Jesus asked His disciples, "Whom do men say that I, the son of man, am?" After the question had been asked the disciples direct, "Whom do ye say I am?" Peter answered, "Thou art the Christ, the son of the living God." That's psychic information, for the Master said, "Flesh and blood hath not revealed it unto you, but my Father which is in heaven." *(see Matt. 16:13-17)*

It's not what we receive from the mental mind. What is psychic cannot be put in the crucible and tested any more than there can be found in the brain the ideas man has respecting anything. Mind is both physical and spiritual, and it is only through the mind that we may be able to attain that something upon which we may lean. The most powerful things in the world are the unseen things, the unseen influences of the soul–the soul being that which is imperishable, that portion of every individual which is the gift of what we worship as a living God. Psychic means pertaining to the soul. Man cannot see God. Only with his soul may he know his God. How do we find that we have a soul? "In patience possess ye your souls." *(Luke 21:19)* Through patience we will understand that we have a soul.

We are worried about many things in this life and about how we are to understand this life, but if we will turn within our own selves, He has promised every man to meet him there! It is our birthright! No one can give it to us–it is ours! If we sell it for a mess of pottage, for the satisfying of our own outer selves, that is our doing. For the will of God is that no man shall perish but that he might come to know Him from within.

Is it possible for one to receive so-called psychic information that isn't exactly straight and right? It *is!* Even though Peter received a message directly from God regarding the status of the Master, in almost the very next breath he received something from the opposite source, and was told "Get thee behind me, Satan, for thou savorest the things of the earth." (see Matt. 16:23)

Now what are the different sources of psychic information? Those things pertaining to the earth and that are earthly come from one source, and spiritual things from another. Those of us who are Christians have been told how to judge such information, and what the standard should be: "Try ye the spirits, and those that declare that God or the Christ has come in the flesh, listen to them–those that declare something else, don't listen to them." (see 1 John 4:1-3)

Psychic information may come from or through discarnate entities, from the Evil One, from an angel in heaven, or it may come from God Himself.

Read the 13th chapter of 1 Kings. A prophet of Judah went down to rebuke Jereboam. He stood before the altar and prophesied as to what was coming to pass. From whence did he receive his information? Shortly afterward, he went against the voice from within and listened to a message through another so-called *prophet*, and it destroyed him, although the things he prophesied before the altar later came to pass. One source of information was from *God, direct through the inner self or soul*–the other was from *outside of himself, directly opposed to the voice from within*.

Most of us listen to the signs from *without* so much quicker than we do to the real from *within*. We use them as excuses because we are not willing ourselves to pay the price, and we are hunting for a shorter way! That's the whole answer, isn't it? We will accept what this one, that one, or the other has to say, rather than going to the trouble to find the truth for ourselves. God has promised to meet us, and yet we will say, "I'm not worthy." Who said you are not worthy? If you say it yourself, you create a barrier that prevents you from receiving Him.

How does God hear people? In the same way the Devil does! There's not a bit of difference. Everything we say or do attracts one or the other! When Jesus Christ physically left this world, in whose hands did He leave the redemption of the world? In yours and mine! When the Devil tries to get the world, does he use somebody else–or just you and me? There is that war constantly going on. God has prepared for *everything* that has come into our experience a way of escape, through the promises made to us and to our children. How? He has promised to meet us in our individual selves!

Where is the temple of God so far as we individually are concerned? It isn't built in stone, nor in any congregation, no matter what may be its creed! Where is it? What is that tabernacle of which that builded in the wilderness was a pattern? It is our own inner self, where God has promised to meet us–as He promised in those outward appearances to meet those people who were called for a definite purpose–in the holy of holies! Where is the holy of holies so far as we are concerned? *It is within!*

That those who have passed on may aid and be aided by us is without question, but who is our Savior? Is it just anybody? Is just anyone that comes along all right?

From whom may we obtain psychic information? How may we obtain psychic information that is practical and workable in our everyday life? Only from that source which answers to the inner conscience! It may come through another individual, a Ouija board, a sign in the heavens, or through a dream. It may come almost any way, but when are we to believe it and not to believe it? Have we put our trust in signs, in numbers, in days? God no longer requires human sacrifice, for the sacrifice has been made once for all. What does He require? Simply that we just be gentle and kind and loving to the man that treats us the worst! He has asked us to sacrifice *self*ishness. But how may we do that? Not by running to church, not by conforming to this ritual, that, or the other merely for the formality of the thing. We must live the real thing, that upon which all the rituals and formalities of the ages have been built! "If ye love me, ye will keep my commandments; and I will come and abide with you, and bring to your remembrance all things . . . even from the beginning." *(see John 14:21-26)*

When Peter made his confession, the Master said, "Upon this . . . (this confession) . . . I will build my church, and the gates of hell shall not prevail against it." *(see Matt. 16:18)* Where is the church? It must be within! For until He is our individual Savior, to us His words and teachings do not become practical things in our everyday lives. Unless we can take hold of that promise, know that it exists and rely upon it, to us it is not practical. Then, most of us think of Him as only being with us when we are having trials, troubles, or tribulations.

Remember, He said regarding John the Baptist, "What went ye out into the wilderness to see? A reed shaken by the wind? The Son of Man came eating and drinking, and ye say he is a winebibber and a glutton." (see Luke 7:24, 34) In other words, what are we looking for? "Seek and ye shall find." (Luke 11:9) If we will seek Him in our joys as well as our sorrows, we shall find Him, and there can be no greater joy than having Him share it with us–for He is the joy of the world. "Be of good cheer, I have overcome the world." (John 16:33) Isn't that enough to make us joyous always, just to know that in such joy we are lifted above the easily besetting things to that place where there is no sorrow, no tribulation, for He is with us? And, "If God be with us, who can be against us?" (see Rom. 8:31)

What was the matter with Enoch, that God took him? Do you know what Enoch preached? (Read the Book of Jude in the New Testament.) He preached that God was coming, and with ten thousand of His angels, to judge man for the way he was treating his neighbor. That was psychic information. Did the people like it? Not very much! Most of us don't like the things we get if we really go into the holy of holies with God and are rebuked within our own conscience for the things we have done and the things we have sought. There's always that other door through which the Devil may slip in and persuade us to choose the easier way, by saying flattering things to us and justifying us in our own weaknesses–that is, justifying us before the Devil himself, not before God.

The mental mind that functions through the body is amenable to suggestions from without and from within, and we must make our choice. And that chosen is that destiny we set before ourselves.

How will we make practical application of psychic information? By living the life that Christ would have us lead, by accepting that our own conscience verifies according to what we are seeking. If we are satisfied to listen to those on this side, that, or the other, then we are forgetting the way that we–deep down within ourselves–know has been set before us.

When Saul was in trouble and God had rejected him through Samuel, he still knew deep down within his soul that Samuel had anointed him and had told him what was coming to pass if he would follow in the way he had been chosen–or what would happen if he didn't. At one time, the spirit of God had shone upon Saul's countenance, for he had been chosen to lead a mighty people. But when he followed the dictates of the outer self rather than from God, he brought about the natural result–there was taken away "even that which he seemed to have"–and he sought Samuel, to try to justify his own conscience. God no longer spoke to him directly, because he had turned himself away from hearing God's voice. Saul asked that there be sought out one who had familiar spirits, and the witch of Endor was found. Not until Saul said, "It is Samuel!" did the witch of Endor know that was who he sought. (see 1 Sam. 28:7-15) Why? She was in the presence of what had been chosen as a divine manifestation of God, which had been promised even before Samuel was born. Why would he come up from the witch of Endor whom many questioned? That spirit of truth is ever present with each one of us! It is only by attunement to any source that we may receive the light thereof. But Saul only saw in Samuel then the same thing that he had seen during his lifetime on earth–it was not a bit different! How could he receive anything different, when he had lived only to justify the prophecy which Samuel made would come about if he continued to go against the inner dictates?

No one individual has any more psychic ability than another. It is simply the *use* of it that makes a greater manifestation in some than others. And the direction in which we use it makes for either a working toward the Oneness with the purposes of God, or toward the gratification of our outer selves which brings death. Only in working towards the manifestation of the Divine within us can we have life and have it more abundantly, through the way which has been set by the One who made the great manifestation and practical application of psychic information.

And how has He shown us is the way? Just being patient, just being loving to those that despitefully use us, to those that are about us day by day. If we will consciously do it, we will consciously know that His Spirit bears witness with our spirit, our soul, that we are children of the Most High.

The human mind is the most glorious thing, and yet the most inconsistent!

What was and is the first command given to man? "Go ye into all the world and preach the gospel–multiply, subdue, replenish the earth." (see Mark 16:15; Gen. 1:28) It is our command today, it hasn't changed. We all stand in the same relationship to God, don't we? He is no respecter of persons. What we have builded we must live by and die by. But "When ye call, I will hear." The provision is within our individual selves always. For He is ours. He is as personal as we let Him be.

The Master said, "Ye are gods." (John 10:34) In the making, yes. For if we do not so live that we can look our worst enemy in the face and find in him what we find in the God we worship, then we are in danger of hell fire! "As ye have done it unto the least of thy brethren ye have done it unto me!" (see Matt. 25:40) That's what God has said, and what He says today! If we have treated our fellow man wrong, how can we go within and ask God to save us, to be merciful to us, if we haven't measured the same to our brother?

The Devil can never be manifested in the flesh except through us. Why? Because Jesus the Christ, our Savior, was manifested in the flesh and overcame flesh and the devil. It is only then, in the imagination of our hearts and minds, that He can enter. And when we have the promise and the opportunity to be on speaking terms with God, why will we be satisfied with or seek any other?

How may we find the soul information–that is, psychic information–and apply it in our daily lives? Only by seeking within, and not from without–by justifying ourselves only with God within–and then our psychic information may be worthwhile. It is within our own souls that God will meet us and direct us: "If ye will be my people, I will be your God." (see Lev. 26:12; Jer. 30:22)

What Is Soul Power?
Sunday, February 3, 1935
Arlington Hotel, Washington, D.C.

What is "soul power"? On this subject I haven't anything new to offer, other than my understanding of that presented by the man Jesus who became the Christ. For I am determined that as long as I live, I will know nothing among men save Jesus Christ and Him crucified! For until we crucify our own personal desires, we can never know whether we have a soul or not!

So what is soul power?

Some years ago, I had the privilege of meeting one of the best-known scientists, a man considered throughout the world as an electrical wizard. He said at that time, "There isn't such a thing as a soul. It is purely the development of the race ideal." Just a few days ago, I had a communication from that same man. He said, "Cayce, I do not know whether I was right in what I said to you in 1910 or not. We do not *know* that man has a soul, we cannot *prove* it with our instruments. Yet when we see the entire world seeking, seeking, seeking, there must be something. And I am convinced that when scientists go to work at studying God, just as they have undertaken to study how to make greater conveniences for mankind, we will learn something about the soul—if there is one."

I had a report from one of the better writers in which he gave statistics on all the wonderful things that had been accomplished—how many new trains set in motion, how many new airplanes, new this, that, and the other, and how many changes had come about. But I am wondering if that is really even civilization. We see *so little* about *how much good* we have tried to do for our fellow man—there's so little being presented!

We as a people are so material-minded that we are thinking of the moment rather than of what we may learn about our inner selves. What is the motivative force with any of us?

I am reminded of what a physician asked me not long ago, in seeking a reading through me for himself: "Would you advise that I affiliate myself with some church that I might increase my clientele?" Isn't that why most of us go to church these days? That we may be well-thought-of—that we may be caught in a crowd thinking along that line—rather than that we might truly worship by communing with God through our inner selves?

If we would truly find the soul, we would let the motivating influence in us be the love of God as it manifests itself in our actions toward men. We and others can tell what our motivating influence is by what it makes us do towards our fellow man.

As Jesus Christ said, the whole gospel is "Thou shalt love the Lord thy God with all thine heart, thine soul, and thine body, and thy neighbor as thyself." (see Matt. 22:37-39) Then the rest of that given in Holy Writ is an explanation of that one sentence, isn't it?

So, whenever we begin to delve into the motivative influence within our inner selves, we will have to turn to our relationship with God, as it manifests itself in our relationship to our fellow man. It isn't of ourselves that we can do this, for "Of myself," (this applies to all of us) "I can do nothing." (see John 8:28)

We have been admonished by this one, that one, and the other to develop our own personality in order to be a power in this direction, that, or the other, but if instead we go rather within ourselves, where the kingdom of heaven is, what has our promise been? "All these things shall be added to you, in their place." (see Matt. 6:33; Luke 12:31) All that is necessary will be added, as we make step after step, for as we use what we have, the next step is given to us. We are all on our way for a development. What did the Master say about our becoming aware of our souls? "In patience possess ye your souls!" (see Luke 21:19) How many of us are patient and know that we are patient with our fellow man? Many of us are not patient even with the fellow who says or does something nice to us, because we immediately begin to think he wants something from us. That's "human nature," we say—but remember it's human nature!

The soul is of God. If we love God and act like it, then we express the soul power. But how many of us really act like it? We say we believe that God is love and that we should love our neighbor, our enemy, but how many of us do? Until we can, how can we become aware that we have a soul?

Let's not confuse the terms "spirit" and "soul," for they are not the same. I believe in the survival of personality, yes. I believe it is possible for us to communicate with those who have passed on, but I'm not preaching that we should do it. I would prefer (hadn't you?) going to "headquarters" for orders, instead of to anyone lower. We had all rather have our orders, our instructions, our promises, from headquarters! Who is our headquarters? To as many as have named His name, He is the headquarters. And His promise has been, "If ye ask in my name, *believing*, that shall I give unto you." (*see Matt. 21:22; John 14:13*) Also, "I will come and abide with you." (*see John 14:16; 15: 4-7*) Do we believe that? If so, then we would not be satisfied with anything less! It is true, "He has given his angels charge concerning thee, lest thou dash thy foot against a stone." (*see Ps. 91:11-12*) But from whom do we want our orders? And how may we receive them? We say receive them through the awareness of that within us which *is* eternal—our soul! Only our soul!

What is the power of the soul, then? All that is within the infinite itself! All of that! It is ours! He has given it to us! What is every man's birthright? What did Esau sell for a mess of pottage? He sold that awareness that he might approach the throne of God itself! For what? To satisfy the cravings of the body for a moment! (*see Gen. 25:29-33*) And that's what we are doing every day, isn't it? That is what keeps us from knowing our inner self. We are so pressed about by the things of the outer self or world. What did the Master say about the seed that was sown in one place? The cares of this world came in and crowded it out, until there was nothing left. (*see Matt. 13:22*)

And that's what is the matter with most of us—that's why we are disturbed and wondering what it is all about. Can't we accept and then live, "In my father's house are many mansions. If it were not so, I would have told you. And I go to prepare a place for you, that where I am there ye may be also"? (*see John 14:2-3*) Does that mean we are to attain to a place? How many expressions or manifestations of God do we see in the world? All the beauty is not in a sunset, although to some of us a sunset might appear the most beautiful thing imaginable. All the beauty is not in a rose, although to some of us a rose might be the most beautiful thing imaginable. But wherever we see life at all, we see a manifestation of that force, that power we call God.

What do we see in the smile of a tiny babe—how does it move the whole world? There are two places in our lives where we come the closer to seeing the soul. One is the smile of a newborn babe—the other is the last word of a mother to her son, though he be a wayward son. We see such manifestations, we *feel* them, we have a reverence for them, we stand in awe of them. When a babe is born or a mother passes, to what are they very close?

If we were as anxious about where we came from as we are about where we are going, we would be in quite a different position as to what we are doing with ourselves now, wouldn't we? And there isn't but one way we can find out or know what the power of that influence is that carries on and on, and that is through the Divine within us as we give expression of it to someone else! We can't explain it to someone else. We have to experience it individually, through *just doing a kindness to another*—one perhaps who cannot do for himself—and *then* we experience it.

In a letter from an individual several thousand miles away whom I had tried to aid with the information coming through me as a channel, she said, "I have regained my health through following the suggestions you gave, but—most of all—my husband and I have found God, and I am now ready to die any day, but—praise God—I'm living *for* something!"

If you know what it is to bring that into the *meaning* of a person's life, you realize—as I cannot tell you—that there is such a thing as a soul. If you just go out and do a kindness, a good deed, it makes something just happen to you, and you feel good about it yourself! And the world looks a great deal better, no matter if you are hungry. And, "The silver and gold are mine, saith the Lord, and the cattle on a thousand hills." *(see Ps. 50:10-12)* Those who serve the Lord and love *Him* shall *not* go hungry! Perhaps it is our job to supply that needed to meet somebody else's hunger—for what?

What is the question that is asked us when we stand before the judgment bar of God in the last day? "As we do it unto the least of these, my brethren, ye do it unto me!" *(see Matt. 25:40)* What is the soul? It is the God-Force in the *weakest* of our brethren, in the *lowest* of our people. And when we do an unkindness to another individual, we do not hurt the individual, but we hurt God and ourselves. If it applies one way, it does another. When do we dishonor God? When do we show that we deny Him? When we do an unkindness, say an unkind word about our fellow man! What will make us aware of the soul? When we become God-minded and conscious of the fact that we are our brother's keeper! What was the excuse of the first man who did a wrong to another? "Am I my brother's keeper?" *(Gen. 4:9)* Many of us try to hide behind something, to prevent our own conscience from hurting, and say, "Well, I don't have to worry about that, that's *his* job." If he is a living being that is wandering, disturbed, then it is *our* job—when we come in contact with him—if we want to know God at all!

How may we use our soul power? By manifesting the fruits of the spirit, which are kindness, patience, long-suffering—just doing these things we would like to have done to us. No matter how many fancy names we give to it, that's what is necessary when we come right down to facts. And if we seek first those fruits of the spirit, to manifest them in our lives towards our fellow man, all other things will be added unto us—and we will be expressing the soul power within us. *(see Matt. 6:33; Luke 12:31)*

"Know ye not that your bodies are the temples of the living God?" *(see 1 Cor. 3:16;6:19;2 Cor. 6:16; John 2:21)* He has promised to meet us in our temple, within our inner self. In what condition is He going to find that temple? Whenever we remain in a prayerful, meditative state, asking Him to meet us there, we may gain that which—if applied in our daily life—gives us the knowledge of the power of God in all its beauty.

Many of us have gone through hardships and have wondered, "If God loves us, why does He allow us to suffer so?" Who brought suffering into the world? Did God? He made man with free will, and when suffering began—after sin had entered—it was only through same that the man Jesus became whole again—became the Christ. "Behold," He said, "I show you a mystery. Without the shedding of blood there is *no* remission of sin." *(see 1 Cor. 15:51; Heb. 9:22)* What does that mean? How will we become aware of our souls without passing through all the experiences even as He?

Can we ever become aware of our soul power by finding fault with someone else? Suppose God found fault with us? Should we wonder

that we suffer when we consider how many hard things we have said
about people? But what has He promised? "If ye will take my yoke
upon you and learn of me, ye shall find rest unto your souls." *(see Matt.
11:29)* He has promised to meet with us and talk with us to bring to our
remembrance all things even from the beginning, if we will only listen
to that voice from within, using what we have today—and that necessary for tomorrow will be added in its due time. *Today* is the acceptable
time! If we will hear, we may become aware of the soul power within
our inner self.

Many of us in our suffering have doubted the ability of the Christ
Consciousness to arouse us to that necessary activity in our daily life.
But the experience of the world has been from the very beginning,
"Know, O Israel, the Lord thy God is *One!*" *(see Deut. 6:4)* What destroyed
the people in Atlantis, or in any nation of which we have any record?
The attempt to promulgate the power of self alone. We are a power unto
ourselves, but our individual self is the only thing that can keep us
away from God. Those that would know God must first believe that He
is, and then just act like it, and they will become aware of the God-
Consciousness within themselves that make all as one.

Then, those things that are spiritual *must* permeate the body, the
mind, the soul, if we would make ourselves one with God—even as the
Father, the Son, and the Holy Spirit are one—thus our soul force and
power is everlasting. How great is the soul power? It is everlasting, for it
is the gift of God to every individual.

Why do we have to justify ourselves when we tell a lie? Because the
soul within us *demands* it! For God has ever demanded, "Thou shalt have
no other God before me." *(Exod. 20:3)* And we all do it every day. We
justify ourselves before whom? Before our inner selves, in the same
place where we find grace and mercy and peace and understanding
with God.

Why is there turmoil and strife in our lives? Because we have justified ourselves when we know we don't want justice! We have a God of
mercy. He doesn't demand sacrifices any longer of this or that, but
merely that the giving of our whole self—body, mind, soul—justifies us
in Him.

Even though we may do things in the name of the Son—and do them for our own gratification—we cannot be justified before Him. Like begets like. We must love Him and keep His commandments, if we would truly know Him and the soul power that is within each of us.

References

Information about events in the life of Edgar Cayce has been gleaned from several Cayce biographical and historical resources, in addition to the readings themselves. Of special value were the following:

Carter, Mary Ellen. *Miss Gladys and the Edgar Cayce Legacy.* Virginia Beach, VA: A.R.E. Press, 1972.

Cayce, Charles Thomas, and Jeanette M. Thomas. *The Work of Edgar Cayce As Seen Through His Letters.* Virginia Beach, VA: A.R.E. Press, 2000.

Smith, A. Robert (compiler and editor). *Edgar Cayce—My Life As a Seer: The Lost Memoirs.* New York: St. Martin's Press, 2002.

Kirkpatrick, Sidney D. *Edgar Cayce: An American Prophet.* New York: Riverhead Books (Penguin Putnam), 2000.

The archives of the Edgar Cayce Foundation and the CD–ROM of the complete Cayce readings and related material provided certain details about events and information of the period, as well as quotes from the readings themselves.

Information about world and local events was found in several reference library resources and at Web sites relating to historical events, facts, and people. Of special value were the following print resources:

American Decades: 1920-1929 (Judith S. Baughman, editor). Detroit: Gale Research, 1996.

American Decades: 1930-1939 (Victor Bondi, editor). Detroit: Gale Research, 1995.

Mansfield, Stephen S. *Princess Anne County and Virginia Beach: A Pictorial History.* Norfolk: Donning Press, 1989.

Twentieth Century Day by Day (Clifton Daniels, editor-in-chief). New York: DK Publishing, 1999.

Yarinsky, Amy Waters. *Virginia Beach: Jewel Resort of the Atlantic.* Dover, NH: Arcadia Publishing, 1998.

A.R.E. PRESS

DISCOVER HOW THE EDGAR CAYCE MATERIAL CAN HELP YOU!

The Association for Research and Enlightenment, Inc. (A.R.E.®), was founded in 1931 by Edgar Cayce. Its international headquarters are in Virginia Beach, Virginia, where thousands of visitors come year-round. Many more are helped and inspired by A.R.E.'s local activities in their own hometowns or by contact via mail (and now the Internet!) with A.R.E. headquarters.

People from all walks of life, all around the world, have discovered meaningful and life-transforming insights in the A.R.E. programs and materials, which focus on such areas as personal spirituality, holistic health, dreams, family life, finding your best vocation, reincarnation, ESP, meditation, and soul growth in small-group settings. Call us today at our toll-free number:

1-800-333-4499

or

Explore our electronic visitors center on the
Internet: **http://www.edgarcayce.org.**

We'll be happy to tell you more about how the work of the A.R.E. can help you!

A.R.E.
215 67th Street
Virginia Beach, VA 23451-2061